I0213296

The Transnational Hero

Juan de la Cuesta Hispanic Monographs

Series: *Documentación cervantina «Tom Lathrop»*, 48

FOUNDING EDITOR
Tom Lathrop†
*University of Delaware*

PUBLISHER
Michael P. Bolan
*University of Delaware*

EDITOR
Michael J. McGrath
*Georgia Southern University*

EDITORIAL BOARD
Vincent Barletta
*Stanford University*

Annette Grant Cash
*Georgia State University*

David Castillo
*State University of New York - Buffalo*

Gwen Kirkpatrick
*Georgetown University*

Mark P. Del Mastro
*College of Charleston*

Juan F. Egea
*University of Wisconsin - Madison*

Sara L. Lehman
*Fordham University*

Mariselle Meléndez
*University of Illinois at Urbana - Champaign*

Eyda Merediz
*University of Maryland*

Dayle Seidenspinner-Núñez
*University of Notre Dame*

Elzbieta Sklodowska
*Washington University in St. Louis*

Noël Valis
*Yale University*

# The Transnational Hero: Re-accentuations of Don Quixote in the Novel

*by*

TATEVIK GYULAMIRYAN
*Hope College*

Juan de la Cuesta
Newark, Delaware

Cover art by Miche Andre.

*Portions of this book are adapted from:*

"On Re-accentuation, Adaptation, and Imitation of Don Quixote," by Tatevik Gyulamiryan, from the book *Don Quixote: The Re-accentuation of the World's Greatest Literary Hero*, edited by Slav N. Gratchev and Howard Mancing, 2017. Used by kind permission of Rowman & Littlefield Publishing Group, Inc.

"Toward a Poetics of Re-accentuation: Don Quixote and His Female Mimeses." *Cervantes ilimitado: Cuatrocientos años del Quijote*, special issue of *ALDEEU*, edited by Nuria Morgado, 2016.

No portion of this book may be reproduced in any form without permission from the publisher.
For permission contact: libros@juandelacuesta.com.

Copyright © 2024 by Linguatext, LLC. All rights reserved.

Juan de la Cuesta Hispanic Monographs
An imprint of Linguatext, LLC.
103 Walker Way
Newark, Delaware 19711 USA
(302) 453-8695

www.JuandelaCuesta.com

MANUFACTURED IN THE UNITED STATES OF AMERICA

ISBN: 978-1-58871-406-0

## Table of Contents

Acknowledgments ........ 7

Introduction ........ 11

1 Re-accentuating Don Quixote ........ 23

2 Readers ........ 50

3 Dreamers ........ 71

4 Adventurers ........ 100

5 Lovers ........ 132

Conclusion ........ 153

Works Cited ........ 163

Index ........ 181

# Acknowledgments

THE IDEA FOR THIS book was conceived during a graduate seminar on Mikhail Bakhtin taught by Howard Mancing at Purdue University. It was there that I completed my first research project on quixotic literature and re-accentuated characters. Inspired by Bakhtin and quixotic novels, I requested to enroll in an independent study with Howard and wrote several short pieces on my findings for that course. Those short essays laid the groundwork for what would eventually become my dissertation. Since writing my dissertation, I never stopped reading fiction without subconsciously thinking of re-accentuations of Cervantine characters. However, it was not until the pandemic that I resolved to mold my previous research and newfound insights into a cohesive form of a book.

Throughout the process of researching and writing, I was lucky to have companionship from friends and colleagues, who also entertained long conversations about literature with me. Foremost among them is Howard Mancing, my mentor and friend, to whom I owe immeasurable gratitude for introducing me to Bakhtin and reading dozens of drafts of my work on re-accentuation. Without him, this book would not have come to life. I am also grateful for the cohort of friends from the Bakhtin seminar, including Felipe Fiuza, Melissa Garr, Massimiliano Giorgini, Laura Ramiro Moreno, and Sarah Gretter, with whom I shared countless cups of coffee and conversations on re-accentuation, *Don Quixote*, and other literary musings. The invaluable contributions from the School of Languages and Cultures and the English Department at Purdue, including Iñigo Sánchez-Llama, Jennifer William, Charles Ross, Yonsoo Kim, Joni Hipsher, Ale Encarnación, and Eilyn Hidalgo, enriched my work immensely. Their insightful feedback and encouragement propelled me forward, shaping the trajectory of this endeavor.

I am indebted to friends, colleagues, and scholars of Cervantes and Golden Age Spain who graciously offered their time and expertise, providing feedback that refined my manuscript. Special mentions go to Carolyn Nadeau, who suggested I consider cutting from eight chapters to my current five; the late James Parr and John Jay Allen for their pointed questions about my project and their encouragement of my work; Steve Wagschal and Charles Ganelin for the illuminating conversations on Bakhtin and *Don Quixote*; Manuel Mühlbacher and Oliver Grill for including me in the panel on adventure at the ACLA symposium and for the fruitful discussions that stemmed from it. I cannot thank enough the generous friends and colleagues who have read and provided feedback on parts or all of my book: Joan Cammarata, Carmela Mattza, Liana Hakobyan, Elizabeth Gansen, Anne Larsen, Lee Forester, and the late Claudine André. I am thankful for my RSA writing group: Elizabeth Kolkovich, Dan Mills, Veronika Polakova, Izis Tomass, and Vanessa Lim, who read and commented on my Chapter One. I am also grateful for Ann Smith, Isabella Furth, and Julie Lind for reading my work during various stages of my writing and helping me find and fix tangled sentences, unnecessary repetitions, and mistakes—big and small.

The support from the Office of the Dean of Arts and Humanities at Hope College and Stephen Maiullo made it possible to publish this book, for which I am immensely grateful. The support and enthusiasm of Michael McGrath, editor of Juan de la Cuesta, has been incomparable and has made the various stages of the publication of this book seamless. Thank you, Mike. The reviewers of this book were encouraging in their comments and challenged me to think about my own interpretations and writing style critically; I thank them for that. I also extend my heartfelt thanks to Michael DeNotto and Michelle Yost for their invaluable assistance in sourcing essential texts for my research.

I am grateful to my students, including Jamie Breyfogle, Miche Andre, Leslie Pérez, Bryan Forrest, Erin Matheny, Stella Hays, and many others, whose interpretations of *Don Quixote* enriched my understanding and teaching of the text. The work of the talented Miche

Andre adorns the cover of this book. I also thank Nuria Morgado of ALDEEU and Bucknell University Press for granting permission to republish excerpts from my earlier versions of Chapters One and Two.

Lastly, my deepest gratitude is for my family, my parents, and my sister for their unwavering support, always. To Kevin, your patience and encouragement sustained me through countless hours of solitary work. I am profoundly grateful for your love and support and cannot be more excited to share with you and Ophelia the joy of holding the final product of my years' work in my hands.

# Introduction

A GREAT DEAL HAS been said and written about the eminent Spanish writer Miguel de Cervantes. His literary heritage is vast and enduring. Even after four centuries since the publication of the first and second parts of *Don Quixote* (1605 and 1615),[1] scholars persist in their exploration of Cervantes's work. Through lectures, articles, and books, they provide fresh approaches to analysis and critique, ensuring the lasting relevance of his literary legacy. I am certain that numerous scholars, writers, and readers will agree with me in that *Don Quixote*, Cervantes's most revisited work, has had undeniable influence on the development and dynamics of world literature. *Don Quixote* is one of the most translated novels and one with an incredibly large number of editions. It is also still used as a textbook, as a guide to writing techniques, as a distinctive bibliographical reference of older works, and as a manual of Golden Age Spanish popular culture, food, music, traditions, and daily life. *Don Quixote* presents the intricate and multi-faceted nature of human life. Cervantes wrote of the past and the present, of human conditions and dreams; Cervantes composed what many call the first modern novel and left a legacy for generations to come.

The novelistic genre takes a new shape with *Don Quixote*. María Stoopen believes that "the *Quixote* laid the foundations of the modern novel" (110). Robert Alter suggests that "[t]he novel begins out of an erosion of belief in the authority of the written word and it begins

1 Throughout the book, I use Quixote or Don Quixote in reference to Cervantes's character, whereas when referring to the novel, I italicize the title: *Don Quixote*.

with Cervantes" (3). Thinkers and writers like Carlos Fuentes have contemplated the experience of reading *Don Quixote*, also regarding it as the "origin but also destiny of the genre" (Fuentes xxxviii). Whether authors consider Cervantes's creation the first modern novel, it is widely acknowledged that *Don Quixote* played an instrumental role in shaping the novelistic genre as we know it today.

Although Cervantes's accomplishments in writing a modern novel are commonly recognized, there are still academics who believe that the rise of the novel did not begin with *Don Quixote*, but with such English novels as *Pamela* (1740), *Joseph Andrews* (1742), and *Tom Jones* (1749). Ralph W. Rader, for example, is convinced that *Pamela* not only establishes chronological priority in the history of the novel, but also enables and conditions "influence on the whole subsequent development of the form" (74). Leslie Fiedler calls Samuel Richardson the first inventor of the true novel (189). Ian Watt, in *The Rise of the Novel* (1957), designates Daniel Defoe, Samuel Richardson, and Henry Fielding as the founders of the European novel. This completely overlooks the fact that, for example, Fielding himself states that he wrote *Joseph Andrews* in imitation of Cervantes.[2]

Critics who favor the English writers of the eighteenth century as the first novelists are ignoring various important elements that make up the novelistic genre. For John Garrido Ardila, these elements are irony, unreliable narrators, autobiographical elements, psychological depth, among others, and all these can be traced back to the Spanish novel of the Golden Age (*History* 54). Garrido Ardila adds: "What Watt termed *formal realism* is perhaps the most defining feature of the novel," and we can find it in *Don Quixote*, replacing "the marvelous and escapist elements of romances" (3). Exploring Mikhail Bakhtin's work helps further differentiate between early iterations of the genre and the modern novel by outlining two stylistic lines of the European novel. Bakhtin begins with the following observations:

---

2 The title of Fielding's novel reads *The History of the Adventures of Joseph Andrews and His Friend Mr. Abraham Adams*, with a proceeding note, *Written in Imitation of the Manner of Cervantes, Author of* Don *Quixote*.

> [T]he novel is a multi-layered genre (although there also exist magnificent single-layered novels); the novel is a precisely plotted and dynamic genre (although there also exist novels that push to its literary limits the art of pure description); the novel is a complicated genre (although novels are mass produced as pure and frivolous entertainment like no other genre); the novel is a love story (although the greatest examples of the European novel are utterly devoid of the love element); the novel is a prose genre (although there exist excellent novels in verse). One could of course mention a large number of additional "generic characteristics" for the novel similar to those given above, which are immediately annulled by some reservation innocently appended to them. (*Dialogic* 8-9)

Bakhtin's description of the novel reveals that it does not have a straightforward definition nor an exact origin or beginning. Instead, the genre has evolved through various literary influences and developed a defining stylistic feature called *heteroglossia*—multiplicity of voices.[3] Bakhtin traces these heteroglot meanings in two stylistic lines, first of which encompasses prosaic works of chivalric, pastoral, and sentimental fiction, among others. In this line, the characters are usually flat, seldom exhibit *autopoiesis* (self-growth),[4] and are often

3 Bakhtin defines *heteroglossia* as the multiplicity of themes and ideas expressed through diverse voices and different speech types (*Dialogic* 263). He identifies the fundamentals of a heteroglot narrative, which include the speeches of author, narrator, and characters, as well as inserted genres all linked through some sort of a relationship in the text, often dialogized (263).

4 Humberto Maturana and Francisco Varela, in their *Autopoiesis and Cognition: The Realization of the Living* (1980), coined a very essential term: *autopoiesis*. The word is derived from Greek and means self-construction, self-production. Although in Maturana and Varela's definition *autopoiesis* is biological, I find its linguistic meaning and value extremely useful in literary analysis, as in numerous novels, the protagonists (and secondary characters) are shaped through *autopoiesis* (the process of self-realization and self-growth). If we examine Don Quixote's autopoietic journey, we can observe his transformation from a simple *hidalgo* to an avid reader, then from an avid reader to a mock knight errant, followed by his evolution into the Knight of La Mancha, and finally, his transition back from the recognized knight

monologic, as opposed to dialogic. In contrast to the first line of the European novel, the second line represents post-Renaissance literary production, beginning with *Don Quixote*. Here, the novelistic genre becomes more dialogic, heteroglot, and polyphonic.[5] It is important to note that not all post-Renaissance works of fiction pertain to the second line of novels. Sentimental fiction, for example, did not cease in production after the seventeenth century. In other words, the two stylistic lines of the novel are not strictly bound to temporal or chronological markers. Rather, what sets the second line apart from the first one is the intentional and natural representation of diverse voices, the "encyclopedic comprehensiveness," the non-literary language, and the "comprehensive reflection" of the era in which these novels were written (410-11). Bakhtin's descriptions of the second stylistic line of the novel are widely accepted among scholars as some of the fundamental elements of the modern novel.

Of post-Renaissance fiction and the second stylistic line of the novel, *Don Quixote* is one of the most referenced examples in Bakhtin. It conveys polyphony (various voices in the text), dialogism (recipro-

to the simple *hidalgo* Alonso Quijano. An autopoietic novel, therefore, has elements that can be traced in the picaresque tradition, as well as later, in *Bildüngsroman*. A good example of a character of picaresque fiction would be that of Lazarillo from *Lazarillo de Tormes* (1554), also considered a precursor of *Bildüngsroman*. In this work, the eponymous protagonist grows from a *pícaro* into a man of the middle class. The changes that Lazarillo undergoes are aided by the difficult life situations he encounters; they shape him, mold him, *build* him into his adult self. Lazarillo's story, his picaresque forming, is inevitable given the need to navigate the situations thrust upon him. In later fiction, Don Quixote consciously and deliberately chooses his identities and creates himself, imposing his self-creation on his contexts and adapting his contexts to the way he identifies himself. See Mancing's "Embodied Cognition and Autopoiesis in *Don Quixote*" for more.

5 *Dialogic*, *heteroglot*, and *polyphonic* are literary (and linguistic) terms redefined by Bakhtin. These concepts refer to characters and works that are non-monologic, characterized by a multiplicity of voices and opinions. While these elements coexist harmoniously within their literary contexts, they do not always present uniformity and can be antagonistic in their values. See Chapter Three, note 23 for more on polyphonic novels.

cal discourses), heteroglossia (blending of world views—fiction and reality—through multiplicity of languages), carnival (mixed identities and masks), and, to add to the list of these Bakhtinian definitions, it also presents *autopoiesis* (conscious and cognitive development of the main heroes and other characters). Howard Mancing points out that:

> [t]hough we can identify in Cervantes' novel all the character-types, motifs, themes, structures, devices, and much more from earlier Spanish chivalric, pastoral, picaresque, and other kinds of fiction, popular and erudite poetry, and various kinds of theater, *Don Quixote* is clearly more than that. ("Bakhtin" 152)

Diana de Armas Wilson, like Mancing, sees Cervantes's novel as literature that grows from and represents "polyglot energies" (54). *Don Quixote* incorporates metafiction in the genre of the novel by including poems, songs, letters, and short stories in its long narrative space, also engaging with previous literary works. As an amalgam of earlier traditions and a hub for various literary genres, Cervantes's novel rises as a new form of fiction in which its own sense of fictionality emerges. Alter asserts:

> Although novelists were by no means the first writers to recognize clearly the fictional status of fictions, I think they were the first—and Cervantes of course the first among them—to see in the mere fictionality of fictions the key to the predicament of a whole culture, and to use this awareness centrally in creating new fictions of their own. (3)

It is with such awareness of fictionality, still deriving from the relatable and real experiences of humans, that Cervantes produces his masterpiece. His work is deeply rooted in the realities his contemporaries knew or experienced—reading, chivalry, love, social class, honor, and more—presenting at the same time a blurred vision between what can be real and what is fiction. With "comprehensive reflections" of his time and beyond, Cervantes wrote an influential novel, one that served as a source of inspiration for many authors, among them, of course, Fielding, Richardson, and Defoe.

My work is inspired by a literary exploration of novels that resemble *Don Quixote* in style, form, and content. I focus mostly on characters who are similar to the protagonist of Cervantes's masterpiece, effectively becoming a re-accentuation of Don Quixote, a recreation of him in another context. This is in no way the first work to view other literary characters through the lens of Quixote-like attributes. In fact, the scholarship on quixotic literature is ever-growing. The novelty of this work lies in the conceptualization and refinement of re-accentuation—useful not only in analyzing quixotic works but also valuable in comparative studies—and a new approach I propose to understand Cervantes's hero through his salient qualities.

Through an analysis of hundreds of quixotic novels, I have noticed that characters who resemble Don Quixote usually highlight four of his defining features. The quixotic traits of a reader, dreamer, adventurer, and lover emerge repeatedly in *Quixote*-inspired literature. In going back and rereading Cervantes's novel through this lens of its eponymous hero's hallmarks, I could see the need for redefining Don Quixote as a literary character through some of his most influential qualities. Don Quixote is an avid reader, a zealous dreamer, an eager adventurer, and an idealistic lover. In quixotic novels, various authors have identified these features and reformulated them in their respective contexts. Manifesting these traits through their characters, authors exhibit a fascination with Cervantes's descriptions of how one can be carried away by reading and be propelled to dream big, how dreams can inspire adventures, and how love can be a most coveted need, yet calamitous at its limits. The subsequent organization of this book is based on these four salient quixotic traits and their expressions in Quixote-inspired characters.

In choosing the novels to analyze in my chapters, I have attempted to include a diverse collection of works. At first glance, the selection might seem arbitrary or even haphazard. However, I have been deliberate and purposeful in determining which novels to discuss as part of the analysis of re-accentuated Quixotes. In the process, I asked myself various questions: Which novels highlight a quixotic trait in a comparable manner? Are these novels also different enough to present diverse geographic areas, time periods, or literary movements? How can

I select three to five novels that can represent something very specific yet do that in the most distinct way possible? In other words, how can I ensure a literary diversity of both well-known and possibly unknown novels, yet works that are of literary importance, especially in the frames of Cervantes-influenced fiction? These questions helped me determine the selection of works included here, ones that represent diverse geographic areas and literary meanings, as well as pertain to various social contexts and eras.

It is not my intention in this book to offer a comprehensive study of theoretical or thematic concerns of *Don Quixote* or quixotic novels. That would certainly be impossible to achieve in one single study due to the sheer number of quixotic novels, theoretical approaches that novels generate, and numerous thematic choices in *Don Quixote* and other works of fiction inspired by it. Instead, I offer a new approach to reading Cervantes's novel and his protagonist in the light of the Bakhtinian concept of re-accentuation as applied to the four quixotic traits. To place my work among other contributions to the field, I offer in this book a detailed study of re-accentuation and focus on several quixotic characters bridging various parts of the world for centuries. I also reconceptualize terms used in Cervantes studies and offer new grounds for further discussions of works that re-accentuate, imitate, adapt, and parody *Don Quixote*.

My work is an extension of Garrido Ardila's well-regarded *Cervantes en Inglaterra: El Quijote y la novela inglesa del siglo XVIII* (2014) and his edited volume *The Cervantean Heritage: Reception and Influence of Cervantes in Britain* (2009). Garrido Ardila's work on the English novel has impacted my research on the influence of *Don Quixote* in England and has impelled me to explore Cervantes-inspired novels beyond the borders of Britain and Europe. In addition to his literary analyses of quixotic works in Britain, Garrido Ardila has redefined terms such as quixotic and Cervantine/Cervantean. His definitions have allowed me to think more deeply about the intertextual relevance of re-accentuation, as well as its potential contributions to the studies of novels inspired by *Don Quixote*.

There are numerous excellent essays and monographs on Miguel de Cervantes's influence on other works of literature: Angel Flores and

M. J. Benardete's edited volume *Cervantes Across the Centuries* (1969), Carroll Johnson's *Don Quixote: The Quest for Modern Fiction* (1990), Darío Fernández-Morera and Michael Hanke's edited volume *Cervantes in the English-Speaking World: New Essays* (2005), and Manuel Durán and Fay R. Rogg's *Fighting Windmills: Encounters with Don Quixote* (2006), to name only a few. These and myriad other excellent works help define and redefine Quixote, quixotic, and quixotism in the literary world.[6] Even with these contributions, we have arrived at a point where the term quixotic can signify something other than the complex and intricate meanings it should convey.

The word *quixotic* is complex, it's chaotic, it's emotional, it's physical, it's never singular. This polyphonic term is used to refer to many aspects that define Cervantes's *Don Quixote* and its eponymous character. Its intertextual meanings can allude to various facets of Cervantes's novel or interpretations of them. Because of the use and abuse of the term, quixotic has transcended its original meaning and can be seen applied liberally to anything vaguely echoing the character from whom the word originated. Even literary works inspired by Cervantes can diminish the legacy of *Don Quixote* and its protagonist by not fully grasping the complex connotations of the word quixotic; as Aaron Hanlon notes, "so long as 'quixotic' is predominantly used in literary studies as a taxonomic term to relate some allusive or structural aspect of a text back to *Don Quixote* as a source text, [it] will be conflated with an unwieldy array of allusions, authorial devices, and structural components" ("Toward" 141-42). This allows for a disarray of interpretations and definitions, alienating the term from its origins.

Much like Don Quixote's transcendence of his literary confines and transformation into a cultural icon independent from Cervantes and his novel, the term quixotic serves as a linguistic example of meaning transcending its original context, evolving beyond the limits of its origin. The term has taken on a life of its own to the extent that it might no longer be seen as necessary to read *Don Quixote* to write a quixotic work; knowledge of its presence in popular culture may seem

6 Quixotism implies irrationality generally observed in dreamers of the impossible (Matooka 133).

enough. A hypothetical author might not feel the need to read *Don Quixote* to create a quixotic work because they might trust the cultural presentations and popular displays of Don Quixote and his world. In consequence, the literary world abounds in works labeled as quixotic that do not live up to their namesake.

The changing values of *Don Quixote* and all meanings derived from it are a natural and necessary part of its literary evolution. But as it evolves further, it becomes increasingly crucial to discern between elements that are vaguely reminiscent of Quixote's adventures and those that are firmly rooted in Cervantes's original work. Hanlon notes:

> Rather than seeking to understand first the character of quixotism as it affects Don Quixote and his 'offspring' in subsequent literary traditions, scholars have overlooked what precisely we mean by 'quixotic' in an attempt to define quixotism as a genre, a collection of texts generally related to *Don Quixote*. (*World* 5)

Hanlon, then, offers meaningful insights about how to define and approach quixotic literature. Still, the changes of perception of *Don Quixote* and what quixotic is affect the way we understand Cervantes's characters and other literary personages inspired by them. And so, I suggest we consider in this book what makes fiction quixotic, focusing on characters.

In Chapter One, I engage with the scholarly tradition of meanings of quixotic, recently redefined by scholars like Garrido Ardila and Mancing, and suggest that, in describing what is quixotic, we also consider several qualities that characterize Don Quixote—those of a reader, dreamer, adventurer, and lover. It is with such Quixote-like features that authors inspired by Cervantes's work tend to adorn their characters and weave a quixotic story. In so doing, they create re-accentuated versions of Don Quixote—characters who imitate, adapt, parody, or resemble Cervantes's hero in some aspect.

The Bakhtinian term re-accentuation is useful in concretizing quixotic features in other characters, but it also can become confusing as it relates to other intertextual meanings. And so, I compare the notion of re-accentuation to such phenomena as rewriting (writing again with little or no changes), adaptation (tailoring something for a new medium), imitation (creating a replica or a facsimile), parody (imitation, usually infused with satire), and, of course, what quixotic is (deriving from *Don Quixote* or the hero). Establishing re-accentuation as the highlighting of a given characteristic in a new context, I offer readings of Don Quixote's four salient traits of the reader, dreamer, adventurer, and lover in quixotic novels.

In Chapter Two, I include an analysis of re-accentuated readers. What does it mean to be a reader in Don Quixote's terms, a quixotic reader? And what implications does reading have depending on the context in which it is practiced? While one often comes across literary characters who are readers, it is a trait that frequently denotes negative habits—or, better said, the type of reading and the manner of reading in which characters engage may provoke adverse reactions or outcomes. This is particularly prevalent among women who engage in quixotic reading, as the historical suppression of reading profane works has often targeted them specifically. The reader's trait in Don Quixote assumes perusing certain kinds of literature and being carried away by fictive horizons in quotidian realities. Re-accentuating this feature in women results in threats such as burning their books or reconfining them to the domestic frames from which they were estranged due to reading. It can also bear catastrophic implications for women who find themselves unable to rectify the mistakes which are seen as choices made because of uncritical reading.

Quixotic reading promises a world full of ideas and imagination. It also propels the reader to dream big. The dreamer's trait in Don Quixote is relentless, driven from a need to make a change—an obsessive quest that often slips away the moment it seems to be achieved. Re-accentuating the dreamer's trait, whether inspired by reading or not, assumes an intense belief in a goal, a dream of the impossible (to paraphrase Dale Wasserman's famous lyrics). In Chapter Three, I look at re-accentuated dreamers who become obsessed by their dreams and argue that these characters let their goals slip away from them because they are unable to differentiate between their dreamed and real lives. Impassioned by their quests, re-accentuated dreamers risk everything to achieve what they desire, but their journeys are often cut short, their ideals unattained.

Dreaming like Don Quixote is an active process. The Spanish *hidalgo* embarks on a quest to bring his literary fantasies to life and seek out adventures. The latter, of course, can be read as a fool's errand, but they also suggest something deeper than that. I see Don Quixote as experimenting with the surrounding world by asking the question *what if*? What if I were a knight errant? What if a peasant woman were to be a princess? What if I brought fiction into reality? Thus, in Chapter Four, I contend that re-accentuating the adventurer's trait denotes not only a journey, some kind of wanderlust, but also an experiment—a sort of spatial, temporal, and ideological negotiation with reality. Re-accentuated quixotic adventurers offer a glimpse into a world of limitless possibilities where the absurd makes sense, where adventures are born from a dream and describe a journey—mad or sagacious—that leads these characters into discovering new realities.

The lover's trait is perhaps Don Quixote's most complicated characteristic. It is as platonic and congenial as it is malformed and problematic. While love, as a feeling and sentiment, is generally perceived as a positive part of human experiences, I see the lover's trait in Don Quixote as a characteristic that exposes various negative expressions of the sentiment, manifested in the form of obsession, mania, and idealism. Re-accentuations of quixotic love reveal the ineptitude of the lover's feelings when they are unbalanced, unconventional, or even, in a way, unorthodox. In Chapter Five, I look into the problematic re-accentuations of quixotic love in literature. I focus on the manic and nonconformist expressions of love studying how Cervantes and Cervantes-inspired authors challenged the idealization of the sentiment.

As Cervantes's novel enters and influences other fictional worlds, homecoming festivals are celebrated in all corners of the globe and in all periods of time.[7] *Don Quixote* and its eponymous character have

7 *Homecoming festivals* is one of the many new literary and linguistic concepts found in Mikhail Bakhtin's work. In his *Speech Genres* (1979), the Russian thinker refers to concepts that never lose their meaning. According to him, we humans keep recycling every concept, meaning, thought, and object. He claims that over half of our utterances are borrowed from others and

given Cervantes a thousand lives: *Don Quixote*—one of the most influential works of all time, and the protagonist—the hero with a thousand faces.[8] Let us now delve into several novels grounded in and influenced by *Don Quixote* and deliberate over their contexts in which readers, dreamers, adventurers, and lovers dwell.

---

are not unique. Also, everything that the human world produces is based on something previously introduced. Every time we return to an older concept or a meaning, we assure its revival in a different context. The revival of any meaning is referred to as its "homecoming festival" (Bakhtin, *Speech* 170). Literature grounded in *Don Quixote* helps make the novel's revival constant. Each time the novel or its protagonists enter a renewed context, they celebrate their homecoming festivals.

8 Joseph Campbell published his book titled *The Hero with a Thousand Faces* in 1949. Although the title is not a reference to Don Quixote, I think that the phrase perfectly describes Cervantes's protagonist and his generative characteristics.

# 1
# Re-accentuating Don Quixote

A PIONEER IN DIALOGIC criticism, Mikhail Bakhtin is often characterized by his interdisciplinary approaches to language and literature. His works convey unprecedented interpretations of literary pieces, linguistic phenomena, philosophical approaches, and cultural practices. They reflect his fascination with what context is and what it does, as the author contemplates the human *pragma* and *idea* through various perspectives. Among the many dialogues that Bakhtin established between literary, linguistic, and philosophical notions, his reflections on the relationships of well-known and new concepts are especially noteworthy.

The Russian thinker delves into the world of links between *the old* and *the new*, as well as the human tendency to reuse and reclaim old trends in various cultural, social, and artistic contexts. Bakhtin highlights the importance of recycling familiar words, ideas, concepts, and even objects to create new ones; in fact, he states that more than half of what we claim to be new has appeared in other contexts previously (*Speech* 87-89). Because of the human predisposition to refine and redefine the known—*the old*—Bakhtin sees *the new* as some sort of a variation or derivation of a preexisting artifact or thought. Almost every discovery made by humans leans on a long chain of prior inventions that serve as a basis for new findings; nearly everything *new* is derived from something *old*.

As we progress through our lives, we come across numerous objects, designs, and notions that are a new version of an old entity. These are *re-accentuations* of previously known materials and ideas. Re-accentuation—a term Bakhtin uses in reference to literary discourses, characters, and works—carries a singular value in comparative studies, as it establishes a connection between an original and a new value. Bakhtin sees it as a phenomenon that emerges from dialogic fusions. It can take place when a given entity is characterized by differing points of views, *autopoiesis*, and adaptability. In literature, re-accentuations of characters and works recur regularly.

A superficial reading of Bakhtin may leave the impression that he refers to any reutterance as re-accentuation. However, theorizing the term and contextualizing it among well-established notions such as parody, imitation, and adaptation will uncover its unique role in comparative analyses. That is the goal of this chapter: to expand on re-accentuation as a literary term as it relates to other intertextual notions, as well as to analyze it in the context of a work that has yielded numerous re-accentuations in literary history, that of *Don Quixote* by Miguel de Cervantes, an example that Bakhtin uses repeatedly.

Re-accentuating *Don Quixote* and its eponymous hero has been a common practice since the seventeenth century. As Bakhtin notes, "The image of Don Quixote has been thus re-accentuated in a variety of ways . . . and interpreted in different ways, for these re-accentuations and interpretations were an inevitable and organic further development of the image" (*Dialogic* 410). Indeed, authors inspired by Cervantes's masterwork often create characters that remind us of the Quixote-Sancho duo, a hopeless quixotic lover, or an adventurer fighting for a good cause. Characters, who seem to imitate Cervantine heroes, also contribute to the "organic further development" of those who inspired them. This, in turn, promotes the process of defining and redefining the original prototypes. Particular characters, reminiscent of Don Quixote, Sancho, Dulcinea, and others, can epitomize re-accentuations of them. Motivated by Cervantes's narrative, authors may also imitate speech, style, and form encountered in *Don Quixote*, but emulations at a character level are a more common occurrence.

Before delving into the world of Cervantine structures and quixotic characters, it is necessary to uphold re-accentuation as a literary concept deriving from Bakhtin's descriptions. To understand better the functions of the Bakhtinian term in literature, as well as in the context of Cervantes's novel and its imitators, it is also essential to expand on its original definitions. This can be achieved by establishing a relationship between re-accentuation and other phenomena such as parody, imitation, adaptation, and other intertextual references.

## What It Means to Re-accentuate

In *The Dialogic Imagination* (1982), Bakhtin briefly refers to re-accentuation as a means of highlighting linguistically and intertextually an existing speech act or image in a different framework. Context bears a central significance in this process, as it delivers a new model that still carries the visible old within. Re-accentuation takes a variety of forms, including those related to linguistics and discourse, as well as characters and novels. In this book, I focus on characters in novels, but a laconic mention of Bakhtin's understanding of language and discourse reformulations will help situate the term in different contexts.

Linguistic re-accentuation occurs when the stress on a spoken word shifts due to added prefixes or suffixes to form verbs, adjectives, and more. Some examples include: áccent/accéntuate, sénse/nónsense, práctical/practicálity, síituate/situátion, hábit/habítual. The root or the base word remain the same, yet the meaning of the word changes. In linguistics, this is an obvious and a common occurrence.

Using this linguistic practice with accents, authors give words a syntactic role as they shape their language of expression, their discourse. Bakhtin provides a detailed analysis of discourse in the novel with its constituents as he considers both form and content of the genre.[1] For him, authors' narrative is a polyphonic and heteroglot phenomenon in which are present written and oral practices of the social groups represented in a given work. Discourse in the novel also includes influences from social, historical, or literary practices that blend reality with fiction. Most importantly, this language integrates authors' intentions synthesized with their characters' thoughts, which lend themselves to varying interpretations by readers.

1 "Discourse in the Novel" is one of the four essays of *The Dialogic Imagination*; see pp. 259-422.

A narrative that carries a hybrid of authors' and characters' words bears re-accentuated discourse within. That is, the speech of a hero coalesces with that of the author in the novel. Bakhtin considers the fusion of the author and hero thoughts and words as the hero's re-accentuation of the author's ideas. In his words: "The author encases his own thought in the image of another's language," while the hero encapsulates a "discourse about himself and about his world" intermixed with the author's view "about him and his world" (*Dialogic* 409). In Bakhtin's eyes, characters are couriers between writers and readers; they re-accentuate the writer's original ruminations through the dialogues, monologues, and thoughts they have. This process is essential for the development of the novelistic genre, as this phenomenon occurs not only within a novel—through the fusion of author and hero discourse—but also within the genre, by way of intertextual influence. Every interpretation of a narrative assumes a discourse re-accentuation by readers. And so, those who read a novel and write fiction inspired by it, re-accentuate certain aspects of the said novel's form.

While Bakhtin mainly focuses on discourse re-accentuation of the author via their characters, it is common in literature to come across characters re-accentuating each other's words as well. One of the greatest examples of this kind of a shift can be found, of course, in *Don Quixote*. When knight and squire are at the house of the Duke and Duchess, they meet Countess Trifaldi, who greets them in a pseudo-sophisticated manner, her speech overflowing with superlatives:

> —Confiada estoy, señor poderisísimo, hermosísima señora y discretísimos circunstantes, que ha de hallar mi cuitísima en vuestros valerosísimos pechos acogimiento, no menos plácido que generoso y doloroso; porque ella es tal, que es bastante a enternecer los mármoles, y a ablandar los diamantes, y a molificar los aceros de los más endurecidos corazones del mundo; pero antes que salga a la plaza de vuestros oídos (por no decir orejas), quisiera que me hicieran sabidora si está en este gremio, corro y compañía, el acendradísimo caballero de don Quijote de la Manchísima, y escuderísimo Panza. (Cervantes, *Don Quijote* II 347)

> ["I am confident, most powerful lord, most beautiful lady, most discerning company, that my most grievous affliction will find in your most valiant bosoms a refuge no less serene than generous and pitying, for it is such that it would be enough to soften marble, and dulcify diamonds, and bend the steel of the hardest hearts in the world; but before I bring it to your hearing, so as not to say ears, I would be most happy if you would tell me if in this group, circle, and company there is to be found that most unblemished knight Don Quixote of La Manchissima, and his most squirish Panza." (Cervantes, *Don Quixote* 705-706)]

Sancho Panza rushes to reply:

> —El Panza —antes que otro respondiese, dijo Sancho— aquí está, y el don Quijotísimo asimismo; y así podréis, dolorosísima dueñísima, decir lo que quisieridísimis; que todos estamos prontos y aparejadísimos a ser vuestros servidorísimos. (Cervantes, *Don Quijote* II 347)

> ["Panza," said Sancho before anyone else could respond, "is here, and Don Quixotissimo as well; and so, most dolorous duennissima, you can say whatever you wishissima, for we're all ready and most prepared to be your most servantish servantissimos." (Cervantes, *Don Quixote* 706)][2]

Sancho parodies Countess Trifaldi's discourse, highlighting her superlatives and applying them not only to adjectives but to nouns and verbs as well.[3] The squire's comic imitation of Countess Trifaldi's words prefigures the multiple re-accentuations that take place between *Don Quixote* and other literary works; Sancho is doing with nouns and

---

2 From here on, quotes from Edith Grossman's translation of *Don Quixote* will exclude the title of the novel and be cited as simply (Cervantes [page]).

3 Sancho's re-accentuation of Countess Trifaldi's words illustrates his attempt to parody her speech, his discourse also being a re-accentuation of Cervantes's thoughts expressed through Sancho.

verbs what many authors will do with *Don Quixote*'s characters and themes in their works.

Re-accentuation, therefore, is not limited to words and discourse. Bakhtin argues that novelistic themes and characters can be re-accentuations of earlier models as well (*Dialogic* 409-22). In the case of the themes, central ideas from an original novel are incorporated into a new work of fiction. To illustrate the point within the context of Cervantes-inspired literature, Graham Greene's *Monsignor Quixote* (1982) is a re-accentuation of *Don Quixote*; the plotline primarily encompasses the adventures of Father Quixote (a re-accentuated Don Quixote) with his squire Zancas (a re-accentuated Sancho Panza) in his limping SEAT 600 (a re-accentuation of Rocinante). Greene's novel offers an imaginative story of a bishop and ex-mayor's travels through post-Franco Spain but lends itself to a quixotic reading due to the grounding of characters and themes in Cervantes's *Don Quixote*. There are various other examples of such quixotic novels that exhibit the Bakhtinian re-accentuation of novelistic themes and fictional heroes. It is in these heroes, however, that one can find Cervantine influences expressed more clearly, especially if the reader has formulated a more definite image, a standard for the prototypes in *Don Quixote*. Thus, shared interpretations of a certain character between readers and authors are important to identify other expressions of them.

To re-accentuate a character, an author takes an original model's recognizable image and places it in a different context. Bakhtin sees characters as images formulated in authors' and readers' minds (*Dialogic* 419-21).[4] In his words: "New images in literature are very often created through a re-accentuating of old image, by translating them from one accentuated register into another" (421). To take it further, a fictional hero transmuted into a new body and placed in a new context, who maintains core qualities that defined its prototype, is a re-accentuation of its model. These characters usually appear in a context other than that of the character on whom they are based, as seen in the

4 Bakhtin also uses the word *images* in more general terms, referring to commonly conceptualized thoughts about characters, novels, and genres. For him, an image is "a symbol" (*Dialogic* 410). Context plays an important role in understanding to what, specifically, image refers in Bakhtin's work.

example of *Monsignor Quixote*. While new characters are grounded in an existing hero—bearing easily recognizable similarities in appearance, traits, or comportment—they are fully independent of their influencer.

As noted by Bakhtin, *Don Quixote* and its eponymous character have been re-accentuated in a variety of ways in the novelistic genre. Cervantes's masterpiece stands as one of the most influential works of fiction, while his protagonist has transcended his literary limits and become one of the most recognizable icons throughout the literary world. It is due to his distinguishable characteristics that Don Quixote has formulated a certain standard for his image. And if we take a look at how Cervantes-inspired authors have reconceptualized the image of Don Quixote through their characters, we will notice that several perceptions of the Spanish *hidalgo* emerge repeatedly in the novelistic genre. Those are the quixotic traits of 1) a reader, 2) a dreamer, 3) an adventurer, and 4) a lover. I suggest that when analyzing characters who exhibit most of these quixotic traits, we call them, as Bakhtin would propose, re-accentuations of Don Quixote. Clearly, there is already abundant scholarship on quixotic literature and innumerous examples of imitations, parodies, and adaptations of *Don Quixote*. So, let us place re-accentuation among these intertextual meanings for further definitions and clarity before looking at specific quixotic traits.

## Re-accentuation: What It Is and What It Is Not

The Bakhtinian term is related to, but not quite the same as, literary processes such as rewriting, parody, imitation, and adaptation. For example, it is different from mere rewriting, since rewriting involves revision or copying without changes in context. Jorge Luis Borges's "Pierre Menard, Author of *Don Quixote*" is a brilliant illustration of the concept of rewriting. Borges's eponymous protagonist strives to recreate Cervantes's novel, not copying it but producing "a number of pages which coincided—word for word and line for line—with those of Miguel de Cervantes" (Borges 91). Menard immerses himself in *Don Quixote* with great dedication and manages to rewrite parts of the novel so accurately that they are almost indistinguishable from the original. As Borges states, "The Cervantes text and the Menard text are verbally identical, but the second is almost infinitely richer" (94). Here, Borges alludes to the experience of reading and rereading, visiting and revisiting, interpreting and reinterpreting *Don Quixote*, which is different every time. The creative act then, according to him, dwells in reading Menard's version, not in writing it (Martín 178). Although Borges states that Menard's *Don Quixote* is far richer than that of Cervantes, the reader realizes that, in Menard's rendition, there have been no textual or contextual changes; therefore, his attempt to recreate the novel results in (ironically unintentional) plagiarism.

Without altering fictional contexts, an author will likely not be able to achieve a completely unique rewriting of a character or a novel. Without changes, an attempt at recreating Cervantes's novel will result in a revision of it (with the same characters) or, optimally, become a sort of Pierre Menard's *Don Quixote*. Indeed, the image of Don Quixote, with his distinctive traits, motivations, and social context, may not seamlessly translate to every cultural or historical setting. His iconic speeches, intricate relationships with friends and foes, and the societal landscape that shapes him are deeply rooted in the specific context of early modern Spain. Attempting to transplant him directly into vastly different cultural milieus like Imperial Japan or Soviet Russia might prove nonsensical. However, with strategic changes to, say, his literary predilections or historical pertinence, a new version of Don Quixote could arise in many contexts. Variations of literary realms—new setting, geographical location, historical period, cultural norms, genre, etc.—will also help create a re-accentuated character. Thus, new settings and attributes are essential for re-accentuation. Only then can fictional heroes become independent, distinct from their prototype, even if some of their characteristics appear to be rewritten. Different contexts assume that characters inhabit a new world and maybe new mind and body, re-accentuating (but not rewriting) their predecessor's persona.

Parody is another concept related to re-accentuation but not synonymous with it. Linda Hutcheon notes that parody is a type of imitation "characterized by ironic inversion" (*Parody* 6). Through this sort of imitation, Hutcheon believes that it creates a "formal or structural relation between two texts" that amounts to "a form of textual dialogism" (22). She cites Bakhtin, who describes the notion as "an intentional dialogized hybrid" (*Dialogic* 76). For example, Jane Austen's *Northanger Abbey* (1818) parodies the genre of gothic fiction that enjoyed great popularity in England during the late eighteenth and early nineteenth centuries. The main character, Catherine Morland, is heavily influenced by these readings, to such extents that they begin to govern her daily life. Juxtaposing gothic readings with lifelike events, Austen establishes a dialogue between fiction and reality throughout the text. The parody in the novel becomes clear when the heroine employs gothic principles in her lifestyle, and these principles fail, embarrassing her. Gothic fiction proves irrelevant and even detrimental for certain fans like Catherine. To contrast that, what prevails in Austen's work is the necessity of a benevolent love as a phenomenon that helps leave endured failures behind. In this manner, *Northanger Abbey* generates ironic inversion and criticism of gothic novels though the lens of parody, while also outlining a narrative that will forerun the romance novel.

To continue, Hutcheon affirms that parody does not always involve satire (*Parody* 6), and Michael Scham sees it as a tool to "salvage and revitalize" former works (81). These definitions can easily be applied to the type of chivalric parody presented in *Don Quixote*, as well as to most of the parodic literature derived from it.[5] It is also important to note that "parodied genres do not belong to the genres that they parody" (Bakhtin, *Dialogic* 59).[6] For example, *Don Quixote* can be read as a parody of chivalric romances; however, the novel itself is not a chivalric romance given that it is also characterized by myriad other

5 Through parody, *Don Quixote* revitalizes *Amadís de Gaula* (1508), which had declined in popularity by the time Cervantes began working on his book. Likewise, any modern work that exhibits quixotic features, whether in the form of (satiric) parody or not, reanimates Cervantes's novel. For more on parody, revitalization, irony, and hybridity in the context of *Don Quixote*, see Schmidt, pp. 250-60.

6 Bakhtin firmly believes that no parodied work represents the genre of the original work. For him, a parodied sonnet is not a sonnet but an "image of a sonnet," and a parodic epic poem is an "image of an epic poem" and not an original or independent epic poem (*Dialogic* 51).

elements that are common to pastoral, picaresque, byzantine, and other types of fiction. By the same token, while gothic foundations constitute a substantial part of the plot and character development in *Northanger Abbey*, it is not common to refer to it as a gothic novel. Another example is Ken Mitchell's *The Heroic Adventures of Donny Coyote* (2003), whose title already indicates the novel's parodic nature. *Donny Coyote* is an adventure novel that also employs re-accentuations of *Don Quixote* and its characters, but it simultaneously parodies comic books as the eponymous protagonist strives to imitate superheroes.

Parody and imitation are closely related to each other,[7] the former being a sort of mimicry with an intention to criticize, dramatize, or satirize a previously known work or genre. Imitation, on the other hand, does not bear an explicit dramatization and criticism; it is principally a replication of an aspect of an influencer. A distinction between these two concepts is that parody derives from a previous work (for example, *Don Quixote* parodying chivalric romances), while imitation is grounded in a previous work (such as Fielding's *Joseph Andrews,* which explicitly imitates Cervantine narrative).[8] Imitation is a

7 Parody and imitation are also related to intertextual influence, since many works show influence from another work without necessarily parodying or imitating it explicitly. For example, *Don Quixote* inspired and influenced Herman Melville, but Melville's works are neither parodies nor imitations of Cervantes's novel (although Captain Ahab in *Moby Dick* is a re-accentuation of the Spanish knight errant; more in Chapter Three). Ludmilla Buketoff Turkevich suggests that "influence may be positive or negative, and may act directly or inversely. The positive effect is far more usual. It occurs when an author, favorably impressed by some feature of an earlier work, uses it consciously or subconsciously in his own" (x). To consider another approach, Harold Bloom sees influence as if there were "*no* texts, but only relationships *between* texts" (*A Map* 3).

8 As mentioned, the title page of Fielding's *Joseph Andrews* indicates that Fielding wrote his novel in "imitation of the manner of Cervantes, who wrote *Don Quixote.*" In addition, the narrative portrays various quixotic characters (including Joseph Andrews, who is an adventurer and lover, and Abraham Adams, who exhibits the traits of a reader and a dreamer; more in Chapter Four).

conscious intertextual reference and emulation that can be achieved through a given character or in the work as a whole.

Imitation, like parody, is similar to re-accentuation, but they are not synonymous literary concepts. The former consists of conscious mimicking of a technique or a persona in an attempt to be or become like something or someone, whereas the latter implies molding a character or work based on a previously familiar image. To illustrate the difference: Don Quixote strives to imitate heroes from chivalric romances, especially Amadís de Gaula.[9] Although he copies Amadís in some ways (for example, his penitence for Dulcinea is a nod to Amadís's in Peña Pobre), Don Quixote fails to become a re-accentuation of him. It is because numerous unique traits define Don Quixote and not the one who inspired him (for instance, Amadís is not a reader like Don Quixote). This, of course, is not to say that imitation, unlike re-accentuation, should always be viewed as something literal, simply copied, and not unique. *Joseph Andrews* is not a novel in which the author copies episodes from *Don Quixote* and other works by its author. Rather, the English writer exhibits deep inspiration, grounding his creation in Cervantes. What Fielding is imitating is Cervantine narrative techniques and certain characteristics of his world of personages (i.e., their names) without necessarily replicating them. A different example of imitation at a character level is Emma Bovary, the protagonist of Gustave Flaubert's celebrated *Madame Bovary* (1856). Emma aspires to imitate the lives of the women portrayed in romance novels. In her imitation, she also exposes quixotic traits, such as those of a reader, dreamer, adventurer, and lover, re-accentuating them in the context of the nineteenth-century France.[10]

Re-accentuation can be equated to adaptation in comparative studies since both terms imply intertextual and dialogic relations

---

9 Amadís de Gaula is the eponymous character of Garci Rodríguez de Montalvo's novel.

10 Note that characters who imitate other literary heroes do not necessarily re-accentuate their traits. Madame Bovary is not a re-accentuation of a popular romantic heroine. Instead, she portrays qualities that are attributed to Cervantes's knight errant, who, in turn, was out imitating chivalric romance heroes.

between something original and something derived. Still, they bear differences. Works can be adapted for different audiences within the same genre, like a children's adaptation of *Don Quixote*, or an adaptation of a movie for different screens, among other forms. This sort of adaptation assumes abridgment or slight modification to comply with the specific standards and needs of differing consumers. However, the kind of adaptation that includes a shift in artistic form—adaptations of novels to movies, movies to TV shows, literature to art, etc.—may foster a belief that a character presented in another medium is not the same but a re-accentuation of an original.

Adaptation, like re-accentuation, is "not simply repetition; there is always a change" (Hutcheon, *Adaptation* 176). And it is generally accepted among critics that adaptations should and do bear the main themes of an original product in the adapted one. Film critics agree that adapting text for screen is an exercise to project familiar themes in another medium. However, there are some scholars, called fidelity critics, who advocate for "a good faithful adaptation . . . with the entire text read offscreen" (Agee 216; qtd. in McFarlane, "It Wasn't" 4).[11] This sort of approach in Cervantes studies would perhaps critique Dale Wasserman's *Man of La Mancha* (1964) as a poor adaptation of *Don Quixote*. Although the musical is inspired by Cervantes and his work, introducing a flesh and blood Dulcinea and giving her a voice, for instance, would be considered a point of digression from the original text. To contrast that, Steven Ritz-Barr and Hoku Uchiyama's puppet film *Quixote* (2010) presents various events from Cervantes's novel with only slight variations that do not seem to violate the author's original intentions.[12] For example, the viewer can see the episode of the burning of the books, the incident with the little boy Andrés, or the scene where Don Quixote watches a puppet show. Unlike *Man of La Mancha*, fidelity critics would say that Ritz-Barr and Uchiyama's

11 See McFarlane, *Novel to Film* (1996), pp. 8-11, as well as Hutcheon, *A Theory of Adaptation* (2006), pp. 2-9, for a brief commentary on the varying views on adaptation by critics.

12 See Ritz-Barr's recounting of how his puppet film came to be, especially, how he ensured that his audience understood the "background of Don Quixote" as presented in Cervantes's novel (210).

film does not take gross liberties, alienating itself from Cervantes's work; *Quixote*, the film, is a presentation of *Don Quixote*, the novel, in a different medium—an adaptation of it.

Bakhtin would challenge fidelity critics. He would say that adaptation generally assumes re-accentuation (*Discourse* 419-21). He believes that, given specific authorial interventions, certain adaptations would look something like this: an artist or director fuses their discourse with that of Cervantes, who ascribed his discourse to Don Quixote. That is discourse re-accentuation. In addition, Bakhtin would argue that with every new interpretation, a renewed image of an original work or character emerges in another context (410). Still, he reiterates, to re-accentuate is to change "the background animating dialogue . . . the composition of heteroglossia" (420). Without that change, there is not re-accentuation, but repetition. And so, Bakhtin implicitly references re-accentuation as a phenomenon that transcends mere repetition, instead being shaped by shifts in background or context.

Concerning repetition in adapted work, Hutcheon believes that it is part of the adaptation process. However, she states that repetition is achieved "without replication" (*Adaptation* 7). Adaptation theorists would agree that changes in discourse—as well as choices made to accentuate certain parts, eliminate others, and add new features—make essential shifts in the adapted project. Nevertheless, even after these changes, the final product does not ultimately present an entirely new plot, context, discourse, or characters—things that are eminent in re-accentuations. Instead, an adapted work concretizes ideas, simplifies selections but also amplifies them, and critiques or shows respect for an original project (3). In this manner, as long as the consumer is acquainted with its original, adaptation is a derivation, a second to a known work, a "palimpsestic thing" (9, 21). And so, on screen, an old adventurer knight errant named Don Quixote of La Mancha is an adaptation of Cervantes's character and not a new invention who resembles Don Quixote or reminds the viewer of him.

Re-accentuation—different from rewriting, parody, adaptation, and imitation—encapsulates the phenomenon in which well-known characteristics of an old artifact are highlighted in a new one in another context. In literature, as mentioned, this occurs when a character or a work is grounded in a previously known one, not necessarily parodying or imitating it. It is like giving new flesh to an old skeleton, where the old and the new entities function in dialogue. In Cervantes scholarship, re-accentuation may be used in reference to quixotic characters or works to account for specific attributes imitated from *Don Quixote*. Quixotic characters and re-accentuated Quixotes, nevertheless, may also bear slight differences.

Works and characters that are grounded in *Don Quixote* and its eponymous hero are often referred to as *quixotic*. According to Mancing, quixotic novels are the ones "grounded directly or indirectly, consciously or unconsciously, in *Don Quixote*" ("Don Quixote" 412).[13] A quixotic novel "most typically is one that involves a character who has some of those qualities we associate with Don Quixote and/or displays an innovative, postmodern, narrative self-awareness that places a work in juxtaposition to Cervantes" (397). Garrido Ardila gives a list of characteristics that make a novel quixotic, several of them being: 1) an incorporation of a quixotic protagonist, 2) imitation of characters, especially of Don Quixote and Sancho Panza, 3) comical irony, 4) parodic and satiric character, 5) narrative techniques, among others (*Cervantes* 55). To reiterate the definitions of quixotic provided by Mancing and Garrido Ardila, a character or a novel that resembles Cervantes's Don Quixote or the eponymous novel in a single or a myriad of ways may be viewed as quixotic.

In literature, occurrences of quixotic characters and novels abound. A versatile and complicated characterization, quixotic originates with Cervantes's creation, referring to one or several traits that make up the personage of Don Quixote or the novel. Various literary works and characters have been donned the label quixotic, yet sometimes, this label does not connote the complex nature of Cervantes's design. Re-

---

13 Quixotic novels and quixotic characters may give birth to *quixotism*, which Wendy Matooka defines as "a parody of reason, satirizing rational authority as a political fiction only as rational as the authority of Don Quixote's lance" (2). And while the adjective *quixotic* characterizes any comportment of Cervantes's *Don Quixote*, *quixotism* is simply used to oppose the term *cervantism*. It takes away the authorial discourse and "gives preference to the hero rather than his creator" (Canavaggio 159; my translation).

ferring to literary personages, the term may be seen used loosely to describe someone's irrational act rooted in idealism. At times, I find that some usages of quixotic diminish the complexity of Cervantes's character, alluding to a quality or behavior of the well-known hero without accounting for others that may be its opposite; and Don Quixote embodies a number of converse characteristics! Often, this adjective is understood in the context of one quixotic state, namely insanity, although it could just as easily assume the contrary meaning of sensibility. Quixotic can therefore be an ambiguous description that, in addition, may turn out to be problematic for denoting the qualities of idealism and irrationality alone (as defined by various dictionaries). Still, it is absolutely sensible to use the term quixotic to signal something or someone *like* Don Quixote or *from* the novel, but without further specification, the label may be interpreted in many possible ways.

And so, to be *like* Don Quixote can refer to a host of different behaviors, from the way he speaks to his demeanor, his zeal for adventures, his platonic love, his lifestyle, the books he reads, etc. But the current vocabulary that scholars use may still be limiting when it comes to fully grasping the intricacies of intertextual references. While many quixotic works or, as Santiago Alfonso López Navia calls them, recreations of *Don Quixote*,[14] have contributed to the significant advancement of comparative studies in the light of Cervantes's work, it is still worthwhile to consider further specifying what makes a work *like Don Quixote*, so as to clarify whether it is due to the parodic elements, characters imitating idols, or other functions. Thus, in character analysis, re-accentuation might prove a meaningful literary tool to elaborate the specific attributes that make a character quixotic, *like* Quixote. For example, if I found a statement like "Madame Bovary is a re-accentuation of Don Quixote," I would need a brief clarification, perhaps in the form of "because she is an avid reader similar to Cervantes's hero." To re-accentuate means to highlight an old aspect in a new entity, thus necessitating a specification of that old aspect. And

14 See López Navia's *Inspiración y pretexto II: Nuevos estudios sobre Cervantes, su obra y su recepción* (2021) for a rich commentary on quixotic recreations.

to repeat, in Cervantes-influenced literature, I consider characters who exhibit the traits of readers, dreamers, adventurers, or lovers as branded by Don Quixote to be re-accentuations of the Spanish knight errant.

Delving deeper into the world of Quixote-influenced personages, I have found that re-accentuated characters are quixotic, but not always the reverse. Given that re-accentuating Cervantes's hero means bringing forth some of his formative features in a new character, who thus bears an attribute *of* Don Quixote, the re-accentuated character can naturally be classified as quixotic. For example, in Mario Vargas Llosa's *The Bad Girl* (2006), Ricardo Somocurcio is a re-accentuated quixotic character, in that he resembles Don Quixote in his enthusiasm for reading, his dreamy persona, and his idealized love for Otilia—all manifested throughout his extensive travels through the Americas, Asia, and Europe. On the other hand, not all quixotic characters are re-accentuations of Don Quixote. Although we may encounter protagonists described as embarking on quixotic journeys or engaging in quixotic fights, it's important to recognize that these characters may not always directly reflect Cervantes's hero. Instead, they might embody an interpretation or perception of what it means to be like Quixote, which could sometimes stem from popularized or dictionary definition of quixotic.[15] For example, in Gail Honeyman's *Eleanor Oliphant is Completely Fine* (2018), the title character is presented as someone who lacks self-awareness and often finds herself in situations in which others judge her for her odd behavior. For her awkward personality, her lack of social savviness, and for cherishing an unattainable dream, (and based on a dictionary definition of the term) Eleanor may be seen as quixotic, but she is not a re-accentuation of Don Quixote.[16] Unlike

15 Note that the Merriam-Webster definition of *quixotic* is "foolishly impractical especially in the pursuit of ideals."

16 It is fitting to mention that Honeyman writes a humorous account to shed light on serious mental health issues, a lens through which various scholars have analyzed Cervantes's character as well. It is due to Eleanor's trauma that she acts a certain way (see Suzanne LaLonde's "Don Quixote's Quixotic Trauma Therapy" for a similar analysis). The parallels shared by these two novels invite intertextual analysis rather than re-accentuated char-

Cervantes's hero, Honeyman's protagonist exhibits a lack of interest in contributing to the common good (although she somewhat reluctantly helps two people and a cat in the novel). Moreover, she lacks the curiosity and imagination that are prominent traits of the Spanish hero.

To recapitulate the meaning and application of the Bakhtinian term in the context of Cervantes's work: re-accentuations of characters in *Don Quixote* occur when an author, producer, or artist identifies the most defining features of Cervantes's protagonists and crafts new personages who embody those traits. Through a reading of hundreds of Cervantes-inspired novels, I have found that re-accentuations of Don Quixote often showcase prominent traits of the Spanish knight errant, like those of a reader or an adventurer. Likewise, in other contexts, Sancho Panzas are loyal friends and employ a unique linguistic style (lavish usage of idiomatic expressions or misremembering and mishearing words). Re-accentuated Dulcineas are idealized, unreachable, and often muted. One may even come across new versions of Rocinantes, like the one in *Monsignor Quixote*, who are old and worn down. Most quixotic novels that present a re-accentuation of Don Quixote also include a Sancho-like companion and a love figure. The image of a re-accentuated Don Quixote, nonetheless, recurs more frequently than any other Cervantine character.

Literary personages who embody quixotic qualities usually undergo adventures as they strive to achieve dreams born due to voracious reading. They may also be enamored of unattainable or unsuitable beloveds, weaving a knotty love story. Let us now delve deeper into the significance of the mentioned quixotic features and explore how they manifest in various literary figures. In later chapters, I focus on separate quixotic traits and analyze characters embodying them in more detail.

---

acter analysis. Eleanor bears certain traits that would superficially be associated with Don Quixote (for example, her finding herself in awkward social circumstances), yet these traits would not be seen as a complex and defining feature of Cervantes's hero's life.

## Quixotic Readers

One of the most famous literary bibliophiles, Don Quixote, is known for his fervent perusal of numerous books, particularly chivalric romances. The trait of the reader in Cervantes's protagonist is not limited to the act of leafing through and delving into a fictional world for personal titillation; it also entails taking out what belongs to that fictional world and materializing it in reality.[17] Cervantes writes: "The truth is that when his mind was completely gone [as a consequence of reading too much], he had the strangest thought any lunatic in the world ever had," which is that of "righting all manner of wrongs and . . . winning eternal renown and everlasting fame" (21). The literary works that inspire Don Quixote turn into a lifestyle for him, as he endeavors to embody the personas and adventures of literary characters in the real world.[18] And so, Don Quixote decides to assume a selfhood of a knight errant and sets out to reenact heroic deeds germane to chivalric worlds.

Given that language, garments, and various other practices have gone through many changes since the age of chivalry, the old man's decision to embody any aspect of it in the seventeenth-century Spanish context appears foolish. His attire and demeanor underscore this anachronistic transformation: his rusty armor appears outdated and out of place, his bookish language sounds archaic and useless, and his chivalric pledges to his lady seem antiquated and bewildering to onlookers. While Don Quixote finds these styles appropriate for a knight errant, he neglects to consider the divide between the chivalric past and his contemporary society, which has long abandoned the trappings of the medieval lifestyle that he has donned. This discrepancy

17 Because of multiple examples of metafiction in this book, I refer to fiction as characters' reality and metafiction as their fictional world. (Don Quixote's efforts to embody medieval knights errant is his attempt to fictionalize his reality—the narrative setup of *Don Quixote*.) I do this in order to avoid overusing the word fiction and to simplify the discussion of multilayered contexts.

18 For instance, he grounds some of his choices of demeanor in one of his favorite chivalric romances, *Amadís de Gaula*. Believed to be first released in 1304, there are no surviving copies of *Amadís* until the year of 1508.

generates laughter, which may well serve as a warning that unrestricted reading can prove dangerous for certain booklovers.

Although Cervantes draws attention to how fiction "dried up" his character's brains "causing him to lose his mind" (21), it is still important to notice how reading has positively affected Don Quixote. Because of it, he has acquired unparalleled eloquence and intelligence mastering the archaic lexicon of books of chivalry. He uses erudite references in Latin and Italian. In addition, he is able to adjust (on occasion, and more so in the second part of the novel) his linguistic style based on the level of education of his interlocutors. The literary works that fill the shelves of Don Quixote's library, as seen in the episode of the burning of his books, attest that the self-proclaimed knight errant is not merely an amateur reader addicted to chivalric romances; the collection points to a versatile bookman, a learned *hidalgo* with a fine taste for contemporary and classic literature, as well as popular fiction of the time.

Re-accentuations of Don Quixote who embody the quixotic obsession with reading usually exhibit a diminished ability to differentiate between reality and fiction. Characters who portray a quixotic reader, usually accentuate the quixotic predilection for one literary genre or category. For example, Arabella, the protagonist of Charlotte Lennox's *The Female Quixote* (1752), becomes enthusiastic about perusing heroic romances. She begins to act like the characters she encounters in literary realms. Like Don Quixote, Arabella begins to see aspects of her own life through a lens provided in books, which is the reason society misunderstands and misinterprets her behavior. Other noteworthy novels with a re-accentuated reader protagonist include Gustave Flaubert's *Madame Bovary* and Jane Austen's *Northanger Abbey*. In these works, too, the heroines exhibit a powerful inclination toward reading. Similar to Arabella and their predecessor Don Quixote, they interpret reality according to fiction, thus jeopardizing their reputations, their social images, and, above all, their judgments.

## Quixotic Dreamers

The trait of the dreamer resides in the unrealistic and idealistic vision of Cervantes's hero (as a result of excessive reading), combined with his endeavor to make the world surrounding him a better place. Alonso Quijano, a simple *hidalgo* who has devoured all the literary fiction available to him, adopts a new identity and sets off on the roads of La Mancha with a goal to "right all manner of wrongs" (21). He espouses an image of a knight errant, appropriates the archaic style of his favorite characters from chivalric romances, chooses a lady worthy of his love, recruits a squire, and leaves home to fulfill his dreams. He often perceives himself and the surrounding world with exaggerated optimism, which in turn affects his ability to evaluate reasonably the consequences of his actions. Don Quixote consistently rejects what others might view as failure and persists in his belief that he can justly resolve the conflicts that he encounters.

Don Quixote's dream of righting wrongs and helping others is not merely a selfless goal inspired by literary examples; the knight errant expects praise and recognition for himself and for his lady Dulcinea. Although in the first part of the novel, Don Quixote is deprived of such acknowledgment (and some of his attempts to right wrongs might better be characterized as wronging rights), he eventually achieves recognition in the second part of the novel. Here, some of the characters are familiar with the said Don Quixote of La Mancha because they have either read or heard about the first part of the novel and his adventures. Still, Don Quixote's dream of righting all manner of wrongs and saving distressed damsels remains unrealized. It even proves to be self-destructive (given the instances in which the Spanish *hidalgo*'s dream causes physical pain and even mutilations, like losing half of his ear).[19] Nevertheless, the dreaming old man leaves a legacy both within the novel and beyond the limits of the text, thus achieving the "everlasting fame" he was so eagerly pursuing (21).

Re-accentuated quixotic dreamers encountered elsewhere in literature exhibit equally skewed perceptions of situations in which

19 Don Quixote's last combat with the Knight of the White Moon (who in disguise is Sansón Carrasco, previously seen under the mask of the Knight of the Mirrors) also contributes to the decline of his health, ultimately leading him to his deathbed. If Don Quixote's physical turmoil caused by his adventures were considered without accounting for his age, then it would be viable to claim that his feats led him to self-destruction.

they find themselves, as well as similar perseverance in achieving their goals. Like Don Quixote, these dreamer characters often fail to distinguish reality from illusions, and their inability to acknowledge the unreasonableness of their goals ultimately leads them to failure. Some literary examples of re-accentuated dreamers include Captain Ahab from Herman Melville's *Moby Dick* (1851), Jay Gatsby from F. Scott Fitzgerald's *The Great Gatsby* (1925), and Daniel Quinn from Paul Auster's *City of Glass* (1985). The central characters of these novels develop dreams that later mutate into obsessive goals. Ahab searches for a white whale called Moby Dick in order to take revenge for his lost limb; Gatsby spares no effort to reunite with his beloved Daisy; and Quinn is determined to solve a family mystery and protect Stillman Jr. from Stillman Sr. Despite these characters' almost deranged exertions, their respective quests fail, and their dreams remain unrealized. Ahab's encounter with Moby Dick takes a deadly turn, as the whale attacks and destroys the captain's ship leaving only one member of the crew alive; the day Jay Gatsby anticipates a new beginning with Daisy comes to a close with his murder; and Quinn believes he has finally identified the place where Stillman Jr. has been taking refuge, only to find an empty apartment. As in *Don Quixote*, the moment the protagonists of these novels feel they finally have come close to realizing their dreams, the narratives twist in a sudden *peripeteia*, and the novels end in a minor key; Don Quixote renounces his identity as a knight errant in his deathbed, Ahab and Gatsby are killed, and Quinn simply vanishes from the novel.

### Quixotic Adventurers

The trait of the adventurer is perhaps the strongest and the most recognizable characteristic of the Spanish knight errant. Don Quixote, after having read an excessive number of books, has set for himself the goal of wandering through the world and rectifying all situations gone wrong. Because of his dimmed perception of reality, he labels most everything that he comes across as adventure. Largely impartial in choosing adventures in which to engage and volunteering himself in most situations, the knight errant is rather unsuccessful in these quests. Episodes such as the combat with the windmills/giants and the finding of his *baciyelmo*, among others, demonstrate that Don Quixote's understanding of an adventure may be limited to fighting (both literally and metaphorically) for personal and common good. It also seems as though Don Quixote is experimenting with what can be possible in his world. These experiments, in turn, invite the readers to explore the liminal spaces between reality and imagination, madness and sanity, roles and identities.

Because the adventures of the Spanish *hidalgo* are inspired by his literary models, who roam the roads and chance upon situations in need of the aid of a strong and benevolent nobleman, Don Quixote assimilates himself to the *modus operandi* of the chivalric order, thus alienating himself from the norms adopted by his contemporary society. This alienation, at first, triggers the act of *othering* of the knight errant from his contemporaries—his adventures at times resulting in verbal or physical contests between him and others. While Don Quixote may appear oblivious to the physical and mental disparities and perseveres in his search for adventures to fulfil his dream of aiding those in need, his quests often take an ironic turn as others attempt to rescue him from his "woe from wit" (to borrow Alexander Griboyedov's play title for this context). In order to restrain Don Quixote from engaging in dangerous adventures, characters like the priest, barber, housekeeper and niece, devise escapades for him to embark on, which deter him from the ones he would seek out (i.e., the encounter with Princess Micomicona). Through ploys of this kind, the friends intend to save Don Quixote from his own imagination and bring him back to his home. On the other hand, and more so in the second part of the novel, characters who have read or heard about Don Quixote's quests create situations in which he can engage in adventures and showcase his imagination and wit. (The Spanish *hidalgo*'s stay with the Duke and Duchess, for example, results in such adventures for him.) Most characters seem to embrace the spirit of adventure in Don Quixote, be it in a mocking, empathetic, or genuine way. The characters who devise adventures for Cervantes's hero, plan their steps to convince him of the spontaneity and reliability of the gimmicks that they carefully put together. But because of the impertinence of Don Quixote's image in various contexts, the plans devised for him are either for their entertainment or to bring him back to his home.

Various authors who have re-accentuated Don Quixote have captured and recapitulated one of the core definitions of the Spanish hero's life: his adventures. In such characters, the adventurer's trait is usually insatiable, voracious, experimental, and most of the times driven by an overambitious dream. Because finding adventure generally signifies being outside of domestic confines, in most literary works, such quests are defined by extensive travels.[20] Many re-accentuated adventurers, thus, are travelers like Don Quixote and are usually consumed by a dream they want to realize. Works like *The Adventures of Tom Sawyer* (1876) and *The Adventures of Huckleberry Finn* (1884) by Mark Twain, *The Savage Detectives* (1998) by Roberto Bolaño, as well as *The Heroic Adventures of Donny Coyote* (2003) by Ken Mitchell are comprised of exploratory voyages. The heroes of these novels brilliantly re-accentuate the image of Don Quixote-the-adventurer as they travel extensively, stumbling upon various emprises along the way. While the adventures undergone by Twain's characters may not be defined by one single dream, Mitchell's and Bolaño's characters are on voracious searches for their singular ideals, searches that carry them through their respective countries and even across their borders to fulfill their goals.

## Quixotic Lovers

The trait of lover is one of Don Quixote's most versatile feature, encompassing romanticization, obsession, and obliviousness, as well as

20 It is fitting to mention here that not all quixotic adventurers weave a story of a hero's journey, as branded by Joseph Campbell. The hero's journeys include a departure from home (seen in quixotic adventurers), a material reward (which is not always the case for quixotic adventurers), power and powerfulness (which does not define all quixotic adventurers), and a triumphant return home (not always outlined in quixotic adventure narratives). Also, while many adventurers perform heroic deeds in their contexts, they do not necessarily rise to the stature to be referred to as heroes.

loyalty and commitment to an ideal.[21] The Spanish *hidalgo*, having decided to become a knight errant, immediately and actively begins his transformation: "Having cleaned his armor and made a full helmet out of a simple headpiece, and having given a name to his horse and decided one for himself, he realized that the only thing left for him to do was to find a lady to love" (Cervantes 23). Aldonza Lorenzo, whom he names Dulcinea del Toboso, seems to Don Quixote a fitting choice. Without confessing his refound infatuation to the lady of his dreams,[22] our hero resolves to devote his allegiance to Dulcinea, albeit unreciprocated. Dulcinea's imaginary presence in the old *hidalgo*'s life thus plays a crucial role in his successful embodiment of a knight errant. Don Quixote's lover-like trait develops into idealized yet platonic feelings towards Dulcinea, a type of sentiment that resembles those highlighted in medieval and chivalric romances. Although Don Quixote never once encounters his sweetheart in the novel, he remains devoted to her—better said, the idea of her—until the end. Dulcinea's image serves Cervantes's hero as his muse (like in the episode with the Basque merchants), a guardian angel, and in some ways, even God (as when Don Quixote evokes Dulcinea before an adventure). The knight of La Mancha adulates his beloved in so many ways that he eventually becomes obsessed with the creation of his own imagination—a certain depiction of literary pygmalionism that proves damaging not only to the prized creation, but to the creator as well.

Don Quixote's urgency to find a person to whom he can pledge loyalty and affection initiates a problematic love journey. What Dulcinea represents for Don Quixote is not what her enigmatic presence in the novel signifies. First, the princess Dulcinea is a peasant woman named Aldonza Lorenzo, whom Sancho and his master remember in

---

21 See Carroll B. Johnson's *Madness and Lust: A Psychological Approach to Don Quixote* (1983) for a strikingly different point of view on Don Quixote's love life.

22 Cervantes mentions that Don Quixote was previously in love with Dulcinea: "It is believed that in a nearby village there was a very attractive peasant girl with whom he had once been in love, although she, apparently, never knew or noticed" (23).

very distinct manners.[23] The uncertainty about Aldonza Lorenzo's true identity brings into question the veracity of the descriptions of her and raises speculation as to whether Don Quixote's choice of a lady to enshrine was arbitrary. What is also peculiar about the lover trait in Don Quixote is that his romantic feelings conceal self-serving motives, as the knight fails to acknowledge that love is a dialogic phenomenon that can be sensitive and conditional. The old *hidalgo*'s pledge to Dulcinea for the purposes of maintaining a viable image as a knight errant without contemplating the possible effects of potential [non]reciprocity of fondness by his sweetheart illustrates the flawed essence of the monologic attachment—fondness that characterizes quixotic love.

Most re-accentuated lovers exhibit the quixotic definition of the sentiment: obsessive, ideal, and illusionary. At first, their infatuation may come across as a personal interest and affection. However, characters exhibiting quixotic love or love-like emotions can develop their admiration into something that dwells on the extreme ends of feelings toward someone, like mania, lust, and overprotectiveness. Leo Tolstoy's *Anna Karenina* (1877), Vladimir Nabokov's *Lolita* (1955), and Vargas Llosa's *The Bad Girl* (2006) are examples of novels that present re-accentuated quixotic lovers. The enamored characters of these novels recapitulate the quixotic single-minded pursuit of their ideals and the single-sided perception of their romantic lives. Each of the characters of the mentioned novels expresses their fondness in a distinct manner; Anna Karenina's love may mostly be defined by passion, while Vargas Llosa's Ricardo Somocurcio may be perceived as naive and obsessive. Nabokov's Humbert Humbert is one of the most controversial lovers in literature, given the immoral implications of his lust and the psychological harm he causes to the one he claims to love. The antagonist's feelings take notorious forms of affection—obsessiveness, overprotectiveness, and possessiveness—all expressed through erroneous and neglectful convictions about his beloved. The amorous characters of the aforementioned novels illustrate that monologic or self-serving

23 Note how Don Quixote's numerous praises of the "incomparable Dulcinea" are contrasted by the descriptions of Sancho: "I can say that she can throw a metal bar just as well as the brawniest lad in the village" (Cervantes 255; 199).

interests toward an idealized partner takes love's most extreme form: obsession, which threatens to destroy the lover's and beloved's mental or emotional well-being. Re-accentuated romantics, thus, do not necessarily have to demonstrate pure and platonic sentiments toward an ideal. They may express different forms of love that question the overdramatization of this very term, as they explore the dysfunctional extents of both selfless devotion and selfish needs for affection.

## Conclusion

Reading Cervantes's *Don Quixote* through a comparative lens allows us to see some aspects of the knight errant that have captured the attention of writers and creators for centuries. With many works being branded as quixotic literature or quixotic works, it is becoming more and more imperative to define what exactly this sort of production comprises and what it is that groups diverse literary and artistic works into such category. Looking into novels that have traditionally been called quixotic, as well as identifying others that resemble Cervantes's hero in various ways, I have noticed that, at a character level, certain individualities of Don Quixote keep resurfacing and continue being emphasized in different contexts. Analyzing these similarities can inform us of new ways of interpreting Cervantes's novel and the eponymous protagonist. In addition, clarifying what relates *Don Quixote* to succeeding works that imitate, parody, re-accentuate, or adapt aspects of the novel can help us further analyze Cervantes's masterpiece as part of a connected network of the literary world.

We come across quixotic readers, dreamers, adventurers, or lovers in literature (and in our lives) virtually every day, and we are constantly reminded of the prevalence of *Don Quixote* in various aspects of our lives even after more than four hundred years since the novel's publication. With almost every rising quixotic novel, film, or any form of art, the image of Don Quixote becomes more and more popularized in Spain and beyond. Don Quixote is like Homer's No-man (222-24).

He can stand at his tower of faces, don the mask of a chosen character, and be reborn in any context.[24]

As versions of new Quixotes keep reappearing in literary and other realms, Bakhtin provides us with an important tool that allows us to define certain quixotic appearances in literature. Thanks to the Bakhtinian notion of re-accentuation, we can refocus on Cervantes's creation, bring the spotlight to the origins of the novel, and to quote Bakhtin again, collectively celebrate Don Quixote's "homecoming festivals" every time we see the character reborn in another context.[25] Let us now examine what re-accentuations of quixotic readers, dreamers, adventurers, and lovers communicate within literary works published in the past few centuries and how re-accentuating Cervantes's masterpiece and characters has shaped the novelistic genre as we know it.

---

24 Compare this image to the Faceless Man in *Game of Thrones* (2011-2018).

25 See note 7 of Introduction for the Bakhtinian definition of homecoming festivals.

# 2
# Readers

THE TRAIT OF A reader is a hallmark of Don Quixote. The Spanish knight errant is known for his passion for chivalric romances and his extensive library, reflecting his deep immersion in the world of literature. While he dutifully tries to adhere to the codes of conduct depicted in fictional realms, often earning him the label of a madman, he also develops a profound understanding of philosophy, religion, Latin, and more through reading. This pursuit of knowledge of the fictional and erudite worlds enriches his intellectual breadth and depth, shaping him into a character of remarkable complexity and insight. Re-accentuations of the reader's trait of Don Quixote usually appear in many contexts. They can be manifested in postmodern or romance fiction,[1] found in readers who are young girls and those who are queer middle-aged men; they can appear in varied locations such as Mexico or China and can reflect societies of the seventeenth century

1 It is fitting here to make a distinction between romance as a pre-novelistic genre and fiction of romance. I follow Bakhtin's descriptions of romance and novel laid out in *The Dialogic Imagination*—the comprehensive novelistic genre being formed by *Don Quixote* in imitation of chivalric, pastoral, picaresque, and sentimental romances. Fiction of romance (such as the quixotic romance novel discussed in this chapter, *The Female Quixote*) is a subgenre within the novelistic genre; it is that which, to overly simplify, recounts the romantic adventures and encounters of its heroes and heroines. So, again, *romance* here is a pre-novelistic genre; *romance fiction* is fiction containing a romantic plot.

or our world today.[2] The re-accentuated quixotic reader does not only read a lot; he or she also takes that "ephemeral existence" experienced in the moments spent reading and makes it a permanent part of his or her life (Doubinsky 95). Reading, as modeled by Don Quixote, is not mere literacy; it is a lifestyle, a zeal for change, an imitation, and, sometimes, a form of escapism. Quixotic readers peruse what is available to them, develop specific predilections for certain genres, and live by the ideals set in fiction.

Fictional bibliophiles were rare in literature before *Don Quixote.* With his predilection toward chivalric romances and his bookish acts, Cervantes's groundbreaking character sets a precedent for the many later literary characters who enjoy reading, thus also shaping the metafictional form of literature.[3] Don Quixote's approach and response to literature precedes many literary theories that would emerge centuries after the knight sat in his oil lamp-lit room to consume the literature available to him.[4] It is possible that Don Quixote and re-accentuated readers created in his image planted the seeds for reader-response criticism. The Spanish knight stands out as perhaps the first literary figure known for avidly delving into chivalric romances and interpreting their content with such deep admiration that these books spark within him a desire to imitate their heroes of romanticized realms. The

2 References to works such as Paul Auster's *City of Glass* (1985), Charlotte Lennox's *The Female Quixote* (1752), Roald Dahl's *Matilda* (1988), Andrew Sean Greer's *Less* (2017), José Joaquín Fernandez de Lizardi's *La Quijotita y su prima* (1818), Dai Sijie's *Balzac and the Little Chinese Seamstress* (2000), respectively.

3 Though Don Quixote is not the first fictional character who engages with literature, nor is he the only reader in Cervantes's novel (consider the priest, Sansón Carrasco, the Duke and Duchess, etc.), the nature of his reading is distinct. Don Quixote's interaction with literature is transformative: he reads, finds inspiration, begins to dream, feels compelled to enact the tales he consumes, and ultimately seeks to improve his surroundings by embodying the ideals he encounters in books. In doing so, he embraces a bookish lifestyle that reshapes his entire identity. Quixotic readers often mirror this trajectory, adopting a similar pattern of engagement with literature.

4 See Garrido Ardila's "Cervantes y la novela moderna" for a commentary on Cervantes, the evolution of the novel, and literary criticism.

act of reading, especially subjective reading as depicted by Don Quixote, plays a significant role in the novelistic genre, following the model set forth by Cervantes's "literary man" (Bakhtin, *Dialogic* 413). The trend of literary readers has become so pervasive that when perusing recently published novels, encountering at least one fictional character engrossed in reading is almost expected.

Reading and the response of the reader to the text can bear various interpretations in different contexts. More specifically, artistic (created by the author) and esthetic (realization carried out by the reader) interpretations of texts are manifested in different forms based on the socio-cultural context the readers represent.[5] For example, gendered reading and gendered quixotic reading immediately assume a commentary on social norms, gender equality issues, and gendered consequences for the reader. Academic and intellectual reading allow for a glimpse into the intellectual and theoretical trends of a given place and time. And of course, any bookish predilection offers a distinctive understanding of a reading character, since giving preference to a certain genre often reflects personal hobbies, background in education, emotional needs that almost always conform to the social standards of the time and the place where reading occurs. In Don Quixote's case, he prefers books about chivalry, a genre that has seen its golden age and has declined in popularity by the time the old *hidalgo* sits down to sample *Amadís de Gaula.* Yet the fading popularity of this genre does not seem to pose an issue for Don Quixote, as he becomes carried away by the chivalric values penned in fiction and deems it necessary to revive chivalry by reenacting what he reads. But his new identity causes a "literary otherness" among other characters (López Navia 37; my translation). Don Quixote fails to recognize fiction as "a relation, a form of engagement" that changes over time (Dimock 1062). His chivalric reenactments, of course, are not always true to the fictional presentations he has read. Two reasons for his fallacious reenactments are easy to observe. First, Don Quixote does not live in a fictional world designed in a chivalric context; he is not Amadís, nor is he Galaor or

5 See Wolfgang Iser's "The Reading Process: A Phenomenological Approach" for more on artistic and esthetic responses to texts.

Belianís.[6] And second, Don Quixote's socio-cultural context has long transcended medieval trappings and chivalric norms to be bothered by what Amadíses and Galaors have to offer (if only in fiction). Iser beautifully defines literature and the act of reading as follows: "Literature simulates life, not in order to portray it, but in order to allow the reader to share in it. He can step out of his own world and enter another, where he can experience extremes of pleasures and pain without being involved in any consequences whatsoever" (*Prospecting* 29). Yet, Don Quixote and subsequent quixotic readers defy the conventional approach of passive reading; instead, they carry out active reading and act out the reading based on their idiosyncratic interpretations of the text, thus inflicting upon themselves whatever consequences this active reading may bring.

Don Quixote breaks various social norms as a consequence of reading. He is considerably old, and the societal conventions of his time would typically prescribe that he remain at home, perhaps attending to his land. Yet the old man merges past and future, befriending thinkers and storytellers of yesteryears and dreaming up prospects based on his reading. Education, books, reading, and knowledge of literature were not so widespread in the Spanish society of Don Quixote's time; thus, an erudite elderly bibliophile *hidalgo* was a rarity in and around La Mancha. (Sancho Panza's character would be a more typical representation of an early seventeenth-century villager.) But reading seems to rejuvenate Don Quixote; it invites him to dream, to yearn for adventure, and it awakens in him the desire to idolize a lover. Passion for reading is a trait that changes Don Quixote: it makes him an unusual character for his time and incites in him the noteworthy traits of a dreamer, adventurer, and lover.

Re-accentuations of Don Quixote who represent the trait of a reader are usually seen as somewhat peculiar, as well. Women booklovers are seen as especially peculiar, because until recently, women who were avid readers were disapproved of in their respective patri-

6 Galaor was Amadís's brother and Belianís is the protagonist of Jerónimo Fernández's novel *Belianís de Grecia* (1545)—all referenced by Don Quixote as bearers of various chivalric values.

archal societies, and in some, they still are.[7] Women readers were already seen as estranged from their roles; acting based on the bookish norms of the literature they consumed would put them at risk of complete alienation from the society. A woman reading fiction would be recognized as someone sinful allowing the profane world to corrupt her mind.[8] Again, fiction was considered to be alluring for women estranging them from their domestic and societal duties. Iser explains this concept in his reader-response theories, noting that "In the act of reading, having to think something that we have not yet experienced does not mean only being in a position to conceive or even understand it; it also means that such acts of conception are possible and successful to the degree that they lead to something being formulated in us" ("The Reading" 67). The male-controlled fear was that women who read fiction would develop curiosity and pursue knowledge, thus endangering the stability of the social patriarchy. The consequences of women having unsupervised access to literature are well depicted in the novelistic genre, from young readers like Matilda to teenagers like the Little Seamstress to young adults like Caroline to adults like Emma—characters who challenge the constructs of patriarchy and exemplify lives of women bibliophiles.[9] Let us delve into the worlds of several women readers who neatly represent re-accentuated quixotic readers.

7 There are numerous examples of women readers in literature before and after *Don Quixote,* although not all of them can be classified as quixotic readers. Oftentimes, early modern women readers have been depicted as members of a literate group of the society, but also as ones who should be or are limited to reading only a certain type of literature. For more on women readers (not quixotic), see, for example, Lombardi and Triplette. For more on women's literacy and readership in Cervantes, see Vollendorf and Bernández Rodal.

8 While it was generally acceptable for women in the Early Modern era to read texts oriented toward spiritual and moral growth, reading entertainment-oriented genres was believed to encourage "idleness and vice" in women (Triplette 135).

9 The mentioned characters appear in the following novels: Roald Dahl's *Matilda*, Dai Sijie's *Balzac and the Little Chinese Seamstress*, Jane Austen's *Northanger Abbey*, and Gustave Flaubert's *Madame Bovary*.

## When Women Read

Numerous quixotic works featuring women readers have garnered both widespread recognition and critique. Among such novels are *The Female Quixote* by Charlotte Lennox, *Northanger Abbey* by Jane Austen, and *Madame Bovary* by Gustave Flaubert. I consider this selection of novels for examination in this chapter as apt due to their enduring popularity among readers and scholars. These classics have been extensively analyzed, and while much of the discussion in this section builds upon existing scholarship, the novelty lies in the perspective from which they are approached. Rather than offering entirely new interpretations, my forthcoming analysis aims to offer a fresh angle by examining these novels through the lens of Bakhtinian re-accentuation. By viewing the protagonists as re-accentuated readers within broader quixotic contexts, we can gain more insight into the characters and themes of these narratives.

Lennox, Austen, and Flaubert show the profound influence of Cervantes and depict a re-accentuated quixotic protagonist in their novels. To recapitulate what was stated in the previous chapter, novels can be quixotic if 1) the protagonist is identified as a kind of Don Quixote, 2) the protagonist is explicitly based on or inspired by *Don Quixote*, 3) the protagonist duplicates Don Quixote's basic premise of a fantasy or alternative reality inspired by books, or 4) the protagonist is dissatisfied with his or her life and circumstances and attempts to change them in some way (Mancing, "Don Quixote" 413-14). Re-accentuation, in turn, assumes that salient quixotic traits are embodied by characters at least to some degree: the protagonist may be presented as a reader, a dreamer, an adventurer, or a lover. The three novels that I will examine in this section are quixotic and their protagonists are re-accentuated Quixotes. *The Female Quixote* introduces Arabella, a fan of heroic romances who pretends to be a heroine out of such books. However, as a woman in her historical and social context, she is destined to face reality and enter into marriage. The same fate awaits Catherine, the protagonist of *Northanger Abbey*. Flaubert's protagonist has no other choice but to take her own life, as her illusions and mistakes, stemming from uncritical reading, have led to financial and emotional devastation. Lennox's, Austen's, and Flaubert's re-accentuated characters, like their predecessor Don Quixote, have consumed what turns out to be damaging to them, and their authors seem to imply that their reading habits resemble a malady requiring a remedy. As Patrick Brantlinger notes, the act of reading—a sort of Socratic *pharmakon*, medicine and poison at the same time—needs to be treated in these and other women readers (8-9). While the effects of reading can be unprecedented, treating this obsession usually takes the form of marriage, marriageability, or an adaptation to a familial life; and if there is no treatment, like in *Madame Bovary*, the damage to self becomes final. It seems, thus, that Lennox, Austen, and Flaubert create their protagonists in the image of the Spanish bibliophile to warn against quixotic reading—that, which influences minds and makes readers see fiction as a possible reality.

## Romance and Madness

*The Female Quixote; or, The Adventures of Arabella* is one of the first attempts to re-accentuate and feminize Cervantes's protagonist Don Quixote in an English novel.[10] Influenced by Cervantes's novel and early quixotic works such as the French *Mock-Clelia, or Madam Quixote* (1670) by Adrien Thomas Perdou de Subligny (translated into English in 1678), Lennox builds a world of parody and satire with a protagonist striving to imitate heroines of romance. Amelia Dale sees Lennox's work as a construct of simultaneous "gendering and universalizing of quixotism" (24). Susan Staves considers Lennox's *The Female Quixote* a quixotic novel that intends to incorporate humor, satire, and the burlesque, following the example of Cervantes (204). And following the example of Cervantes, Lennox does more than present mere satire or parody of the French heroic romances. Various scholars of English literature, Laurie Langbauer among them, have referred to *The*

10 Note that in England, the first references to and imitations of Cervantes appeared earlier on in the dramatic genre. Such works as Francis Beaumont's *The Knight of the Burning Pestle* (1607), Benjamin Jonson's *The Alchemist* (1610), and William Shakespeare's *Cardenno* (1612; now lost), are among the first ones to show the influence of Cervantes. For a more comprehensive list, see Dale Randall and Jackson Boswell's *Cervantes in Seventeenth-Century England* (2009).

*Female Quixote* as a revision or a representation of a romance (Langbauer, "Romance" 514). Others believe that Cervantes's influence on Lennox played an instrumental role in popularizing quixotic themes in eighteenth-century British literature.[11] But above all the thematic influences that Lennox presents in her novel, her protagonist Arabella stands as a re-accentuation of Don Quixote in the way she recapitulates quixotic traits, especially that of a reader.

Like her predecessor Don Quixote, Arabella is greatly inspired by the books she reads. She speaks and acts as if she were living in a fictional world described in a heroic romance. Neither Don Quixote nor Arabella lead a lifestyle deriving solely from the rules set by their literary predecessors; according to Amy Pawl, "they expect to be immortalized among them" (168). Don Quixote's wish to win "eternal renown and everlasting fame" by the righteous deeds he sets off to accomplish is parallel to Arabella's conviction that her history "will be written after [her] death" (Cervantes 21; Lennox 110). Neither of them sees the point of literature as passive personal enjoyment. Rather, they expect literary revivals, homecoming festivals.

Unveiling the story of a young daughter of marquis who enjoys perusing French heroic romances, Lennox's novel, again, demonstrates Cervantes's significant influence. As Langbauer notes, "*The Female Quixote* both mocks and lauds the heroine's quixotism, and the way it ridicules romance actually exposes the attractions of what that form represents" ("Diverting" 65), which imitates the presentation of Don Quixote and his obsession with chivalric romances. Of course, there is a key difference between readers of different genders and consequent quixotism because of the common belief of the time that if women read for pleasure they will become estranged from their social roles. Arabella is a mock example of such estrangement, typifying romance reading that, as Scott Paul Gordon notes, "leads young women to fail (if not resist) the expected practices of courtship and marriage" (38). Like Don Quixote, Arabella interprets other people and her surroundings according to her imagination inspired by romances. She appro-

11 See Staves.

priates the image of the heroines of the books she enjoys reading—a threat to her marriageability.[12]

Arabella posesses both exquisite intelligence and charm, yet her manner of presenting herself in society often leads to moments of awkward confusion. She frequently references heroic romances, their characters, and passages, which causes her to often be misunderstood. Her cousin Mr. Glanville, who is in love with Arabella, repeatedly fails to capture her heart due to his inability to meet her bookish expectations. As Lennox observes, he falters in entertaining her with matters of gallantry, leaving "so poor a figure" in her eyes (30). But Arabella's nonconformist eccentricities eventually lead to her "cure" from her fictional obsessions (368-82). Consequently, she willingly embraces the prospect of a comfortable married life with Mr. Glanville, relinquishing her literary allurements.

As in Cervantes, reading and the consequences of reading are central to the narrative throughout Lennox's novel. Don Quixote's brains are said to be "dried up" from so much reading (Cervantes 21); Arabella is seen as someone who "talks very oddly, and has the strangest Conceits!" due to her bookish interests (Lennox 64). Due to the perceived detrimental effects excessive reading inflicted upon the protagonists of Cervantes and Lennox, their books are deemed necessary for destruction: Don Quixote, who is seen as a victim of leisure reading, loses almost all of his library; Arabella's father, enraged by the rudeness she shows to her cousin Glanville, vows to "commit them [her books] all to the Flames" (55). Protagonists with similar fates, Don Quixote and Arabella resemble each other as avid readers, exaggerated dreamers, enthusiasts for new adventures, and inexperienced lovers. Both are believed to lose their sanity after reading a large number of books. Both begin leading a lifestyle trying to replicate episodes from literature they have read.[13] Both characters persevere in their illusory

12 The works she mentions most frequently are *Artamenes; or, The Grand Cyrus* (1653-1655), *Clelia* (1678) by Madeleine de Scudéry, and *Cassandra; the Fam'd Romance* (1652) by Gauthier de Costes de La Calprenède.

13 See Cristina Garrigós's "Las mujeres quijotes" where the author makes a statement that thinking of Arabella merely as a madwoman is as complex as considering Don Quixote simply a madman (460).

worlds, imitating concepts from their favorite books, and they both have a series of adventures throughout the respective novels. The two protagonists encounter unfriendly or mocking attitudes most of the time when they use their literary vocabulary or mention their heroes. Each of them also exhibits some contrasting behaviors that bring attention to the gender differences and the constructed societal confines that their gender inhabits. For example, Don Quixote sets out searching and initiating his adventures, while Arabella prefers to wait for an adventurous hero to come along.[14] Don Quixote praises the beauty of women, and Arabella expects men to praise her beauty.[15] Still, both protagonists come to grips with reality, accepting their identities with-

14 Deriving from the fact that the adventures of Arabella are mainly romantic, Langbauer claims that Lennox's intention was to show that a woman can only have sexual adventures. She claims that: "when Arabella *does* hear the adventures of other characters, as she does about Miss Groves from her maid and about people at the ball from Mr. Tinsel, what she hears is scandal. The sharp-eyed Miss Glanville points out that the madness romance has caused in Arabella is definitely sexual. Arabella's romantic behavior is a way of "exposing" herself, of displaying sexual signs. Miss Glanville's jealous solution is to keep Arabella not from romances but from men" ("Diverting" 79). But Arabella's motives do not really seem consciously self-exposing and sexual. In parallel with Don Quixote, Arabella's behavior is largely a consequence of consuming fiction, while she fails to realistically assess how her behavior can have potential to be misinterpreted. I see Lennox's portrayal of the heroine reader as an instance shedding light on the consequences women face when they deviate from conventional societal norms.

15 These emphasized differences also approximates Arabella's image to Don Quixote's Dulcinea. In fact, Ronald Paulson asserts that Lennox's intention is not to present a feminized version of Don Quixote, but to make Dulcinea the protagonist of her quixotic novel: "Lennox's radical departure is to have Dulcinea change places with Quixote and become the protagonist" (171). Arabella, therefore, "embodies the two Dulcineas—the ideal and, in the manner of the ideal travestied, the real" (171). It is true that Arabella can be seen as Dulcinea in her feminine image as she embodies a woman who waits to be courted by a virtuous gentleman. However, I am more inclined to believe that Lennox chose to portray a female Quixote from a woman's perspective, exploring the potential realities of quixotic reading as experienced by a woman in a patriarchal context.

in their social situatedness. Don Quixote reclaims his identity as an *hidalgo* named Alonso Quijano, and Arabella's doctor, who is familiar with her obsessions, brings her back to her senses. Both characters denounce books claiming that they can be damaging.

## Quixotic Readings of Gothic Fiction

"Oh, Mr. Tilney, how frightful!—This is just like a book!" exclaims Catherine Morland upon hearing Henry Tilney's descriptions of Northanger Abbey (Austen 162). Catherine imagines the Tilneys' family estate being an enigmatic space which holds the mystery tied to the death of Mrs. Tilney. Yet, it symbolizes what Catherine shows no interest in at the beginning of the novel—a domestic space charged with the gendered social norms of her time. And so, Jane Austen's protagonist, a reader of gothic fiction, becomes immersed in this world of domestic and social obligations while she persistently searches for gothic meanings. Catherine's reading of gothic fiction shapes her perception of the surrounding world, a world that keeps offering her domestic and social functions far separated from any gothic significance.

Jane Austen's *Northanger Abbey* reflects her deep inspiration of Cervantes and his influence on her work. Catherine, a seventeen-year-old woman, is a re-accentuated Don Quixote distinctly exhibiting the reader's trait. The quixotic heroine lives her life in a bookish world constructed through a reading of gothic fiction popular at the time, particularly *The Mysteries of Udolpho* (1794) by Ann Radcliffe. While characterizing the books she reads as "only a novel" (Austen 31), Catherine begins to perceive the people who surround her to be similar to the heroes of gothic fiction. Natalie Neill notes how Catherine also incorporates "idiomatic language of sensibility romance," which "not only parodies the emotive heroines of Gothic fiction" but also highlights the differences between their "fictional adventures and the more mundane kinds of 'adventures' a 'real' adolescent girl might expect to experience at the turn of the nineteenth century" (181-82). Ultimately, what Austen weaves through *Northanger Abbey* is a narrative in which female quixotism, influenced by gothic readings and combined with sensibility and impressionability as elements of gendered identities of the English society of the time, creates a world of adventure and romance that are accompanied by suspense and perturbations (Dale 52; Tandon 73-74).

Catherine sees reading as not only enjoyable, imaginative, and full of new discoveries, but also as an escapist activity that frees her from her gendered obligations and takes her into another realm. "'You have been abroad then?' said Henry, a little surprised. 'Oh! no, I only mean what I have read about. It always puts me in the mind of the country that Emily and her father travelled through, in the *Mysteries of Udolpho*'" (Austen 107). Her thoughts on reading and the works she reads are often shared with other characters in the novel for further commentary and analysis. For example, her friend Isabella is a character with whom Catherine shares many similar observations regarding the literature they consume. There is also John, Isabella's brother, who has diverging opinions about some of the books that Catherine reads. John's critique of reading and categorization of reading activities as intelligent or unintelligent, depending on the work, quite resemble the comments of the priest in *Don Quixote*, who, a reader himself, deems certain types of reading as more worthy than others. Note John's response to Catherine: "Novels are all so full of nonsense and stuff; there has not been a tolerably decent one come out since Tom Jones, except the Monk; I read that t'other day; but as for all the other they are stupidest things in creation" (43). Brantlinger reads this episode as meant to ridicule not Catherine but John, who is "so lacking in critical discrimination as to lump Fielding's realistic novel with Lewis's Gothic romance" (34). Indeed, John's comment may come across as uncritical and superficial, yet his [lack of] literary critique bears no visible effects on his perception of his surroundings. Conversely, the non-critical reading affects readers like Don Quixote and Catherine, who, engrossing themselves in the world of fiction, find it difficult to interpret their realities as separate from fiction.

As Catherine navigates the social circles of Bath, it becomes clear that her innocence, coupled with her bookish ideas and expectations, will hinder her reputation. She is expected to comply with the image of an already over-stigmatized ideal of an English woman, but that image is antagonistic to Catherine's character. Introducing her as an innocent adolescent with a "mind about as ignorant and uninformed as the female mind at seventeen usually is" (Austen 10), the writer brews a satiric and parodic story in which the girl's innocence trumps her intellect as she tries to make sense of books and real life.

The mix of parody and imitation of gothic fiction in *Northanger Abbey* highlights Austen's influence and masterful reading of Cervantes—a reading that in Alter's words is conscious of "a world at once marvelous and credible," but burdened or blessed with a character whose actions "bear within them the visible explosive freight of their own parodistic negation" (25). In Catherine's society and time, women of her age were expected to be more preoccupied with sustaining social norms and living idealized romantic encounters at balls. That she would rather read gothic fiction for entertainment does not only create a satiric image of a character so far from the norm, but also a parody of gothic genre which heavily influences Catherine's perception of the world. Like *Don Quixote*, *Northanger Abbey* stands as another example of a work written as a parody of another genre, in which characters imitate their heroes, create an unconscious parody, yet dwell in a world free of such imitative and parodistic habits. "A novel about novels, and novel reading" (Neill 163), *Northanger Abbey* parodies gothic fiction, yet pertains to the genre of romance fiction, following faithfully the traditions of the English novel of Austen's time. Susana Nicolás Román views the protagonist and her romantic illusions as an "assault on the romance" (160), but I see Austen's presentation of a protagonist lacking the basic traits of a romantic heroine as deliberate, calculated, and thoughtful. That initial perception of an anti-heroine of Austen's romance novel is what makes the protagonist even more quixotic.

In Chapter Ten of *Northanger Abbey*, Henry's confrontation with Catherine regarding her imagination marks a turning point: "The visions of romance were over. Catherine was completely awakened" (Austen 204). Like her predecessor Don Quixote, Catherine renounces her fanciful ideals and resolves to embrace a life more in accordance with the gender norms dictated by society. Whether Austen is criticizing the consequences of unguided reading or satirizing the perception of what reading for pleasure begets, she seems to imply that education—women's education above all—can prevent the overexaggerated literary influence on readers and challenge the views of moralists toward leisure reading. I agree with Hutcheon in that "in *Northanger Abbey*, Austen . . . succeeds in reinvesting the 'female gothic' with authority derived from the interaction of parody and satire: the true cause of women's confinement is shown not to be walls or financial dependency but miseducation" (*Parody* 79). I see Austen's novel as an attempt to shed light on the lack of appropriate resources to allow women to grow into their roles in society not simply as an asset to the patriarchy but as educated and knowledgeable people, aware of their realities and capable of enriching those realities by savvy reading. By re-accentuating Don Quixote's trait of a reader, Austen satirizes the image of a non-inquisitive reader, one who puts her reputation under scrutiny not just as a naive bibliophile but also as a woman reader. And while Austen might seem to scrutinize miseducated reading, Flaubert, another author heavily influenced by the image of the reader Quixote, suggests looking into domestic monotony as another problem causing quixotism.

## Don Quixote in Skirts

*Madame Bovary* is another classic literary work that presents a feminized re-accentuation of Don Quixote. The heroine of this novel resembles the Cervantine protagonist by spending her free time reading and imagining an ideal life based on the books she reads, a resemblance so obvious that José Ortega y Gasset calls her "a Don Quixote in skirts" (162). But Flaubert's character's life trajectory is quite different than that of other women Quixotes like Arabella and Catherine. Madame Bovary's idealistic endeavors drive her to self-destruction. While *The Female Quixote* and *Northanger Abbey* present a patriarchal world in which reading novels is dangerous for women, and in which successful are those who enter into marriage, *Madame Bovary* questions the role of a married woman at home as the protagonist alienates herself from all domestic responsibilities.

Emma Bovary is a desperate reader like Don Quixote, and like him, she thinks life should reflect what books describe. Interested in romantic novels, Emma resorts to reading as a way of escaping her monotonous domestic life and imagining what another life could look like. But Emma is not the only character in Flaubert's novel who reveals an interest in reading. As Soledad Fox observes, "In both works [*Don Quixote* and *Madame Bovary*], the social center is an inn —the *venta* of La Mancha, and the Lion d'or in Yonville L'Abbaye. Both are places of reunion, and in both inns, respectively, the figures of Don Quijote and Emma serve as catalysts for discussions of literature" (153). While inns serve as places that seem to welcome certain literary conversations, most other confined spaces are not the safest places for Madame Bovary and Don Quixote to effectuate their book-influenced ideas. Madame Bovary's reading-inspired lifestyle can come to life in her love affairs outside of her home. Her time spent at home with her husband is presented as mundane—devoid of the excitement she craves for herself. The juxtaposition of her life inside and outside of her house depicts two quixotic spaces; the inside restrains the adventurous spirit, yet the outside is full of adventurous offerings. For Don Quixote, peril exists at home, as his presumed image is under threat every time he returns. His home, for example, is the place where his books are burned. For Emma Bovary, also, home presents a menace to her idyllic life. Her mother-in-law (Madame Bovary senior) resembles Don Quixote's housekeeper. She claims that novels are evil, and that a woman should not spend any time reading fiction. She tells her son:

> "Do you know what your wife really needs?" resumed Madame Bovary senior. "What she needs is hard work, manual labour. If she was obliged to earn her living like so many have to do, she wouldn't suffer from these vapours, which come from all these ideas she fills her head with, and living such an idle life."
>
> "Still, she's always busy," replied Charles.
>
> "Huh! Busy! But doing what? Reading novels, wicked books, books against religion, full of speeches from Voltaire that make fun of priests. This is no laughing matter, my poor boy; someone who has no religion always comes to a bad end." (Flaubert 112)

Madame Bovary senior's criticism of books is not anecdotal; her contemporary society was fundamentally anti-literature, as was that of

Don Quixote (Fox 120). Whether at home or out among others, Quixote and Emma repeatedly face conflicts within their communities. The only difference in their actions is that Madame Bovary has to keep her adventures secret because she will be condemned for her actions, while Don Quixote is perceived a madman, who through ridicule and mocking continues his reading-influenced adventurous quest.[16]

Cervantes's and Flaubert's protagonists are misunderstood because of their book-inspired acts, which evoke certain aspects of satire in the image of uncritical readers. Both novels seem to go beyond the conventional critique of social hypocrisy by not just offering criticism, but also shaking these conventions. The way the reader-protagonists construe their realities suggests that there might be possible alternatives to their social standards. In this way, the authors also allow for various literary interpretations of their characters and their purpose. For example, Remi Clignet explains how *Madame Bovary* would be seen as immoral, reading it through the perspectives of the France of Napoleon III. But of course, a contemporary reader understands that Flaubert's work is more than a novel about a woman who persistently seeks love affairs. This protagonist is looking for "beauty out of place," as much as Don Quixote does (Blackmur 486). Madame Bovary represents a woman who is able to escape from domestic life through novel-reading and romantic affairs. As mentioned, home for both Quixote and Emma is a place where their real and ideal worlds collide, their minds are misread, and their lifestyle is influenced by others. On the other hand, the public space is where their illusions and fantasies have a promise to be fulfilled. Don Quixote yearns to be identical to Amadís de Gaula or Belianís de Grecia, and Emma Bovary impulsively turns to a fictional world that she creates for herself derived from her

16 Note that Cervantes's hero also undergoes a lot of pain because of his adventures. Max Ubelaker Andrade, in "*Don Quixote:* Pain, Space, and Artifice," goes through the performative context of *Don Quixote*, looking at the protagonist's adventures and their painful outcomes. While physical pain is a primary result of our male reader's bookish behavior, it is not the most experienced outcome of the adventures of Emma, Arabella, and Catherine. The three women experience less physical and more emotional pain, especially in the form of guilt and shame.

readings. Flaubert, like Cervantes, creates a protagonist in imitation of other fictional heroes to present the conflict between the two realities—novelistic and worldly. As Fox affirms:

> Even the character's names resound with the similarity of their authors' mission to amalgamate the unlikely; the prosaic and the poetic. *Emma*—a typical name for romantic heroines—loses all its romanticism when combined with *Bovary*, a name more suggestive of the earthy, vulgar word *bovine* than anything else. *Don Quijote de la* could be an auspicious name, as fitting for a chivalric knight as Emma is fitting for a sentimental damsel—until it is attached to *Mancha. Mancha* ("stain" in Spanish) deflates the name's (and the character's) pretensions. (100)

Both Cervantes and Flaubert seem to play simultaneously with such literary notions as parody, satire, and imitation, but their novels transcend the mere critical approaches that these notions may offer, as the authors experiment with a possible alternative through idealistic readers.

Similar to Don Quixote, Emma Bovary stands out for her sentimental chimera, while the society in which she struggles to exist has certain expectations of her. This makes Flaubert's text a story of a clash of universal values, as is *Don Quixote* (Johnson, *Don* 26). The clash, of course, is a consequence of literary imitation that is not validated in the context of Flaubert's character. And while in both *Don Quixote* and *Madame Bovary* the reader character is the one imitating models set by fiction, the writers of these novels achieve their goals by imitating other authors—classical or contemporary authors in both cases (Nadeau 30). Cervantes wrote *Don Quixote* as a parody of chivalric romances, just as Flaubert crafted his novel as a parody of sentimental fiction. Both novels successfully depict characters whose reading habits and attempts to reenact the books they read create a world where unquestioned and uncritical reading fosters an illusion that reality can be altered if individuals impose their bookish ideals upon it. Don Quixote's immersion in his reading and the enactment of his book-inspired ideals led to him being labeled a madman, whereas Emma met a tragic end due to her pursuit of her desires.

## RE-ACCENTUATED AND GENDERED READING IN PATRIARCHIES

The protagonists of *The Female Quixote*, *Northanger Abbey*, and *Madame Bovary* reveal quixotic characteristics and concepts, many grounded in the reader's trait of Don Quixote. Still, as various critics have commented, the significance of the novels in their relative cultures and particular historical and literary moments is much more than an embodiment of a Don Quixote in skirts.[17] Among other themes, the authors experimented with the concept of quixotism induced by reading and its impact on women readers. The results of these experiments are unsurprisingly predictable across all the contexts the novels represent, arising from uncritical reading and resulting in social estrangement.

Fox points out that "*Don Quixote* deliberately incorporates and plays with elements of both chivalric and picaresque traditions, and the literary and social circumstances of Cervantes's epoch are as present in his work as they are rejected and upbraided" (6). The rejection of these traditions results in a sort of satire. *The Female Quixote*, *Northanger Abbey*, and *Madame Bovary* also satirize certain literary genres, but according to Pawl, "each work rapidly reveals that it has an equal if not greater investment in satire, as the 'real' world of text is paraded before the reader and made to look petty, foolish, and even grotesque" (170). Arabella is a member of Gregorian era English society, well beyond the period when heroic romances were popular; in like manner, Catherine's gothic construction of reality does not correspond to the blooming social world of Bath, nor the domestic confines of Northanger Abbey. Lastly, it is Emma's romantic endeavors that estrange her from her family and all that domestic life can offer her. These discrepancies between what the characters' worlds actually *are* and what they wish they *could be* becomes a focal point in the three novels, satirizing the *could-be* image in a place where it simply *is not*.

17 See, for example, Staves, Neill, and Fox.

Fictitious depictions of what a woman's life could be were ever present in the books that the heroines of this chapter consumed. For example, *The Female Quixote* was published at the time when romance and romanticism prevailed in English literature. As Brean Hammond points out:

> Lennox's *The Female Quixote*, a work which Fielding himself praised as superior to *Don Quixote* in certain respects, offers the most fully developed representation of a key contemporary image: that of a young woman led astray by reading too many French romances. . . . For, by contrast to the situations that subsisted in early seventeenth-century Spain, in eighteenth-century Britain the reading of romances was identified almost entirely with women. Emulating Cervantes's tale of "the bad Effects of a whimsical study" (as [Lennox's] opening chapter heading puts it), *The Female Quixote* thus portrayed romance-reading as the modern woman's quixotism. (100)

That "modern woman's quixotism," as opposed to quixotism itself, brought in the concept of transcending various limitations imposed upon women by the domestic and the outside worlds. It was common for women to be restricted to the domestic and the private. But Arabella's quixotic imitation of mock heroines, just like the woman protagonists of Austen and Flaubert, is out in public, marking a clear distinction between private and public spaces (Boyd and Kvande 19). That very trend in romance reading instilled in Arabella a belief that, as a woman, she may as much belong in the public spaces as she does in the private.

Still, the patriarchal belief that women belong at home is prevalent in the works of Lennox, Austen, and Flaubert. In Catherine's case, her confinement to home life notably emphasizes that even in her gothic fantasies, all hidden messages are intricately intertwined with the domestic environment. As Paul Morrison points out:

> Catherine, of course, conceives of the carceral only the most highly "gothicized" sense: she is thus mortified when her search for evidence of the fate of Mrs. Tilney culminates in the discovery of

> the famous "inventory of linen," the most mundane and domestic of all possible "texts." Gilbert and Gubar, in a reading that is now largely canonical, suggest that Austen is pointing to the "real threat" to women's happiness when she describes her heroine finding the list. (12)

Austen adeptly explores the contrast between "threats to women's happiness" perceived in reading versus those in domestic life. Her reader protagonist, when confronted about her bookish illusions, ultimately feels ashamed of her imagination. Following her remorse, she is described as finding happiness in a newlywed life with Henry Tilney. According to Neill, the ending of *Northanger Abbey* is equivocal, because in addition to mocking the "formal didacticism of conventional endings of feminocentric Gothic fiction," it also parodies and challenges the typical endings of quixotic novels with a female character, like Lennox's novel (183). Neill sees Catherine's marriage to Henry as a reward for being "persuaded to change her course of reading" (183-84). Yet, the marriage is still a result of a woman persuaded or forced to leave her fantasies and tend to her wedded life, thus emulating the conventional endings of feminizied Quixote novels. What concerns Catherine's gothic illusions, it becomes clear that "this projection of a Gothic framework on to a situation in her life is no more than a temporary fantasy in the course of her assimilation of the new and unknown" (Howard 165). Catherine's fantasies due to her enraptured reading, like those of Arabella and Emma, generate some sort of quixotic escapism—a life imagined in a world that is not, an illusion that inevitably ends. Like Don Quixote, the re-accentuated readers create a story which springs thanks to reading but reaches its *peripeteia* framed by specific social demands. Thus, while these women readers' books indicate that a life outside of the domestic is a luring possibility, their realities remain confined within the norms of patriarchy.

## Conclusion

When quixotized and re-accentuated, women readers risk their social reputation, their present or future family life. (This is something that Don Quixote does not quite face given his gender.) Neill argues that

Lennox's, Austen's, and Flaubert's "equivocal treatment of the supposed dangers of novel reading serves to interrogate the logic of female improvement and reform that undergirds much female Quixote fiction" (164). By introducing new beliefs in already established ones, the perceived madness of Arabella, Catherine, and Emma, just like that of Don Quixote, can be seen as "the expression of all that is new, the future instead of the past, self-creation instead of determinism, liberation instead of conformism, a slap in the face of the established order, but also the source of inevitable conflicts" (Johnson, *Don* 11). These conflicts can be resolved in favor of or against the protagonists when the re-accentuated Quixotes identify as men, but in the case of the three women re-accentuated readers discussed here, this quixotic liberation is short-lived and what they read ends up being just as Catherine describes them: "only a novel." By re-accentuating the image of Don Quixote, the three authors discussed in this chapter suggest a new platform of possible socio-historical interpretations for contemporary readers. Even someone unfamiliar with the social and historical context of eighteenth- and nineteenth-century England and France can perceive the presence of issues concerning a male-dominated society. By creating an image of a re-accentuated quixotic reader, these authors contemplate on (mis)readings of fiction, gendered realities of a reader in a society that categorizes good and bad readings, and the consequences that (mis)readings can bear.

# 3
# Dreamers

The trait of a dreamer in Don Quixote speaks to the tenets of idealism and utopianism, promising to throw off the shackles of conventionalism. Cervantes challenges conservatism in myriad ways—from the image of his main character to the criticism of religious freedom (or lack thereof).[1] The hero that Cervantes creates offers almost nothing typical to his contemporary society: an old man of lance and shield here to rescue distressed damsels and bring chivalry back to life in a world that has long left the medieval trappings. Don Quixote's dream to change society challenges the conventional norms, creating a sense, even if illusory, that utopia is attainable.

José Antonio Maravall turns to Don Quixote's utopian quest in his *Utopia and Counterutopia in* Don Quixote (1976). His main argument is that while Don Quixote yearns for a more just society—a utopian quest—Cervantes dismantles all belief that his dream is achievable. Don Quixote embodies the dreamer of utopia and Cervantes the utopia cynic. Although some of Maravall's points have generated viable counterarguments,[2] there are many insightful analyses in his work,

---

1 See Carroll B. Johnson and Joe Brockmeier's "Ricote the *Morisco* and Capital Formation" for commentary on religious freedom in *Don Quixote.*

2 See, for example, Myriam Yvonne Jehenson and Peter N. Dunn's *The Utopian Nexus in Don Quixote* (2006), in which the authors argue that for Maravall, utopianism in *Don Quixote* seems to be perceived as fantasy, whereas it is multifaceted and can be seen as "the alternative world" (the authors cite Cioranescu), "cultural ideologies subject to criticism" (they mention Louis Marin), or even "carnival" (they follow Bakhtin's definition) (23-

one of them being his discussion on the juxtaposition of the character's utopia with the author's counterutopia—the promise of a hopeful vision followed by disillusion. In this realm of misguided thinking and ultimate self-deception, the image of the dreaming Don Quixote stands out prominently. Despite all indications that his dream is indeed impossible, the knight errant persists in his fantasies. Thus, the novel proposes two antagonistic slants—that of deceptive thinking, in which Don Quixote insists that his dreams are viable and carries on in pursuit of them, and that of ultimate deception embodied in Don Quixote's renunciation of knight errantry on his deathbed. Re-accentuations of the dreamer's trait are built upon this very conflict of pursuing the unattainable, built upon quixotism. This quixotism finely defines the Spanish Golden Age notion known as *engaño / desengaño* (illusion / disillusionment),[3] the *engaño* being Don Quixote's conviction that he can bring back chivalric values, and the *desengaño* lying in his defeat and renunciation of knight errantry. Whether approached through the lens of *engaño / desengaño*, Maravall's utopia / counterutopia, or another concept, the dreamer's trait in Cervantes's character and his re-accentuations invite for an analysis of the antagonistic values of a promise and the outcomes that it generates.

The quixotic trait of a dreamer stands out in a society in which people have succumbed to conventional norms. Re-accentuations of this trait presume an image of an outlier, a crusader of a sort, who fights for a personal cause driven by an ideal despite all the odds. Hanlon views these characters from the perspective of exceptionalism, claiming that "for the quixote, the exception is the example, and the example is the exception" (*World* 19).[4] In addition, being exemplary in early modern Spain comprised much of the didactical and political premises of

24). In response to Maravall's views, the authors claim that the novel does not present someone's "reformist principles" and is not simply "a satirical distortion of any plan by an *arbitrista*" (96).

3 For more on the concepts of illusion and disillusionment, see Sánchez Sarmiento and Presa Díaz.

4 Hanlon refers to characters who resemble Don Quixote as "the quixote."

the society,[5] and to lead by example in Golden Age communities presumed some sort of repute. As Maravall notes, "fame functioned as a factor in moral-social reform" and the idea of renown confected the "psychological conception of example" (83). Perhaps that is why Don Quixote's dream to bring chivalry back to life is accompanied by "winning eternal renown and everlasting fame."

Don Quixote and his re-accentuated counterparts exemplify their set ideals through leading by example. In other words, while they may recruit others in pursuit of their own dreams, it is they who take the lead in the quest for these dreams. For example, Don Quixote, who dreams of reestablishing the norms of chivalry, adopts an identity of a knight errant but cannot fulfill his dream without recruiting a squire, who will directly contribute to realizing his dream. Don Quixote's quest, of course, is also incomplete if he fails to procure a lance and a shield, name a woman worthy of his love, and lay hold of a noble horse before he sets out for adventures. Similarly, a re-accentuated quixotic dreamer—say, Captain Ahab from Melville's celebrated *Moby Dick* (1851)—cannot fulfill his dream of catching and killing the white whale unless he recruits a whaling crew, who, again, will directly contribute to realizing his dream. Don Quixote and re-accentuated dreamers might not operate alone and are not socially isolated in the quest for their ideals, yet they understand that the achievement of their goals will ultimately depend on their own actions. Hanlon refers to this sort of leadership as "quixotic exceptionalism," which is "founded on a sense of urgency not only to realize an ideal but also to understand oneself as the key to realizing that ideal, as the moral center of some type of reform" (*World* 28). To regard dreamers as leaders, thus, it is essential to recognize in them not only a fervent pursuit of seemingly unattainable goals but also an ability to act as guides, inviting others into their world of illusions.

Don Quixote dreams of bringing chivalry back to life; other characters who re-accentuate the dreamer's trait similarly and obsessively follow their cause. As mentioned, Captain Ahab is after the white

5 Literature reflects this pedagogical theory of leading by example as seen in, for example, the *exempla* (examples) of Don Juan Manuel's *Count Lucanor* written in 1335 and first printed in 1575.

whale named Moby Dick. Looking into other twentieth-century American novels we can find prominent examples of re-accentuated dreamers in Jay Gatsby, who pursues Daisy in hopes of reuniting with her; in the Buendías, who through generations are invested in decoding Melquíades's manuscripts; in Dr. Francia, whose dream is to be the most supreme ruler of all time; and in Daniel Quinn, obsessed with solving the case of the Stillmans.[6]

Re-accentuating the dreamer's trait, authors explore the impact of illusory thinking on goal-driven and determined characters. In the worlds of these characters, reality is deceptive and falsified (Martinez-Bonati 158). Don Quixote and quixotic dreamers themselves create fabricated worlds to justify their pursuit, often distorting reality, spellbound by their end goal. Misconstruing the possible consequences for their zealous quests, the dreamer characters, then, go through disillusionment. For example, Don Quixote renounces knight errantry after his defeat and physical decline. With Don Quixote's transition from a knight errant back to a simple *hidalgo*, Cervantes constructs a "utopian world resting on the transformative willpower of his protagonist," then, twists this world and "looks at his creation through the prism of irony, and makes it the opposite of what it might have been. He makes it, in a word, a counterutopia" (Maravall 180). The dreams of Don Quixote remain unattained, yet the knight errant comes tantalizingly close to fulfilling major parts of what he sets out to accomplish. Similarly, other quixotic dreamers are portrayed in a narrative *peripeteia* just as they believe they have come close to their long-dreamed goals: Ahab perishes after his encounter with Moby Dick; Gatsby is killed on the day of his presumed elopement with Daisy; the last of the Buendías is swept away the moment he deciphers the manuscripts; Dr. Francia passes away achieving the very opposite of his dream; and Daniel Quinn disappears the moment he believes to have found Stillman Jr.'s apartment. Delving deeper into the novels that depict these characters will provide a clearer understanding of them within the context of quixotic dreaming.

6 These are characters from F. Scott Fitzgerald's *The Great Gatsby* (1925), Gabriel García Márquez's *One Hundred Years of Solitude* (1927), Augusto Roa Bastos's *I the Supreme* (1974), and Paul Auster's *City of Glass* (1985), respectively.

## Obsession and Quixotism

*Moby Dick*, one of the most prominent representatives of the North American canon, is deeply rooted in the Cervantine incipience of illusory ideals, adventures, relentless dreaming, and deceptions—all coming together in its main character. Captain Ahab is a flawed romantic like Cervantes's Don Quixote, sharing with him "single-minded obsession with an ideal that is larger than life" (Mancing, *Encyclopedia II* 476). Ahab's fanatism centers on one thing: to catch and kill the white whale Moby Dick, a fixation comparable to Don Quixote's incessant desire to embody a chivalrous knight errant and bring justice to the world. The main characters of Cervantes and Melville often overlook their immediate contexts in pursuit of their goals, leading to deviations from the path to success. Ahab is a full-fledged re-accentuation of Don Quixote bringing forth the quixotic characteristic of a dreamer. He epitomizes the trait of obsessive dreaming through his perseverance followed by failure and destruction, while Melville successfully employs "the Cervantine principle" of a man possessed by his dreams who fails to foresee his own destruction in pursuit of his goals (Johnson, *Don* 19).[7]

Captain Ahab's story is narrated from the perspective of one of his crew members.[8] The narrator Ishmael joins the whaling crew of Ahab's ship and witnesses the chase after Moby Dick. Once Ahab makes his

---

7 Johnson refers to "the Cervantine principle" as something that novelists experiment with and exploit by creating characters who have a dream and who set out to realize that dream (*Don* 19).

8 *Moby Dick* opens with a statement that immediately generates mystery: "Call me Ishmael" (Melville 25). The mysterious "call me"—not "my name is"—opens room for a debate about the credibility of the narrator. The beginning of the novel already suggests possible implausibility of the story told by Ishmael. However, the narrator keeps reassuring the reader that all he tells is based on true stories and acknowledges that, to some, it might seem unbelievable. This narrative trick is present in *Don Quixote* as well, in which the reader is informed that the author is the Arab Cide Hamete Benengeli. The narrator proceeds to say that Arabs are notorious for manipulating facts but assures the reader that the story of Don Quixote is true to the original one, rewritten without adding or removing one single word (Cervantes 67-68).

first appearance on the deck, he is observed to be a tall, powerful man who seems to be "made of solid bronze," exposing a scar like a "lofty trunk of a great tree" and "an ivory leg replacing the one he lost in his fight with Moby Dick" (Melville 131; Durán and Rogg 195). He is a "dictator" and a "supreme lord," one who inspires awe among his crew (Melville 130). A heavy smoker and a "hot old man," Ahab is described to be "consumed with the hot fire of his purpose" to find the white whale and take revenge (134, 210).

Like his predecessor in *Don Quixote*, Ahab recruits a sidekick. Both the knight's and the captain's sidekicks serve to indicate reality to their obsessed masters, but their indications usually bear little value. Ahab's sidekick Starbuck gives advice to the captain and tries to bring him to his senses in moments of ardent and obsessive searches—all unsuccessfully. Carl Van Doren describes Melville's captain as someone "in the grip of a passion so single and inveterate that his mind cannot admit the possibility of giving up or turning aside" (58), which explains why he will not listen to anybody's pleas. "Oh, Ahab, . . . not too late is it, even now, the third day, to desist. See! Moby Dick seeks thee not. It is thou, thou, that madly seekest him!" Starbuck pleads, but Ahab follows his dogmatic vision and perseveres in his hunt for Moby Dick (535). Similarly, in *Don Quixote*, the sidekick anticipates the inevitable outcome; "Didn't I tell your grace to watch what you were doing, that these were nothing but windmills . . . ?" Sancho admonishes his master after the ill-fated attack on the windmills, as he had previously warned him against it (Cervantes 59). Sancho Panza, like his spinoff Starbuck, intends to talk sense into his master during various occasions. Sancho not only accompanies him through their adventures, but also serves as the "reality instructor" of Don Quixote (Mancing, *Chivalric* 49). While Sancho demonstrates goodwill by cautioning his master about the potential consequences of his reckless adventures, his concern also stems from a desire to safeguard his own safety, reflecting his more grounded and realistic worldview. Similar to Starbuck, who is afraid of the risks an encounter with Moby Dick could posit, Sancho is not convinced there can be positive aftereffects of fighting a flock of sheep or disputing with the Basque merchants. As predicted by their sidekicks, Captain Ahab's and Don Quixote's visions often fail to materialize.

The obstinate dreamers of *Don Quixote* and *Moby Dick* convert their irrational thoughts into fervent desires, often seen by others as a sign of madness. Cesáreo Bandera notes that "The desire of the obstacle, the transformation of the obstacle into an object of desire, is an unavoidable possibility of the internal logic," and it governs the development of both protagonists' *mimetic desire* (247).[9] These obsessive goals bring the two protagonists together who resemble each other in various ways: they are dreamers, they are persistent in their pursuits, and they tend not to second-guess their decisions, even if those seem impractical and dangerous. During the pursuit of their dreams, Don Quixote and his re-accentuation Ahab encounter myriad challenges, some real and some perceived as real. Like Don Quixote's resistance against invisible foes and enchanters, Ahab's misconstrued reality revolves around Moby Dick, who "with that malicious intelligence ascribed to him" is believed to bear "malignant intents" against the captain (Melville 517; Furui 608). For this, Don Quixote and Ahab are often perceived as mad, "yet they are mad in very different ways" (Durán and Rogg 193). Ahab calls himself "mad" on various occasions in *Moby Dick*, and Ahab's folly creates awe and fear in the reader (H. Smith 183). Durán and Rogg note that "Ahab . . . is prey to a serious, intense madness that increases dramatically towards the end of the novel, a madness that inspires awe, not laughter" (194). On the contrary, Don Quixote's insanity incites laughter—sometimes piteous, and cruel at other times.[10]

Melville's work, mysterious for some and adventurous for others,[11] proposes an exploration of possibilities in achieving a goal through

9 The term *mimetic desire* comes from René Girard and refers to that desire that we borrow from others. For example, Don Quixote's desire is to become a knight errant through mimesis of various heroes of chivalric romances, among them Amadís de Gaula.

10 For more, see Allen, "Smiles and Laughter in *Don Quixote*."

11 For example, Gleim calls *Moby Dick* a novel of mysteries. He argues that the novel is a conjunction of various riddles put together by Melville: "He also treated his subject in a mysterious manner; he wrote in riddles; his method was indirect and ambiguous; he sought to convey ideas, without giving them definite expression; to hint; to suggest; to imply; to present the

unwavering perseverance. Because of this promise of reaching an ideal, some critics have compared *Moby Dick* to the persistent American Dream. Harry Slochewer, for example, states that "Melville is among those who question the ethic of expansionism. His *Moby Dick* at once continues the American Myth of unlimited possibilities and expresses disenchantment with it" (225). Yet, Harold Bloom views the novel as "the fictional paradigm for American sublimity, for an achievement on the heights or in the depths, profound either way" (*How* 236). Other Melville scholars approach the novel through the scope of American hunting culture in the mid-nineteenth century,[12] since whaling in nineteenth-century industrial societies is closely paralleled with what the petroleum industry is today (Durán and Rogg 198; Fussell 106-10). Yet, like Cervantes's novel, *Moby Dick* is also read for entertainment, without diving into the deeper layers of possible meanings. William Gleim claims that by entertaining the reader with the adventures of Ahab, the narrator is able to avoid questions about the obscurities in the narrative of the story. With that method, the narrator is able to keep the reader's attention focused on the superficial story "without stopping to question the obscure passages which surreptitiously expose, for an instant, the deeper meaning of the book" (10). Gleim's point on Melville's narrative methods, in reality, invokes the narrative structure of *Don Quixote*. A precursor to Melville's work, Cervantes's novel unveils various narrative levels—unreliable narrators, plot twists, and disparities—but for some readers entertained by the amusing story of Don Quixote's adventures, these narrative nuances that reveal Cervantes's genius might remain undiscovered.

Cervantes's and Melville's characters serve as synecdochical archetypes of their societies to demonstrate the inability of change, madness, and the destructive outcomes of dogmatic views. Even though

---

enigma of life in an enigmatic way, and to emphasize the mystery of the ineffable mysteries, for he believed it is 'but vain to popularize profundities'" (11). Also, for Gleim, Starbuck represents Platonism (53), Stubb stands for Epicureanism (54), Flask represents Stoicism (55), Water is the truth (79-81), and Ocean is the metaphor for life (79-81).

12 For more on whaling and what events inspired Melville to write *Moby Dick*, see Nathaniel Philbrick's *In the Heart of the Sea* (2001).

the novels represent two societies that are different from each other, both novels present culture and nature. In *Don Quixote,* knight and squire go adventuring and experience rural and urban Spain; in *Moby Dick*, cultures diverge from ship to ship, and the captain and his crew's social encounters are based on their short communications with the ships they stumble upon in their search for the whale. According to Vladimiro Rivas, this is the peculiarity of *Moby Dick*: the novel does not present a love story or friendship, politics or family; the novel is focused on the universe (24).[13] It also teaches us that there is one expected end but that there is really nothing at that end. Ahab's zeal "turns into helplessness and is eventually transformed into nihilism—or better, nihilistic literary proposal" (24; my translation). For Rivas, "reading *Moby Dick* is attending a prodigious spectacle of nature, experiencing the vertigo of unlimited space, deciphering long metaphors, watching a drama of a mind in its narcissistic state . . . and understanding the masks and borders created by the writer that lead to a disaster" (35; my translation). *Don Quixote* precedes *Moby Dick* by centuries but explores very similar worldviews and explorations of the boundaries of what seem to be limitless possibilities. Cervantes's novel uncovers most of Spain and its profuse and diverse cultural, political, and economical states, while Don Quixote serves as a guide who walks the readers through real spaces in a fictional world, landing at an end that rejects all dreams. Both Don Quixote and Ahab serve as catalysts for their readers to explore broad cultural practices and beliefs through their respective microcosms as the two look ahead to a future that holds no promise.

## Demystifying the American Dream

*The Great Gatsby* (1925), one of F. Scott Fitzgerald's most popular novels, portrays a re-accentuated Don Quixote, painting a prime example

---

13 Rivas's statement on universal values presented in *Moby Dick* corresponds with points made by Antonio Caso about Cervantes's novel. The latter claims that Cervantes is the lord of sensing the Earth and that his writing beats in every Spaniard's heart and defines the spirit of the age. Caso also sees Dulcinea as a universal understanding of an ideal woman and Sancho Panza as the incarnation of justice (Caso 60).

of a quixotic dreamer and lover. Jay Gatsby, the protagonist, has an insatiable desire to win the heart and attention of Daisy, his erstwhile lover from whom he is separated. Throughout his quixotic quest to reenter Daisy's life, Gatsby's goal is to accumulate wealth and draw the attention of Daisy, now married to Tom Buchanan. Gatsby's dream to win Daisy over again turns into an obsessive quest when he learns that his beloved's new partner has substantial financial power. So, Gatsby does his utmost to reach indefinite wealth to attract Daisy through affluence. Gatsby is struck by the dream of having his love back and tries everything for this quest. Yet the pursuit of his happiness results in a disastrous end.

Fitzgerald's protagonist bears resemblance to Cervantes's Don Quixote, embodying a fervent obsession with love that leads to irreparable mistakes and eventual downfall. Gatsby features the quixotic image of the lover, the adventurer, and the dreamer portraying a re-accentuation of Don Quixote who also illustrates some of the realities of the American context of the early twentieth century. Through his protagonist, Fitzgerald questions the meaning of life and on what terms people can live together, illustrating also how the twentieth-century United States answered these questions (Voegeli 69). But in the crux of the novel also lies the disenchantment with the American Dream.

The American Dream, a multifaceted and problematic ideal, has been romanticized by many. Fitzgerald, along with various compatriot thinkers, Melville included, deconstructs the myth of the American Dream, specifically pointing at its inferred futility especially when viewed through the lens of economic prosperity alone. Together with portraying his contemporaries' growing disillusionment with the American Dream, a promise for the future, Fitzgerald tackles a problem antagonistic to this mythos: the glorification of the past. Like Don Quixote, who yearns for the "[f]ortunate age and . . . times called golden" (Cervantes 76), Gatsby clings to the idea of reviving his past with Daisy. "I'm going to fix everything just the way it was before," he insists (Fitzgerald 117). This romanticization of the past often leads to disillusionment, highlighting the frustration with the wish to revive an old ideal as something unattainable in reality.

The protagonists of Cervantes and Fitzgerald guide their lives by their dreams driven primarily by the hope of bringing back what was once lost (Donaldson, "Trouble" 136). However, to revive a point in their stories and histories, both characters first need to break away from parts of their own past, parts that would now nix the dreamed success. And so, Don Quixote and Jay Gatsby "change their names; they leave their home and reject the ordinariness of their home and of everyday life; they play a role; they have a vision, a vision of themselves (Gatsby has a Platonic conception of himself) in order to transform themselves and/or the world" (Selig 129). By breaking with parts of their real stories, Don Quixote and Gatsby create an identity based on an imagined past, which will ensure the successful pursuit of their dreams. It is through books, according to Sebastian Groes, that Gatsby constructs parts of this imagined past, with his library being a projection of a man "boring his way through endless shelves of knowledge" (131). And it is through the transformation from an *hidalgo* to a knight errant that Don Quixote goes through an old identity change to be able to create a future he has charted for himself—all influenced by books, as well. Adam Meehan addresses the issues of new and old realities in *The Great Gatsby* focusing on Gatsby's conviction that, of course, one can change one's past, contrary to what the narrator suggests. By attempting to relive his affair with Daisy, "Gatsby epitomizes the repetition compulsion," refusing to give up on the ideal of being together with his beloved again (Meehan 84). Yet this old romance cannot be the same; it cannot be repeated, but only re-accentuated, neither of which Gatsby manages to achieve just like his predecessor dreamer who, unable to revive what is lost, renounces his ideals.

Jay Gatsby's quest ends tragically; he dies dreaming as he lived dreaming. "In love with love," like Don Quixote, Gatsby's urge for success to get closer to his dream ultimately remains unachieved (Durán and Rogg 223).[14] Fitzgerald depicts such a character in his novel to exemplify various socially unaccepted traits of individuals, at the same time dramatizing the concept of love and obsession. Don Quixote

---

14 Lionel Trilling compares Great Gatsby's love to the American ideal. He claims that Gatsby's love was tender and unique to Americans depicting a failed quest because of this uniqueness (15).

presents an image of an idealizing lover; Jay Gatsby is the incarnation of a possessive and obsessive lover. As William Voegeli states:

> Like Don Quixote, Jay Gatsby moved from the romantic love of a woman to the romantic conviction that the hard realities of this world can be made to yield to a steadfast heart and a vaulting spirit, to one's "Platonic conception of himself." . . . No woman of flesh and bone *could* be worthy of such idealization, and both men turn out to be more in love with love than with their beloved. (70)

The idealization of this and other sentiments in *The Great Gatsby* evokes a quixotic reading of people, times, and places. It evokes Don Quixote's incessant pursuit of the "fortunate times" as a result of its idealization and a push to "not seeing [Dulcinea, but still] believing, confessing, affirming, swearing, and defending that truth" as a result of his Pygmalion-like creation (Cervantes 76, 39). This sort of idealization carries on in *The Great Gatsby* in multiple layers. Like Fitzgerald's narrator Nick romanticizes the image of Gatsby (Lynn 79), so does Gatsby to Daisy, wrapped up in the whole concept of enchantment with the American Dream. Ultimately, what Fitzgerald adverts to is what has also been prominent in Cervantes: the well-known concept of the Golden Age disillusionment. Here, like in Cervantes, dreams remain to be only dreams.

Even with such strong resemblances to *Don Quixote*, *The Great Gatsby* remains an American classic. (Such is the nature of quixotic re-accentuations—generative because of the well-known traits of Don Quixote but new because of the flexibility granted by this generativeness.) William Cain recognizes *The Great Gatsby* as tantamount to Melville's *Moby Dick* and other milestone American books where readers are invited to reflect on "what it means to be human, bodies ensnared by time, consumed by desires destined never to be fulfilled" (469). Indeed, Gatsby, along with Ahab, is a re-accentuated quixotic dreamer, who, similar to how Don Quixote represents the essence of being Spanish, is "rooted in a time and place and nation," embodying an "American through and through" (469).

## Postmodern Vagaries of a Quixote

*City of Glass* is the first book of Paul Auster's *The New York Trilogy* published in 1985. Critics have referred to it as the best novel of the *Trilogy* and as one of the most outstanding contributions to the American postmodern literature.[15] Inspired by a real phone call the author had received, Auster goes on to confess that *Don Quixote* was another source of inspiration for him to create a novel "about a kind of passionate excess" (*The Art* 271, 291). Auster's protagonist, Daniel Quinn, is a re-accentuated dreamer who embodies this "passionate excess" in his quest to untangle the mystery around the Stillmans and help Peter Stillman Jr. A detective writer who becomes entangled in his own detective reality, Quinn refuses to cede until his otiose quest consumes him, obliterating every trace of him but his red notebook. Quinn, who pretends to be detective Paul Auster to save Stillman Jr., finds himself on his quest thanks to the former policeman Michael Saavedra, whose name clearly reminds us of Miguel de Cervantes Saavedra.[16] Auster's widely acknowledged work thus shows influence of techniques seen in Cervantes, with a protagonist also grounded in Don Quixote.

Quinn's quixotic quest begins with a phone call. The caller wants to speak to a detective named Auster but has mistakenly been dialing Quinn's number. The latter, after receiving the same call at various times, decides to play Auster and accept the caller's request to protect Peter Stillman Jr. from his father. However, what starts off as a novel about preventing a potential murder turns out to be a story about the puzzling nature of language, a postmodern case of a detective obsessed over the mysteries he encounters along his way.[17] Finding himself entangled in solving Stillman's mystery case, Quinn decides to find Auster-author and ask him for advice. This encounter creates

15 See, for example, Drumm, Espejo, and Urbina.

16 For clarity, Daniel Quinn will here on be referred to as Quinn-Auster when he is under the guise of the detective. Similarly, Auster-author is used in reference to Paul Auster, the character in *City of Glass*. Auster, without added clarification, is the real-life Paul Auster who wrote the novel.

17 Joseph Tabbi describes Auster's work as "cognitive fiction," as the reader is submerged into the brain-draining quest of Quinn trying to protect Stillman Jr. (xxi).

tension, promising a climactic turn of events, because it prompts a solution which, nonetheless, never comes (Gersdorf 145). Auster-author insists that Quinn's searches are all in vain, and he will not be able to protect Peter Stillman Jr. because he does not need his protection. What Quinn fails to understand as a fictional character is that he is unable to save Stillman Jr. simply because he is fictional, created, made up, and manipulated by the author, the real Paul Auster, writer of *City of Glass*. As noted by William Lavender: "Peter has sent for Auster his author to save his life. Without his author, he must remain in darkness, unknown, off the page; his name cannot be 'real.' But Quinn is only a character; he cannot save him" (226-27). Auster allows Quinn to embody a character that he himself created and brought to life through his words (Musarra-Schronder 223). Quinn will never know the extent of his manipulation as he strongly believes he is in charge of the development of Auster's novel, just like Don Quixote in the second part of Cervantes's novel.[18] The meeting with the fictional Auster-author serves to illuminate Quinn's destiny, while also delving into the authorial dilemmas reminiscent of *Don Quixote*. This thematic resonance underscores the complexities of identity and narrative construction that permeate the novel.

The encounter of the detective Quinn-Auster and the fictional Auster-author reveals other parallels between *Don Quixote* and *City of Glass*, bringing up problems of authorship, as well. The author, the real Auster, has thrown himself into the text and has fictionalized himself to now have a direct dialogue with his literary figure (Gersdorf 145). In *City of Glass,* Auster-author appears to be no detective, but a

18 At the beginning of the second part of *Don Quixote*, the Manchegan hero is not quite ready to set off for more adventures. It is Sansón Carrasco and Sancho Panza, mainly, who convince him to go out of his house once again and do what he does best: engage in adventures. The main reason Don Quixote is convinced is because Sansón tells him about the first published part of a novel about Don Quixote and his squire Sancho and reveals that there will be a sequel to it if both Don Quixote and his sidekick continue their adventures. Don Quixote believes he alone creates his own story as he embarks on new adventures, yet it is Cervantes who is the author of all the stories Don Quixote thinks he is creating.

writer like Quinn. There are three real and fictional writers up to this moment: Auster is the one who wrote *City of Glass*, fictional Auster-author has written about *Don Quixote*, and Quinn-Auster is a novelist who has also been taking notes on his mystery case in his red notebook. But all three writers seem to coalesce into one character at the end of the novel, when Quinn is exposed to the reality that the case he is investigating is nothing more than fiction.

Throughout the novel, Quinn appropriates several identities: himself, his pseudonym William Wilson, his detective character Auster, and his author. It is not coincidental that Quinn, like his predecessor Don Quixote, changes his name to adjust and make his new identity fit in the different pursuits on which he embarks. Alonso Quijano changes his name to Don Quixote, and Daniel Quinn chooses to be William Wilson, later also to wear a mask of pretentious detective-writer Paul Auster—an identity adopted due to his dream of embodying a real-life detective and protecting Stillman Jr. As the writer notes:

> He had not really lost himself; he was merely pretending, and he could return to being Quinn whenever he wished. The fact that there was now a purpose to his being Paul Auster—a purpose that was becoming more and more important to him—served as a kind of moral justification for the charade and absolved him of having to defend his lie. For imagining himself as Auster had become synonymous in his mind with doing good in the world. (Auster, *City* 82)

Quinn's new identity confers on him the power to change the world into a better place. Like Don Quixote's dream to "[right] all manner of wrongs and . . . [seize] the opportunity and [place] himself in danger and [end] those wrongs," Quinn-Auster sets the goal of "doing good in the world" by taking on the task of protecting Stillman Jr. (Cervantes 21; Auster, *City* 82). Don Quixote plays the role of a knight, although he is an *hidalgo*, and Daniel Quinn takes the job of a detective, although he is known only for his detective fiction (Jofré 127).[19] And

19 Note that Don Quixote and Daniel Quinn have the same initials: DQ, which Quinn soon takes notice of, wondering whether it is simply a coin-

while Quinn, like his predecessor Alonso Quijano embodies different identities, builds an idiosyncratic "world of fluid identities" (Espejo 156), Paul Auster, author of *City of Glass*, deconstructs this world like Cervantes does with *Don Quixote*. The characters cannot succeed in these worlds, however persistent they may be in trying to achieve their dreams. In *City of Glass*, Quinn is lost not only in the city, but within himself, and not only in the story, but within the story as well (Auster, *City* 8).

Auster weaves a postmodern narrative at one end and unweaves it at the other. The whole novel is a deconstruction: "it deconstructs the form of the novel, the canons of criticism, theory, and tradition, and it deconstructs itself, as it literally falls apart in its progression" (Lavender 200). The more Quinn finds dead ends throughout his quest, the more he becomes antagonistic to his own success, disappearing, in the end, without a trace. Eduardo Urbina compares the disappearance of Quinn to Don Quixote's reflection in the Knight of the Mirrors, whose obsessions are reflected in the glass and who fades away in his own world of madness (30). In the end, Don Quixote's and Quinn's failures are a result of their inability to relate to their surroundings in pursuit of their dreams. It is a "lack of understanding of vagaries" and what these vagaries can represent (Hennings 137). Looking at *City of Glass* through the lens of Maravall's utopia and counterutopia, it becomes obvious that just like his predecessor Cervantes, Auster weaved a story of an oblivious dreamer, who struck by his quest, creates a world of counterutopia while searching for an idyllic end.

Quinn is a re-accentuated Quixote because he represents the following characteristics. First of all, he is a writer interested in mystery and detective novels. He presents an image of a dedicated reader, and *Don Quixote* is mentioned as one of his favorite books (Auster, *City* 150). He shows sincere dedication to studying detective stories. His enthusiasm and interest in such stories are especially revealed when he has a chance to be a hero in a detective story himself and investi-

cidence: "He thought through the question of why Don Quixote had not simply wanted to write books like the ones he loved—instead of living out their adventures. He wondered why he had the same initials as Don Quixote" (Auster, *City* 198).

gate the mysterious case of the Stillmans. Quinn is a dreamer, like Don Quixote, and similar to him, he does not give up on his quest when others try to open his eyes to reality. Fictional Auster-author warns him that the entire story is a sham and that there is no end to it. But Quinn is determined to solve the puzzle and protect Stillman Jr. as the latter's wife requested of him. Similarly, Don Quixote is warned many times by Sancho that his quests as a dreaming knight errant will have a disastrous end. Don Quixote persists in ignoring his squire's warnings and fails every time, as predicted, also disappointing Sancho, for Don Quixote's dream to be a famous knight errant holds a promise for his squire as well (Durán and Rogg 95). Quinn acts likewise. He refuses to believe in Auster's warnings. He perseveres to reach his desired goal, but instead, he disappears at the end of the novel, unable to find the answers he seeks.[20]

Don Quixote and Daniel Quinn are dreamers because they have imagination which does not comport with reality. Don Quixote dreams of people, places, and concepts of chivalry such as castles, knighthood, and Dulcinea, while Quinn's dream is to carry out his task as a detective successfully, like his favorite character Max Work would. Writing mystery novels also allows Quinn to recreate a world of his fictional fantasies, where he can find the answers to all problems and resolve the existing chaos in the Stillman family (Lázaro Larraz 442). Both Don Quixote and Quinn have been drawn to irrationality by believing in fictional stories and trying to resemble a fictional

20 Elizabeth Drumm gives a different interpretation to the ending of the novel, reading it through the lens of Foucault. Comparing Quinn to Don Quixote, she suggests that the two characters become immortalized within the text. Auster's protagonist, for instance, "having discarded all the rules that would identify him to the world . . . becomes writing and exists only as the words in the red notebook that have been incorporated into the text we are reading" (28). This interpretation is very relevant within the structuralist and postmodernist reading of these characters, but directly opposes Bakhtin's concept of re-accentuation, in which text is viewed as a tool the author uses to gives life to an independent character—one that may reappear in other texts and contexts, adapted, modified, rewritten, parodied, or imitated, like Don Quixote is in Paul Auster's novel.

character in real life. Don Quixote refers to his favorite books of chivalry to build his ideal world, and Quinn refers to his favorite works of detective fiction to achieve the same. Both Don Quixote and Quinn live in their literary and idealistic realms, and both eventually become characters of their own fictional worlds (Gersdorf 146). All these quixotic traits found in Quinn build up a re-accentuated Quixote in an obscure noir context.

Auster's postmodern novel, paradoxical and moving, is as innovative as *Don Quixote* was when it was published (Aguilera Serey 79). It is a novel that puts forward rich literary and contextual versatility whether or not approached through a quixotic lens. Among many things, it constructs and deconstructs a world of possibilities, and does so simultaneously. It also questions the viability of certain masks and identities in the light of deterministic elements in a given place and time, questions that readers have seen emerge in Cervantes, as well.[21]

## Stories and Histories

*Yo el Supremo* (*I the Supreme*), published by eminent Paraguayan author Augusto Roa Bastos in 1974 and translated into English in 1986, is a celebrated work representing the Latin American Boom. Although plotted quite differently than a number of works by Julio Cortázar, Gabriel García Márquez, and other writers of the Boom era, Roa Bastos's novel has been acclaimed as the equal of such works as *One Hundred Years of Solitude* (Martin 280). The main character of the novel is Dr. Francia, a real historical figure fictionalized in the work of Roa Bastos. The historical events portrayed in *I the Supreme* target two dictators who ruled Paraguay, the first from 1811 to 1840, known as José Gaspar Rodríguez Francia, or Dr. Francia. The second is Roa Bastos's contemporary Alfredo Stroessner, who ruled Paraguay from 1954 to 1989. The latter was known to exercise the same forms and practices of dictatorship as Dr. Francia. Stroessner, although not the main character of the book, shared considerable similarities with the antagonist of *I the Supreme*. Writing a fictional biography of the Dictator Francia

21 The exploration of masking and performance in Paul Auster is reminiscent of Bakhtin's concept of *carnival*, which he outlines in detail in his *Rabelais and His World* (1965).

was only an excuse to raise the issue of having power and its consequences (Tovar 28). The publication of the novel, not surprisingly, was disapproved of by the government of the dictator, which resulted in the exile of Roa Bastos (Rowe and Whitfield 245).

The novel is based on the story-history of the Paraguayan dictator, Dr. Francia.[22] His supremacy lies in his regime and his writing. He believes that he confers more power on himself and others by writing his own story. However, this authority is pilfered from him, since his scribe Policarpo Patiño writes what the tyrant dictates, and once again later, when notes and comments are inserted into the main story by an unknown compiler. The compiler reveals that the dictator wanted to imitate Cervantes and create a novel about himself comparable to *Don Quixote*, an act that will make him as grand and immortal as the Spanish writer:

> The rumor has leaked out, however, that these withdrawals to his *hortus conclusus* are for the purpose of writing a novel imitating the Quixote, for which he feels a fascinated admiration. To our novelist Dictator's misfortune, he is not missing an arm like Cervantes, who lost it in the glorious battle of Lepanto, and at the same time he is more than lacking in brains and wit. (Roa Bastos 67)

The three voices narrating the same story craft polyphony that we also find in *Don Quixote*.[23] Dr. Francia's version of his story, Patiño's inter-

22 The term *story-history* encompasses the dual significance of the equivalent word *historia* in Spanish. While Roa Bastos's novel draws from historical events, it presents an imagined narrative of Dr. Francia's life as interpreted by his scribe Patiño, with additional records attributed to an anonymous fictional writer.

23 Polyphony in literary studies was first introduced by M. M. Bakhtin. In his *Problems of Dostoevsky's Poetics* (1963), Bakhtin introduces the polyphonic novel as one that bears several voices. Those voices, as the author states, come together to form one entity, and together as one affect the direction of narration. Bakhtin claims that Dostoevsky is the creator of the polyphonic novel (7), and defines the term attributing the authority to the Russian writer in the following way: "A plurality of independent and unmerged voices and consciousnesses, a genuine polyphony of fully valid voices is in fact the

pretation, and the compiler's notes grow into a harmonic narration, and bring the novel to its unitary form, generating a polyphonic novel. Nevertheless, this narrative is problematic since the verisimilitude of the true story-history becomes debatable. *Don Quixote* and *I the Supreme* both represent several disputable truths stated by different narrators, with one noticeable difference: that the main character of Roa Bastos's novel is one of the narrators of his story. On one hand, Francia is the dictator, the individual who assumes all the powers of the state; on the other hand, he is the dictator, the one who tells Patiño his biography to be written (Gallo 435; Raúl 60). In both Cervantes's and Roa Bastos's works, the story evolves through several narrative layers. Both novels present an omniscient narrator, who however is only interpreting, rewriting, and redelivering what he has found in writing already.[24]

---

chief characteristic of Dostoevsky's novels. What unfolds in his works is not a multitude of characters and fates in a single objective world, illuminated by a single authorial consciousness; rather a plurality of consciousnesses, with equal rights and each with its own world, combine but are not merged in the unity of the event" (6). And although Bakhtin asserts that Dostoevsky was the first to write polyphonic novels, he agrees that the "early buds of polyphony ripened" in the works of Shakespeare, Rabelais, Cervantes, Grimmelshausen and others (34). So Dostoevsky was the "culminator" of the polyphony that rose up in European literature in the nineteenth century (34). In fact, Cervantes's novel is far from being monologic (another term Bakhtin develops in the same work; opposite of polyphonic), and all the specifications that Bakhtin ascribes to Dostoevsky's novels, describe *Don Quixote* as well.

24 It is fitting to quote Helene Carol Weldt-Basson here for details on writing in Roa Bastos: "There are several types of writing in the narrative: (1) transcribed dialogues in which El Supremo dictates to his secretary, Policarpo Patiño (there are also dialogues between the dictator and other characters); (2) entries in the 'private notebook' in which El Supremo reflects on many personal matters, especially his problems with writing and splitting of his personality into two halves, 'I' and 'He,' that correspond to his private and public selves; (3) installments of the 'perpetual circular' in which El Supremo narrates Paraguay's history, dating from the Revolution of the *comuneros* (1717) through his own rule (1814-1840), with allusions to the future; (4) the 'logbook' on pages 270-75 of the novel, in which El Supremo

In Cervantes's case, a translator intervenes in the process of the creation of the final product. The omniscient narrators of both novels are unreliable. In *Don Quixote*, the narrator claims to decipher everything found in a certain document that will ensure the truthfulness of the story. However, since the story was first recorded by Cide Hamete Benengeli, it is said to be untrustworthy. In *I the Supreme*, the omniscient narrator, or the compiler, contradicts himself various times, thus also making the reader question the credibility of his acclamations.

Beside the narrative similarities, *Don Quixote* and *I the Supreme* share various characteristics. One of those is, of course, the re-accentuation of the knight errant in the image of Roa Bastos's dictator. Dr. Francia is a character grounded in Cervantes's Don Quixote and transmuted in the context of nineteenth-century Paraguay. While the dictator reads a lot and creates his story by writing, Don Quixote reads and reenacts episodes of his preferred novels in order to create his story by acting. It is also not coincidental that the dictator of Paraguay, who is trying to write his story in imitation of *Don Quixote* (Roa Bastos 67), has a unique copy of Cervantes's novel on his desk: "The *Quijote*, also lying open in the middle, in a handsome edition with a purple page marker and gold galloons on the cover, lay on a stand" (135). Dr. Francia compares himself with Cervantes and alludes to the famous reference to "arms and letters" that appears in *Don Quixote*.[25] Although he

---

speaks of his origins, genealogy, and relationship with his father; (5) the 'tutorial voice' on pages 282-84, El Supremo's father's narration of his military exploits during a boat trip when El Supremo was fourteen years old; (6) two documents—the anonymous pasquinade demanding El Supremo's decapitation and the hanging of his functionaries, which serves as the narration's catalyst and a leitmotif to which El Supremo returns throughout the novel, and Pueyrredón's draft suggesting the invasion and subjugation of Paraguay by foreign forces. An 'unknown handwriting' interrupts some of these discourses (usually the 'private notebook) to criticize El Supremo's actions" (2-3).

25 Don Quixote's famous discourse on arms and letters covers the beginning of Chapter 38 of the first part of the novel, where the knight errant claims that it is as important to be a soldier as an educated man, since one defends kingdoms, and the other cultures (Cervantes 330-32). Dr. Francia's reference to lance as a pen and vice versa underscores the exact allusion to Don Quixote's discourse. The dictator notes: "I can't remove the fly that's

thinks of himself as tantamount to God, he still acknowledges that he falls short of the experience that writers like Cervantes had. As he mentions to Patiño: "Cervantes, one-armed, writes his great novel with his missing hand," and proceeds to question himself as a writer, as well as his overall identity (66). He also wonders whether or not Patiño can be his Sancho, in his attempt to imitate not only the style and the expertise that Cervantes shows in *Don Quixote*, but also the novel's protagonists: "Who could deny that his fat secretary-squire is less real than you; mounted on his mule, plodding along behind his master's old nag, more real than you mounted on the basin, awkwardly bridling your goose quill?" (66).

Dr. Francia is a keen reader like Don Quixote. He also enjoys comparing various literary characters in his writings. Dr. Francia is a dreamer, the most prominent quixotic trait in his re-accentuated persona. Unlike Don Quixote, however, his quest does not constitute seeing evil vanish from the world; neither does he try to right any wrong by fighting for what is just. What he yearns for is the acknowledgement of his authority by the people of Paraguay, envisioning them not only recognizing his control but also yielding to his power and commands. He dreams of that "everlasting fame" detached from the chivalrous ideals that Don Quixote promises to bring forth. Like many re-accentuated Quixotes, Dr. Francia's image becomes immortalized among other literary-cultural products. However, while Don Quixote's figure becomes more idealized and celebrated in Spain, Dictator Francia's persona comes to stand for the contemporary political rut where Paraguay finds itself (Rodríguez Alcalá de Gonzales Oddone et al. 51).

In *I the Supreme*, there is also the image of Patiño, who brilliantly represents the figure of a loyal friend, who is more rational and realistic, and who makes the protagonist's image complete. It would be hard to think of Dr. Francia without his scribe Patiño. It is the latter who takes care of the dictator, who writes down what Dr. Francia dictates, and who serves him unconditionally, embodying a re-accentuated

---

getting soaking wet in the flicker of the candle, the way I removed the flies drowned in the inkwell with the point of my *lance-pen* in time gone by" (Roa Bastos 319).

Sancho Panza. Patiño possesses the same language interpretation flaws as his predecessor. He misspells and misremembers words and phrases that Dr. Francia dictates, frustrating him. Helene Carol Weldt-Basson notes that the linguistic similarities are "indicative of a certain mutual interpretation of language styles and ideas between Patiño and Dr. Francia, which can be observed in the novel and which relates to their reenactment of a Sancho Panza/Don Quixote-like relationship" (43). In the same manner, Dr. Francia uses some Cervantine and quixotic language—for instance, when he refers to Patiño as his Sancho Panza, stating: "My Sancho Panza's reasoning is not at all unreasonable" (Roa Bastos 411).[26] In these linguistic and interpretative realities, Dr. Francia-Patiño relationship makes them even more human, even more relatable, and even more quixotic.

In addition to obvious quixotic themes in *I the Supreme*, Roa Bastos's novel also strikes the critics for the protagonist's double identity. Dr. Francia consistently brings up his two-faced image. He refers to himself as "He" in writing on several occasions. In this manner, the dictator assumes the identity of "I"—his voice, and "He"—the written evidence of his self (Raúl 64). The references to I, He, and the Supreme also allude to the theological trinity that Dr. Francia believes he embodies. Considering Roa Bastos's depiction of Dr. Francia, *I the Supreme* is not an attempt to validate all that the dictator did. Doris Da Rosa claims that "In the last chapters the many political and philosophical themes" that the Paraguayan writer upholds throughout the novel "come together in a kind of dialogue between the 'yo' and the 'él,' the two aspects of Francia's soul. This permits Francia to consider, for himself and the reader, what he has failed to achieve" (174). Da Rosa then clarifies that Francia's failure lies in his experiment in absolutism (175), something that can be claimed about Don Quixote as well. However, their failure also lies within the way that others perceive the ruler or the knight within their culture-contextual hegemonies. Readers may sympathize with Dr. Francia as much as they empathize with

26 Surely this sentence alludes to *Don Quixote*'s famous first chapter and the protagonist's favorite reference to love: "The reason for the unreason to which my reason turns so weakens my reason that with reason I complain of thy beauty" (Cervantes 20).

Don Quixote, even knowing that both characters lack rationality and take risks to delineate their dreamed identities. Both the protagonists of the respective novels of Cervantes and Roa Bastos are in search of their identities, acceptance, and the truth.[27] The real identity of Don Quixote may be Alonso Quijano, who is a simple *hidalgo*. Nevertheless, Don Quixote's adopted identity and vision do not comport with the vision of his contemporaries. Similarly, Dr. Francia might be a mere mortal equal to everyone else in his country and the world, but he envisions himself as the God, the most Supreme of all.

As mentioned, *I the Supreme* is a fictional historical work. Although the novel conveys historical characters and facts, it does not fully comport with history. Weldt-Basson points out that "[s]ince much of the history written about Doctor Francia is actually myth, the novel questions the reliability of historical sources on Doctor Francia in an attempt to approach the truth about this historical figure" (10). Roa Bastos suggests to view this myth as "the revealing strength of social life" and focuses on it through the fictional lens, writing his *I the Supreme* as a novel inspired by history, and not biography (Rodríguez Alcalá de Gonzales Oddone et al. 20; my translation). The fact that the protagonist dictates his life, thus making his narration a history, juxtaposes Roa Bastos's *Quixote*-inspired novel to García Márquez's *One Hundred Years of Solitude* discussed below, in which the protagonists are living the history of their lives predetermined long ago.

## History and Palimpsest

Gabriel García Márquez, a Colombian writer born in 1927, is one of the most celebrated Latin American literary figures. García Márquez has often been compared to Cervantes for various reasons,[28] and his *Cien*

27 J. Bekunuru Kubayanda looks at the novel of Roa Bastos as a labyrinth and a paradox of the truth, stating that the paradox in the novel lies in the representation of the search for the truth, any truth, even if the truth is absurd (119).

28 For example, Michael Bell claims that García Márquez's and Cervantes's works have significant similarities not only at the narrative level but also in respect with their authors. He states: "*Hundred Years* is an overtly Cervantean book in its fundamental device of the fictitious foreign historian.

*años de soledad* (*One Hundred Years of Solitude*), published in 1967, has been called the *Quixote* of Latin America (Mancing, "Don Quijote" 313). Like Cervantes's novel, *One Hundred Years of Solitude* immediately captivated the attention of literature lovers upon its publication. Editions, adaptations, and translations followed forthwith after the first edition of the novel, and shortly, it became a global contemporary masterpiece. In Ilan Stavans's opinion, "there are only two novelistic masterpieces written in Spanish whose influence radically revamped our understanding of Hispanic civilization" (*Gabriel* 2). Stavans, of course, is referring to *Don Quixote* and *One Hundred Years of Solitude*.

In his renowned novel, García Márquez employs the notion of solitude and solitariness shared by the members of the Buendía family. What I will call cyclical quixotism—the portrayal of quixotism through generations of the Buendías—leaves a sense of mystical, unapprehended, and fallacious reality in which each male Buendía abides. García Márquez weaves a story in which reality and fiction intermix, also blurring the lines between the dreaming and the conscious minds. He creates a parable reminiscent of *Don Quixote* and quixotism, highlighting the fallacies of quixotic dreaming. Bloom notes:

> In the subsequent story of the Buendías it becomes evident that they have lost their proper access to this other realm of sleep; a realm which is commonly expressed, within the terms of daytime consciousness, through magical and dream images. But the fundamental narrative trick of the book, as fundamental as Alonso Quijano's imagining himself as the fictional character, Don Quixote, is

---

But the Cervantean parallel has a deeper significance with implications for his *oeuvre* at large. I have suggested that *Hundred Years* is Márquez' most substantial and representative work and yet is also, in important ways, untypical. In this respect, *Hundred Years* stands in the same relation to Márquez' *oeuvre* as *Don Quixote* does to Cervantes's and for essentially similar reasons. If Cervantes had died immediately after completing the second part of *Don Quixote* 1615), or if Márquez had died after *Hundred Years*, their respective *oeuvres* would not just be shorter, they would have, or would appear to have, a significantly different meaning" (117).

> that Márquez goes on to tell their story at the level of the Buendías' repressed selves. (*Gabriel* 99)

García Márquez draws a line between the fictitious and the real by the means of opinions of neighbors, citizens of Macondo, and visitors, but the Buendías themselves live in some sort of oblivion. They seem heedless of the outside real world, they seem unable to control their urges and feelings, they persist in searching for their ideals, and they all fail in their respective quests in one way or another. Most Buendía men are a re-accentuation of Don Quixote, José Arcadio Buendía being the one who opens the family's cycle of quixotism, and Aureliano, the one to close it.

José Arcadio Buendía has an uncontrollable desire to invent, experiment, and discover. Influenced by a gypsy named Melquíades, he follows the latter's suggestion to come up with something new and awe-inspiring. José Arcadio Buendía frantically waits until the next arrival of the gypsies, as they always bring a new object that will captivate his attention and trigger his imagination. The old man eventually loses his mind after spending too much time in his laboratory, reading the parchments and books that the gypsy hands him and experimenting continuously with various objects. Soon, he completely loses touch with the real world, and his irrational behavior leads his family to tie him to a tree for years, where his health gives out. Once he is untied, he has already given up all his dreams and his wish for new experiments, so he leaves the world.

Next in the family cycle of quixotism is Colonel Aureliano Buendía, whose quixotic life features his irrepressible love for Remedios Moscote. It also features his revolutionary fixations and his adventures at war, as well as his later obsession of spending his time in his father's laboratory making goldfish statuettes and reading Melquíades's papers. His death parallels his father's, both finding their peace at the tree in their courtyard. Each generation of Buendías includes a man who partakes in the dream of fully deciphering the manuscripts and inventing something new in the laboratory, including José Arcadio Segundo and Aureliano. The novel concludes with the birth of Aureliano and Amaranta Úrsula's son, named Aureliano as well, who is devoured by ants. By that time, father Aureliano has deciphered all the manuscripts and discovered the end of the story, which reveals the final destiny of the Buendía family as it unfolds.

*One Hundred Years of Solitude* is a palimpsest. Stavans notes: "Like Cervantes's opus, which is purportedly written by a Moor, García Márquez's novel is presented as a palimpsest: a manuscript drafted by a gypsy" (*Gabriel* 2). As opposed to Cervantes's heroes, who undertake adventures that are being compiled in a novel as they are acting, the history of the Buendías was already written in Melquíades's manuscript, and the generations keep uncovering each page of the paper while living the life described in it. It is Aureliano who reaches the end of the writings. He finds out that all he has been trying to decipher is the history of his own family and its end is emphasized by his son's and his own death.

The examples of the characters of *One Hundred Years of Solitude* reveal that the most prevalent quixotic trait nested in most Buendías is dreaming and doing so obsessively. While several characters might be infatuated with the image of a woman and others with war, incessant quixotic dreaming seems to prevail in almost every member of the Buendía household. Most central to the theme of dreaming in the novel, still, remains the deciphering of Melquíades's parchments. As soon as this goal is achieved, however, the Buendías' story comes to its end.

It is remarkable that notwithstanding their failures or an indication to unfortunate outcomes, all Buendías persist in their fanatisms. For example, José Arcadio Buendía's obsession with Melquíades's novelties never ceases, although there are various indications of his detachment from reality. Similarly, Colonel Aureliano Buendía perseveres in going to wars, ignoring his defeats. Looking at *Don Quixote*, despite his injuries, mocking, and failure, Cervantes's protagonist maintains his identity as a knight errant until the last pages of the novel.

Reading these works, we encounter two separate worlds—the one that the authors describe, and the one in which the protagonists dwell. In Edwin Williamson's words:

> Like Cervantes, García Márquez realized that the novelist must start by making a very clear distinction between fact and fiction, by drawing a line between his novel and the real world; but once this distinction is made, the creative imagination can be brought into play to explore the boundaries between fiction and reality within the narrative itself. ("The Quixotic" 119)

This follows the trend seen in other novels that bring forth the trait of a quixotic dreamer—from *City of Glass* to *One Hundred Years of Solitude*. All these novels contain a world constructed and deconstructed at the same time, something that goes back to Maravall's notion of utopia and counterutopia, again.

Michael Bell notes that in *One Hundred Years of Solitude*, the characters "live out their obsessions in the real world" and allow the readers to follow them (119). He continues: "Márquez is reversing the literalism of the Buendías in their actual lives. With Don Quixote, the problem strictly lies not so much in the unreality or anachronism of the models he tries to follow as in the literalism with which he understands them" (119). With the narrative techniques derived from Cervantes, a cyclical plot and re-accentuated Quixotes, García Márquez's *One Hundred Years of Solitude* develops into a well-rounded quixotic novel. The Colombian writer shows deep understanding of human nature and psychology, like Cervantes did. It is perhaps this profound sensitivity toward the condition of humankind that allowed both Cervantes and García Márquez to create such masterpieces that will keep defining Hispanic literature for centuries.

## Conclusion

It is fascinating to see into how many personas Don Quixote can morph and in how many contexts he can be validated. In this chapter alone, the re-accentuated image of Don Quixote has entered the social context of the nineteenth-century United States and twentieth-century Colombia, among others. In one place, the quixotic protagonist can be interpreted as a madman in pursuit of revenge, in another, he may exemplify men trapped within the confines of their own circumstances, seeking answers to their questions in war and peace, mystery and love. We see re-accentuations of quixotic dreamers deconstructing the mythos of the American Dream and constructing a postmodern society, where questions rarely lead to answers. We see the re-accentuated image of Don Quixote recreating history. In Dr. Francia's case, the quixotism is revealed in a ruthless manner, while the protagonist creates history and becomes history. In *One Hundred Years of Solitude*, as opposed to *I the Supreme*, the quixotic characters live their predestined history, victims of determinism. The two South American writers present quixotic figures in the context of history and how history has failed in their protagonists' quixotic endeavors. Analyzed through the lens of a quixotic dreamer, this chapter's novels demonstrate the thousand faces Don Quixote can appropriate and enter a new context, become re-accentuated. Thus far, re-accentuated Quixotes have been able to posit critical-analytical points on obsession and idealization, among innumerous psychological aspects of human nature. It is through *Don Quixote* and these kinds of quixotic works that readers are reacquainted with the real human being, its universal values, deeds, and needs, also encountering the disillusionment that limitless dreaming may engender.

# 4
# Adventurers

A VERY WELL-KNOWN characteristic of Don Quixote is his fervor for adventure. Cervantes's hero believes that to imitate knights errant successfully, he needs to fight evil and bring justice to the world. To do this, Don Quixote chooses a peculiar method: he puts on rusty armor, takes up an old lance and a shield, and goes out into the world where there are "evils to undo, wrongs to right, injustices to correct, abuses to ameliorate, and offenses to rectify" (Cervantes 24). Of course, Cervantes masterfully satirizes the adventures that his knight errant undergoes while trying to right wrongs, often mixing mockery and cruelty into the amusing occurrences that result from Don Quixote's misinterpretations of the world. The mockery and cruelty may stem from a distortion of the realities surrounding him, an inability to meet contemporary standards, and simply being too different in a society that has long departed from traditional norms. The reader may find Don Quixote's adventures absurd, far removed from those a chivalrous hero would undergo in seventeenth-century Spain. In this context, the often cruel and mocking responses of other characters may not seem shocking. But did Cervantes really mean to bring forth the mockery of a knight errant with dreams and an adventurous zeal?

This question has been a subject of debate for a very long time, generating seminal works by scholars like Oscar Mandel and John Jay Allen, whose analytical readings of academic interpretations of *Don Quixote* have contributed immensely to a better understanding of the novel. It is now widely accepted that interpreting characteristics of

Don Quixote in singular terms, such as viewing him as a Christ-like hero, like Miguel de Unamuno did, is viable but not altogether warranted, since *Don Quixote* is a heterogeneous novel, one that fundamentally defines the principles of perspectivism.

Building upon the rich tradition of Cervantes studies—where critics have established a range of "soft" or "hard" approaches towards the novel, treating Don Quixote as a "hero," a "fool,"[1] or somewhere in between—I see Cervantes's depiction of adventures not simply as a parody of medieval romances of chivalry, an imitation of knight errantry with a dream to bring it back to life, but also as an experiment. As such, Don Quixote's sally, adventures, and return do not connote a hero's journey as defined by Joseph Campbell; they each comprise experiments in themselves. These experiments are designed *by* him (prevalent in Part I; i.e., attacking the windmills) or *for* him (prevalent in Part II; i.e., the flight to the Kingdom of Candaya). Rather than a mere consequence of knight errantry and of the dream to bring justice to the world, the experiments in *Don Quixote* also ask *what if?* What if giants were fought? What if prostitutes were treated like damsels? What if peasants became governors? The consequences of the actions propelled by such inquiries may be branded as misadventures, or perhaps as heroic deeds, but that all depends on readers and the angles through which they approach Don Quixote's quest. Each adventure that Cervantes writes about proposes a hypothesis—or better, a perspectivist hypothesis—posed and pondered by individual readers.[2]

To re-accentuate Don Quixote's adventurer trait does not require writing about feats that a character undertakes outside of their home. It is not the Odyssean journey of an exemplary hero after which the voyager will return triumphant and be rewarded, as Campbell defines such journeys. In fact, Don Quixote and his re-accentuated counterparts represent quite the opposite, but, in their limited contexts, they

---

1 See Mandel's "The Function of the Norm in *Don Quixote*" for soft and hard approaches and Allen's *Don Quixote: Hero or Fool?* (1979) for approaches to Cervantes's character as either a hero or a fool.

2 The word perspectivist here does not relate to Leo Spitzer's study of *Don Quixote* through the lens of linguistic perspectivism, but rather refers, in general terms, to the philosophical principles of perspectivism.

may achieve some sort of heroic stature because of their quests. Like Don Quixote, their feats may be seen as heroic or foolish. Yet, these characters are rather ordinary people, frequently described as less than capable of successfully setting out on a journey with a mission. As they pursue their missions and dreams, their adventures are comical, often misunderstood, and largely self-serving, although they may claim that they are for the common good. Like Don Quixote, they are also readers, dreamers, or lovers, and their respective novels are products of visible Cervantine influence.

The overarching story of these quixotic creatures is quite philosophical. Like Don Quixote, the adventurers that succeed him ask *what if?* "What if poetry were revolutionized?" ask Bolaño's poets. "What if superheroes were real?" asks Mitchell's dreamer. "What if we humorized life's misfortunes?" asks Sterne's narrator. "And what if," ask all of the adventurers, "we went out into the world and embodied our dreams?" Each novel examined in this chapter presents lengthy travels, discoveries of places, and the *autopoiesis* of re-accentuated Quixotes, while the writers, true Virgils, guide us Dantes through their chaotic worlds.

## Quixotic Adventurers of England

The rise of the novel has been a topic of great debate among various scholars. Some, Watt included, have insisted that the novel as a genre took its shape within the works of Fielding, Richardson, Defoe, and their contemporaries. But those familiar with the process of the rise of the novelistic genre in Spain—from *La Celestina* to romances (sentimental, picaresque, chivalric, pastoral, and others) to *Don Quixote*—have disagreed with the claims regarding the eighteenth-century English novel. In fact, various prominent works of eighteenth-century England are not clear semblances of what the novelistic genre would become, but rather seem influenced by what is widely accepted to be the first modern novel, Cervantes's *Don Quixote*. One can hardly add to the extensive work carried out in this sphere over the past decade by scholars like Garrido Ardila, who have studied Cervantine influences in English novels in scrupulous detail.[3] Considering these influences, let us look at two prominent English works of the eighteenth century, *Joseph Andrews* and *Tristram Shandy*, through the scope of re-accentuated quixotic traits, especially that of the adventurer.

*Joseph Andrews* (1742) by Henry Fielding is regarded as one of the earliest modern English novels. It is also one of the best examples of Fielding's quixotic novels, showcasing the deep inspiration that *Don Quixote* brought to his literary career, an inspiration that is also prominent in several other of his works, including *Tom Jones* (1749). The technical resonances and similarities between Cervantes's and Fielding's characters exhibit an imitation of manners (as Fielding states on the title page of *Joseph Andrews*), as well as of structure, plots, and heroes (Church 11; Garrido Ardila, *Cervantes* 126). In effect, the profusion of quixotic characters and Cervantine techniques across Fielding's writing has often led him to be called "the English Cervantes" (Paulson 58).

There are several stylistic similarities between *Don Quixote* and *Joseph Andrews*. Both include various unrevealed details, such as the setting "Somewhere in La Mancha . . ." or "Leonora . . . lived with an aunt of hers in a town in the north of England" (Cervantes 19; Fielding, *Joseph* 103). The acclamation of telling a true story also forms a remarkable part of each. In addition, just like *Don Quixote*, *Joseph Andrews* contains numerous embedded stories. Both Cervantes and Fielding sometimes address their readers directly, which suggests that both writers were conscious, at all times, of the audience who would judge their literary production: "Idle reader: without my swearing to it, you can believe that I would like this book, the child of my understanding, to be the most beautiful, the most brilliant, and the most discreet that anyone could imagine" (Cervantes 3); " . . . I shall leave to my good-natured reader to apply my piece to my observations, and will detain him no longer than with a word concerning the characters in this work" (Fielding, *Joseph* 37). Giving comical names to characters is yet another narrative technique that Fielding may have adopted from Cervantes.

3 Garrido Ardila's *Cervantes en Inglaterra* (2014) and *A History of the Spanish Novel* (2015) represent some of his extensive work on Cervantes in England and the rise of the novel.

For both writers, names can be grotesque but provoke laughter at the same time, as exemplified in Cervantes's Caraculiambro and Micomicona and Fielding's Slipslop and Didapper. Caraculiambro, a monster, is made up of *cara* ("face"), *culi* or *culo* ("butt"), and *ambro* (which, like *ambos*, means "both"). Meanwhile, in Fielding's Slipslop, *slip* and *slop* bring to mind disgusting, watery food. Margaret Church claims that these and other similarities indicate Fielding's "adherence to outward symmetry, polish, and consistency in comparison with Cervantes's structure,[4] which is almost always closely tied in with the inner and often chaotic motivations of his characters" (15). Although Fielding may seek to formulate a critical narration that would be in accord with the culture and values of his society, his original intent, according to Ronald Paulson, is "to focus on the imitation of the book, or what he calls 'affectation'" (59). Fielding's narrative "affectations" remind the reader of Cervantes's novel in many ways, but most noteworthy are the protagonists Joseph Andrews and Abraham Adams, who make up a prominent part of the novel's quixotic reading.

Various critics have claimed that Parson Adams is the character who most resembles Don Quixote in *Joseph Andrews*. For example, Mark Spilka argues that Abraham Adams, like his predecessor Don Quixote, "cuts a bizarre figure outwardly, but, at the same time, his inner dignity remains unassailable;" while his peculiarities might be funny, he is presented in this manner "so that he stands half within Fielding's theory of humor and half without" (81). Church compares Parson Adams's sally to Don Quixote's, claiming that although the two protagonists travel for different reasons, Fielding imitates most of Cervantes's narrative aesthetic to invoke a funny but sympathetic presentation of his characters. She proceeds:

---

4 According to A. A. Parker, Fielding gave the modern novel flawless shape and structure, as opposed to Cervantes, whose *Don Quixote* presents "formless and haphazard structure" (2). Parker believes that *Don Quixote* is not composed as a unified text but rather is a compilation of chapters that are not a flowing continuation of each other. Fielding, imitating Cervantes, worked on the techniques of his novel and applied to them "the rules of the epic structure" (2).

> For example, Adams sets forth from his parish in order to sell his sermons so that he can better support his family, and Joseph (somewhat like Sancho) goes forth merely in servant capacity in the retinue of Lady Booby. Their withdrawal to their parish is not in the nature of a retreat or defeat in purpose: Adams returns because he finds he has left his sermons at home (as Don Quixote has left at home his purse, some clean shirts, and a box of ointments in his first sally in the 1605 *Quixote*, a sally that does not mark an inner turning point for the don), and Joseph returns to see his beloved Fanny. (Church 14-15)

In addition to Adams's oddities and his sallies, his offer to instruct Joseph in Latin is comparable to Don Quixote's promise to grant Sancho an island (Ziolkowski 66). It is true that Adams and Don Quixote have much in common: for example, their unconventional manner of dressing and their wish to rescue damsels.[5] Although these characteristics are persuasive evidence that Abraham Adams does resemble Don Quixote, there is also the title character of the novel, who exposes other similarities with Cervantes's hero.

5 Church provides a detailed list of similarities between these two characters and the novels: "If we are to stress one of these, surely it must be *Don Quixote*; for innumerable parallels, not only of structure but of plot, incident, and character, abound. Just for examples we could cite: Adams's inappropriate dress and Don Quixote's armor; Adams covered with hogs' blood, Don Quixote with curds; Adams's stumbling horse and Rocinante; Adams's rescue of Fanny and Don Quixote's rescue of various damsels in distress; the bird batters and the group of netting small birds in *Don Quixote* (1615; chap. 58); Adams's devotion to Aeschylus and Don Quixote's to *Amadis of Gaul*; the mock epic melee in the Tow-wouse inn and the mock epic melee in *Don Quixote* (1605; chap. 45); the battle between the squire's dogs, Adams, and Joseph, and that between Don Quixote and the sheep; the bedroom scene at Booby Hall and the attic scene in *Don Quixote* (1605; chap 16); Slipslop and Maritornes; Mr. Wilson and the Gentlemen in Green; Adams's witchcraft and Don Quixote's enchanters; Adams's 'roasting' by the Squire and Don Quixote's 'roasting' by the Duke and Duchess; Joseph's love song to Fanny and Don Louis's love song to Doña Clara; the story of Paul and Leonard and 'The Tale of Foolish Curiousity'" (35).

Joseph Andrews also exhibits comparable characteristics with Don Quixote. One explicit quixotic aspect of Joseph is his idealized love towards Fanny, a trait that propels Joseph to undergo various adventures to reach his beloved woman. But Joseph's love, Fanny, is real and appears in the novel, unlike the love of Don Quixote, Dulcinea, who is imagined and never once makes an appearance (although it is known that her image is based on a peasant woman named Aldonza Lorenzo). Joseph's feelings for his beloved become the reason for his travels, essentially turning him into an adventurer as he stumbles upon various feats along his way.

Thinking of Joseph as the re-accentuated quixotic lover and adventurer and Adams as the reader and dreamer, it is a little difficult to assert that Fielding wanted to create a single re-accentuated Quixote in either of his heroes. According to Church, the differences between Joseph Andrews and Abraham Adams are part of a comic pattern, whereas the differences between Don Quixote and Sancho come from deeper psychological sources, which suggests that Cervantes's characters are more prototypical than Fielding's (29). Raimund Borgmeier brings forth the opinions of various critics who present quixotic characteristics as a split between Parson Adams and Joseph Andrews: "Gilman . . . thinks that 'Parson Adams' function in the novel was to resemble that of Cervantes's pair [i.e., both Don Quixote and Sancho Panza].' Ballesteros . . . gives the opinion that, 'In Fielding's novel, the quixotic attributes are divided between Joseph Andrews and Parson Adams'" (56). According to Jean Canavaggio, however, the split and mixed quixotic characteristics shared by Joseph and Abraham create a sort of mismatch in the quixotic sense of the novel (124). Considering all these observations, I believe that Fielding's intention was to quixotize his main adventurers to some extent in order to create a polyphony of satiric imitation in his narrative discourse—an amalgam of parody and satire, re-accentuated characters, the linguistic and stylistic complexity germane to Cervantes, and of course, imitation, as he states on his title page.

Cervantine scenes also seem to influence Fielding's novel. One example is the inn. As in *Don Quixote*, the inn in *Joseph Andrews* is the place where people meet, where conflicts brew and are solved. The use of a public space—the road for much of the novel, which inevitably leads to adventures—also shows inspiration of Cervantes. Fielding's adventure-inspired scenes, of course, are not only a product of mere imitation and influence. He borrows Cervantine concepts and adapts them to his contemporary context, something that leads to varied interpretations in readers. For instance, gathering at an inn in the context of Cervantes does not necessarily carry the same connotation in Fielding's England. And so, finding meanings in such similar scenes raises curiosity toward Fielding's intentions to imitate Cervantine narratives.

The aspects of *Joseph Andrews* that coincide with *Don Quixote* do not limit the reader's immense platform of possible interpretations of the English novel. As *Don Quixote* has garnered a vast array of evaluation and criticism of the intentions of the author, *Joseph Andrews*, too, enjoys different interpretations by critics. This novel, written in eighteenth-century Britain, bears didactic intents and represents the human being, according to C. R. Kropf (114). Drawing support for his arguments mainly from the conversations between Joseph and Abraham, Kropf is convinced that Fielding intended to represent human nature and his posture towards education (116-17). Spilka, on the other hand, thinks that Fielding wanted to make his readers love his characters like Cervantes made his laugh at his protagonist. As Spilka points out:

> But through his admiration for Cervantes he has unconsciously seized on the principle of the *comic figure*—the whole man who is at once lovable and ridiculous, whose entire character is involved in each of his humorous actions, and whose character must be established through time and incident, in the reader's mind, before he becomes "wholly" laughable. To put it in different terms, when someone we know and like is involved in ridiculous action, then the humor of the situation broadens and quickens to include our identification with and sympathy for that person. A sudden or prolonged juxtaposition of his inner dignity with his outer "awkwardness" produces a state of mixed emotions in us—love, sympa-

> thy, and identification, as well as condescension—and this state is released or resolved, in turn, through laughter. (81-82)

Written in different social and cultural contexts and meant to represent distinct geographical spaces and time periods, both *Don Quixote* and *Joseph Andrews* also serve to point out problematic aspects of their respective societies. Cervantes implicitly referred to controversies of his time, as seen in the book-burning episode that points to the censorship of the Inquisition, the conversation between Ricote and Sancho that offers a window into the possible emotional realities of the Morisco people who were expelled from Spain, or even the episode between Andrés and Juan Haldudo that makes visible the abuse of workers by corrupt masters. For *Joseph Andrews*, Spilka notes that:

> Fielding saw affectation in two of its forms, vanity and hypocrisy, as the "only source of the true Ridiculous," and he hoped to expose these qualities wherever he found them. Accordingly, he also designed his novel along more general lines: three virtuous, good-natured persons—Joseph, Fanny, and Adams—must be thrust through every level of society as exemplars or as touchstones and instruments for exposing vanity and hypocrisy, and, just as important, goodness and kindness, in whomever they meet. (81)

All the events and adventures in both *Don Quixote* and *Joseph Andrews*—whether or not they have a didactic purpose, as seen by Kropf, or offer social criticism, as Spilka notes—contribute to the growth of each character. Don Quixote, Sancho Panza, Joseph Andrews, and Parson Adams all undergo journeys that eventually change them. Joseph Bartolomeo, for example, reads Fielding's novel as an attempt at ridiculization provoked by gender role exchange. As Bartolomeo describes it, Joseph occupies a stereotypical feminine position but gradually manages to assume a masculine role (61). Whether or not one should see a gender inversion in Joseph, his growth in the novel as a character comes forth noticeably. Through characters like him, who do not remain stationary but recompose themselves, I believe that Fielding wanted to create a type of an *autopoietic* novel similar to *Don Quixote*. Like his predecessor, Don Quixote, Joseph Andrews goes through a process of self-discovery and self-realization. The transformations of both characters are no doubt due to the adventures that they undergo. As Cervantes states: "he who reads much and travels much sees and knows a great deal" (625). This statement can describe anyone; yet when one encounters a reader and traveler in literature, who comes to mind first? I think Don Quixote. The Spanish *hidalgo* grew into a knight errant thanks to his reading and adventures, yet through his transformations became one of the most generative characters of world literature. Fielding understood that about the Spanish hero, and in turn, intended to create relatable characters. As he stated in *Joseph Andrews*: "I describe not Men, but Manners; not an Individual, but a Species" (148).

## Misfortunes and Adventures

Laurence Sterne wrote his novel *The Life and Opinions of Tristram Shandy, Gentleman* in nine volumes, the first two of which were published in 1759. The other seven were published in 1761, 1762, 1765, and 1767. The novel became one of Sterne's most celebrated works and among those most appreciated by his contemporary readers. Like Fielding's *Joseph Andrews*, *Tristram Shandy* has various characters who share quixotic traits. A unique work that, as the title suggests, serves as an autobiography of Tristram and presents his opinions relating mostly to the life of his uncle, the novel offers an enthralling quixotic reading.

In the early volumes, the first-person narrator relates Tristram's conception, birth, and baptism, as well as events from his early life. Erroneously baptized by a name that in Latin signifies "sad, sorrowful" (*tristis*), Tristram genuinely believes that all the milestones in his life have been unfortunate. Following the details of his childhood and youth is the story of his Uncle Toby. A wounded veteran, Uncle Toby is obsessed with battle and war strategies and wants to build a replica of the site where he fought. (Sterne gives Toby's and everybody else's obsessions the name "hobby-horses.") Toby spends a great deal of time with his friend Trim while working on rebuilding the fortifications of the site. Trim plays the role of a loyal companion, assisting Toby, giving him advice, and serving as a great conversationalist. Later, Sterne's readers learn about Toby's romantic interest in Mrs. Wadman, a widow, which Toby is too shy to even realize himself; other characters help him come to understand that his sentiments are amorous. Then the reader's attention is shifted back to Tristram, who is on the road, traveling (even here he is unlucky). The last two volumes are dedicated to the love life of Uncle Toby. The novel ends with comments by Tristram's father, Walter, which are presumably intended to shift the amorous turn of the earlier chapters of the novel.

A novel brimful of adventure and satire, *Tristram Shandy* "is very much derivative in theme, structure, and technique from *D[on] Q[uixote]*" (Mancing, *Encyclopedia II* 691). A particular resemblance with *Don Quixote* that might strike the reader is the disordered narration. Sterne, in fact, developed a narrative technique similar to that of Cervantes—he presents an order of events that evolve into disorder. "A world of disorderly notions" is how Hanlon, for instance, describes the microcosm of Don Quixote and his re-accentuated counterparts.[6] Similarly, as D. W. Jefferson states, the phrase "order in disorder" is specifically relevant when describing the structure of *Tristram Shandy*: "Sterne took pleasure in destroying the normal order of things and in creating an exaggerated appearance of disorder, but only to link up the pieces in another and more interesting way" (34). Structurally, Sterne's novel resembles Cervantes's in several ways. First, the novel is divided into nine volumes, and each has short chapters. Like *Don Quixote, Tristram Shandy* presents various intercalated stories and narrations, among them letters, prayers, and short stories, which sometimes occupy a narrative space of various chapters. As Mancing notes, "The narrator Tristram makes his own quixotic effort to bring his narrative, with all its overly Benengelian tone and many references to *D[on] Q[uixote]*, always slipping further and further behind his goal" (*Encyclopedia II* 691). With words of praise referring to "this reverend gentleman," Don Quixote, whom the narrator claims to "love more . . . than the greatest hero of antiquity" (Sterne 22), *Tristram Shandy* also abounds with quixotic themes and aspects: a zeal for perfection (Walter writing a textbook for his son), obsessions (everybody's "hobby-horses," espe-

6 See Hanlon's *A World of Disorderly Notions* (2019).

cially Toby's passion for reading military books and building a replica of the battlefield), love (Uncle Toby and the widow Wadman), and, of course, adventures (Tristram's life reads like an adventure).

Most of Sterne's descriptions of characters and their behavior allude to *Don Quixote*, and many of his literary figures represent some quixotic aspect. Alter proposes that Sterne's incorporation of various re-accentuated characters "suggest[s] an infinite *dédoublement*, for everyone is quixotic in putting some private construction of the mind—some personal lexicon—upon reality, and any other is a potential Sancho to one's own quixotry" (39). According to Mancing, it is Yorick who surpasses all the quixotic characters, especially because his horse resembles Rocinante so much so that he is referred to as his brother (*Encyclopedia II* 691).[7] However, Mancing agrees with Alter that there is not just one quixotic character in *Tristram Shandy*:

> But in addition to the obviously quixotic Yorick, both Walter Shandy and Uncle Toby are D[on] Q[uixote] figures, each with his own "hobby-horse," Sterne's term for a quixotic obsession, which is harmless "so long as a man rides [it] peaceably and quietly along the King's highway, and neither compels you or me to get up behind him." In Toby's case, his hobby-horse is his reading of books of military architecture that is specifically compared to D[on] Q[uixote]'s reading of romances of chivalry. (*Encyclopedia II* 691)

7 As stated in *Tristram Shandy*: "Be it known then, that, for about five years before the date of the midwife's licence, of which you have had so circumstantial an account,—the parson we have to do with had made himself a country-talk by a breach of all decorum, which he had committed against himself, his station, and is office;—and that was, in never appearing better, or otherwise mounted, that upon a lean, sorry, jack-ass of a horse, value about one pound fifteen shillings; who, to shorten all description of him, was full brother of *Rocinante*, as far as similitude congenial could make him; for he answered his description to a hair-breadth in every thing,—except that I do not remember 'tis any where said, that *Rocinante* was broken winded; and that, moreover, *Rocinante*, as is the happiness of most *Spanish* horses, fat or lean,—was undoubtedly a horse at all points" (Sterne 17-18).

Sterne adapts the *Cervantic[k]* technique of assigning his male characters a "substitute" activity or "hobby-horse:" Uncle Toby and Trim have a miniature battle site, Walter is concerned with the Tristapaedia, and Tristram is the writer of his biography and of others' life stories (Narozny and Wilson 142).[8] The protagonist shares his idea about what writing is, which can immediately be associated with Cervantes's style of narrating the story of Don Quixote. In his words:

> Writing, when properly managed, (as you may be sure I think mine is) is but a different name for conversation: As no one, who knows what he is about in good company, would venture to talk all;—so no author, who understands the just boundaries of decorum and good breeding, would presume to think all: The truest respect which you can pay to the reader's understanding, is to halve this matter amicably, and leave him something to imagine, in his turn, as well as yourself. (Sterne 108-09)

Tristram, who also has Bakhtin-defined carnivalesque experiences,[9] like his birth or his accidental circumcision, exhibits quixotic characteristics. He travels, he reads and writes, and he dreams—all building his re-accentuated image of the knight errant. Similar to his predecessor, most everything Tristram does turns out to be wrong, and he is almost never able to receive the expected outcome of his actions.

Toby is perhaps the only character who can be considered a complete re-accentuated image of Don Quixote, representing all the quixotic traits.[10] He returns from war with a wound, which can be seen as

---

8 Sterne coins the term *Cervantick* in chapter 12 of volume I of *Tristram Shandy*. The term became widely used thereafter with a slight spelling change, *Cervantic*. Currently, *Cervantine* or *Cervantean* are used to convey a similar meaning when describing something of, from, or by Cervantes.

9 See Bakhtin's *Rabelais and His World* for an extensive commentary on carnival.

10 Wayne Booth points out: "It has long been customary in literary histories to say that Sterne was influenced by Cervantes" (38). The fact that Sterne cites *Don Quixote* as one of his models on various occasions, and presents "striking similarities between Uncle Toby, with his servant Trim, and Don

an implicit reference to Don Quixote given the meaning of his name.[11] The choice of the alias Quixote by Alonso Quijano can be interpreted as reflecting his impotency, adding depth to Toby's character and narrative parallels between the two.[12] After his return from the battle, Toby becomes extremely immersed in his own world of battle, reading military books and building his battle site replica. Trim, who represents the re-accentuated Sancho, motivates Toby and encourages his pursuit of the miniature battleground. Furthermore, both Toby and Don Quixote find themselves in silly and embarrassing love situations: Don Quixote with Maritornes and Altisidora while idealizing Dulcinea, and Toby with Wadman. In each case, the reader suspects the impotence of these old men, and both, in truth, fail to engage in love affairs beyond platonic terms.

*Tristram Shandy*, like *Don Quixote*, contains several picaresque narrative aspects. As illustrated in Bakhtin's *Rabelais and His World*, picaresque fiction is not simply about hunger, survival, mockery, and adventures. They are similar to *Bildüngsromane*: the protagonist grows into the character he or she is at the end of the novel thanks to the adventures and misfortunes presented throughout his or her journey. In *Don Quixote*, however, the picaresque is most explicitly posited in the character of the captive Ginés de Pasamonte, who writes his own story but cannot bring it to its finish line, as he is still alive:

> "And what is the title of the book?" asked Don Quixote.
>
> "The life of *Ginés de Pasamonte*," Ginés replied.
>
> "And is it finished?" asked Don Quixote.

---

Quixote, with his servant Sancho, have been noted again and again as evidence for the relationship" (38).

11 This detail coincides with an episode of Miguel de Cervantes's life. The Spanish writer himself was a soldier and returned from the Lepanto battle with a disabled left hand, which is yet another indication of Sterne's influence by Cervantes (Durán and Rogg 16).

12 In addition, Quexada, one of Don Quixote's possible names before he reveals his true name, means a shield that covers the upper part of the legs and protects masculinity (*queixada*).

> "How can it be finished," he responded, "if my life isn't finished yet? What I have written goes from my birth to the moment when they sentenced me to the galleys this last time." (Cervantes 169)

In *Tristram Shandy*, meanwhile, the picaresque is presented in the figure of Tristram. His birth, unfortunate circumcision, unfinished education, and trip to France, among other aspects of his life, indicate the author's intention to introduce picaresque features into the novel. Some critics think that *Tristram Shandy* is an imitation and satire of the picaresque. As B. H. Lehman notes:

> One called it a "picaresque of the intellect," and Saintsbury drew on his second language, the first having given out, and called it a "fatrasie." They measured the book by its predecessors and successors; it was "a travesty of the regular novel, the main lines of which had been so carefully drawn at the theory so ably expounded by Fielding." They described it in terms of other things instead of describing it in terms of itself; it was "a mere caricature of the novel" compared with "the serious works of fiction" which preceded it. (167-68)

Lehman also believes that *Tristram Shandy* is not a book written for mere fun and entertainment, which is true about *Don Quixote*, as well. What both novels offer is "philosophic laughter," a casual fun that can be approached critically at the same time, one that exhibits the profound wit of their writers (168). For example, in *Don Quixote,* Rocinante's desire to "pleasure himself" stands out as a highly comical episode (Cervantes 103). Don Quixote's horse, seeing ponies in the field, is filled with desire, and so he goes without asking "permission of his owner . . . to communicate his need" with "the ladies" (103). Cervantes's archaic and well-elaborated language makes this episode especially humorous and memorable. But his intention was not simply to make the reader laugh at his language, the awkward situation created between the male and female horses, or the reactions of their owners. In Rocinante, Cervantes creates a cognizant, humanized character with thoughts and desires pertinent to his own world. The horse is also the one who chooses Don Quixote's route when the latter first leaves his house for adventures: "... he immediately grew serene and continued on his way, following only the path his horse wished to take, believing that the virtue of his adventures lay in doing this" (25). In this manner, while Cervantes creates a funny narrative involving a horse, he allows for his reader to also approach such episodes with thoughtfulness, laughing philosophically.

In *Tristram Shandy*, humor lies both in the way Tristram represents occurrences and in the actions of other characters. One of the first and most amusing long narrations is the description of Tristram's birth. His observations are comical: his mother does not go to London to give birth because she has had false alarms before, the doctor does not arrive on time, the father passes out, and it seems like nothing can go right. And the reader learns of all these events from a narrator who is not omniscient but a character describing his own birth. The credibility of Tristram's descriptions therefore becomes questionable. As Lehman notes:

> The point is that Tristram is a figure in the novel, not a mere projection of Sterne. He has a nature and a quality of his own. In a sense nothing happens to him, certainly no events that can be laid end to end and called an action. Yet he observes everything and reflects on everything, even if often the reflection is implicit in the report. His mind is in continuous activity, under the dominance of its own laws. There is no selection and ordering in terms of an issue raised by an impermanent or local morality, nor in terms of a falsifying line of action called a plot. (173-74)

It is noteworthy that Tristram is absent as a character at the beginning of the novel, yet he establishes a prominent presence with his voice. He tells his story and that of others as if he were involved in the situations he describes, as if he were someone who could observe himself and others at the moment; yet, Tristram has not been physically present in all of the occurrences he relays. A comparable situation occurs in the second volume of *Don Quixote*, when the knight and squire learn about a book written about them and realize that there is a sort of live chronicling taking place as they move along, having adventures.

At that point, both Don Quixote and Sancho Panza have the possibility of creating their own story as though they were the ones telling it. And when they tell a story, of course, they want to be able to highlight or omit some aspects of their everyday lives and adventures, just like Tristram does, thus, yes, "taking away or adding to them."[13]

*Joseph Andrews* and *Tristram Shandy* were both considered popular reads in eighteenth-century England. As we have seen, the novels are unique quixotic works, among the first of their kind, and in them, neither Fielding nor Sterne sought to create a singular representation of a re-accentuated Quixote. Rather, many characters are re-accentuated Quixotes and Sanchos, and several episodes strive to represent a funny, quixotic manner of occurrences. It is obvious that both writers, using generic quixotic themes, have achieved long-lasting literary criticism of the ridiculous, the adventurer, the obsessed, the jealous, and the ignorant—all while offering a reading full of hearty laughs and entertainment.

## Unforeseen Adventures

*Monsignor Quixote* (1982) by Graham Greene is another unique representation of re-accentuated characters of *Don Quixote*. The author imitates almost all the main characters from Cervantes's novel, but Greene's protagonists live in post-Franco Spain and reflect the social, political, and religious life of their time.[14] The depiction of the priest accompanied by a communist, the fights against the *Guardia Civil*, and the conversations two friends have over wine paint a perfect, and

13 The phrase is taken from the episode in which *Don Quixote*'s narrator finds Cide Hamete Benengeli's manuscript in Toledo and asks a translator to translate it for him "without taking away or adding anything to them" (Cervantes 67-68).

14 According to Cayetano Estébanez Estébanez, numerous references in *Monsignor Quixote* allude to *Don Quixote*. Still, the author claims that Greene's novel, although very successful, falls short of the fine humor observed in Cervantes (304).

at the same time funny, presentation of what a late-twentieth-century *Don Quixote* might look like.[15]

The protagonist of *Monsignor Quixote* is Father Quixote, a priest who lives in a small town in La Mancha called Toboso.[16] He thinks he is a descendant of Don Quixote, which makes other villagers believe that he might be a little delusional.[17] His life changes when he encounters and offers his help to an Italian Bishop, after which the Pope gives him the title Monsignor. The Bishop of Toboso, however, does not approve of the Monsignor and wants to dismiss him from town. Realizing that the Bishop has secret plans for his dismissal, Monsignor Quixote leaves himself before the Bishop can make him. In order to hide the real reason for his departure, he claims that he will only be away on vacation, but for an indefinite period of time. Meanwhile, the former mayor of Toboso, Sancho Zancas, who is disappointed by the

15 Alberto Lázaro Lafuente considers *Monsignor Quixote* the best modern recreation of the knight's adventures in the region of La Mancha (269). It is also important to mention that Greene dedicated his novel to the Spanish Father Leopoldo Durán, his friend and companion during his trips around Spain for various years. With Father Durán, Greene learned about Spain, its traditions, and its literature. The experiences and conversations they had in the places they visited are rendered in Greene's quixotic novel. This fact is also recorded in the biography of Greene that Father Durán wrote after his friend's death, *Graham Greene: amigo y hermano* (1996; 269-70).

16 In Cervantes's novel, Toboso is the village of Aldonza Lorenzo, to whom Don Quixote gives the name of Dulcinea del Toboso.

17 While Greene's characters know that Don Quixote is a fictional hero created by Cervantes, Father Quixote is convinced that Don Quixote was a real person and that he is a descendant of one of the most eminent figures of Spanish culture. This concept, introduced by Greene, opens an interesting cognitive interpretation. Father Quixote is unable to differentiate fiction from reality, just like Don Quixote. However, in the case of Cervantes's hero, it was clear that the *hidalgo* desired to imitate fictional characters and become the live embodiment and representation of the chivalric world. In Greene's novel, Father Quixote is not trying to imitate a model; the protagonist shows an inability to categorize Don Quixote as a fictional character; he is unable to tell fiction and reality apart and interprets fictional and real events as equal.

newly elected republicans, shows interest in joining Monsignor Quixote on his journey and becomes the latter's re-accentuated Sancho.[18] Father Quixote agrees to have him along, and the two set off. Their trips throughout Spain are each an adventure, comparable to the experiences the protagonists of Cervantes's novel undergo. As Sancho Zancas points out, the fight against the *Guardia* is like Don Quixote's fight with the windmills, and the rescue of the statue of the Virgin Mary from capitalists is comparable to Cervantes's knight errant's rescue of the lady from the Basques. The novel, as expected, ends by informing us "How Monsignor Quixote Rejoined his Ancestor" (Greene 203).

As mentioned above, *Monsignor Quixote* presents a variety of re-accentuated characters based on Cervantes's novel. Father Quixote adopts Don Quixote's most recognized features. Zancas's nickname is Sancho, eponymous to Cervantes's hero, and as Monsignor Quixote's re-accentuated squire, he becomes his companion throughout his trips and adventures. Father Quixote even refers to his old car, a SEAT 600, as Rocinante to "commemorate his ancestor's horse" (Ziolkowski 217). Greene's novel also adapts the romanticized and idealized figure of a beloved; Dulcinea was Father Quixote's love when he was young.

*Don Quixote* and *Monsignor Quixote* also reference various points in the history of Spain in their respective times (Henríquez Jiménez 317). For example, Cervantes's Sancho is frightened of the *Santa Hermandad*, while Greene's re-accentuated Sancho is afraid of the *Guardia Civil*.[19] The *Santa Hermandad* and the *Guardia Civil* were important parts of Spanish history, each existing in the era when these two novels were written. In Greene's novel, the dialogues on religion between the re-accentuated Don Quixote and the twentieth-century Sancho move away from discussions about new or old Christians to focus on such distinctions as good and bad Catholics. These dialogues contrast with Cervantes's work, where criticism often emerges through metaphoric

18 Note the resemblance the name Sancho Zancas (shanks) bears to Sancho Panza (belly).

19 The *Guardia Civil* (founded in 1844) was based on ideas like those that the *Santa Hermandad* began formulating in 1265. Similar in political beliefs and parallel in functionality, the *Santa Hermandad* is considered its forerunner.

or subtle remarks due to the heavy censorship of the period, including that of the Inquisition.

In addition, Don Quixote and Monsignor Quixote share a number of traits. Both are keen readers, but Monsignor Quixote is fond of theological books, not chivalric romances. As mentioned earlier, Monsignor Quixote is seen as a madman for firmly believing that Cervantes's Quixote is his ancestor. The quixotic features of the old romantic lover and dreamer also emerge in Greene's protagonist, while his life is marked by adventures. Cervantes's re-accentuated cast, along with other characters in Greene's novel, resonate with a number of other aspects of Cervantes's work as well. Monsignor Quixote wears purple socks and bibs that Zancas compares to Don Quixote's famous helmet of Mambrino. As mentioned above, Toboso in La Mancha is the town where Father Quixote and Sancho live in Greene's work and is the village of Cervantes's Dulcinea. Furthermore, Zancas, like other characters in Greene's novel, is well-versed in *Don Quixote*, enriching the narrative with numerous examples, comparisons, and commentaries about the work. All of these comparisons, resonances, imitations, contexts, and characters make *Monsignor Quixote* a unique quixotic novel based on and inspired by *Don Quixote*. Greene is able to make his reader laugh in a manner similar to Cervantes, while he neatly changes the image of the main characters of *Don Quixote* and elegantly adapts them into two adventurers of twentieth-century Spain.

## A Quixotic Superhero

Canadian writer Ken Mitchell's comic imitation of *Don Quixote*, published in 2003, is another novel that brings together various re-accentuated characters in adventure-driven episodes recontextualized from Cervantes's novel. *The Heroic Adventures of Donny Coyote* describes the eccentric exploits of the title character and his companion, Sandra Dollar. The novel describes North American society of the twenty-first century, and the hero is a native of a small town, Moose Jaw, in the province of Saskatchewan, Canada. Donny Coyote represents a re-accentuated Quixote in his spirit of an adventurer, deriving from his dream to recreate a utopian world of fiction. Sandra is his travel buddy and helper, a re-accentuated Sancho, who shares with him similar ideas as they set out together on a quest to change the world. Although she does not always agree with Coyote, Sandra is compassionate and devoted both to him and to his mission to do good. Mitchell's protagonist also has a woman of his dreams, Princess Di, a re-accentuated Princess Dulcinea.

In addition to these characters, the novel represents comical occurences resembling Cervantes's work in theme and structure. First, it offers an order of events comparable to *Don Quixote*; here, too, there is a protagonist consumed with reading fiction. A fan of comic books, Donny Coyote's dream is to become a real-life superhero like the ones he so often reads about. Like Don Quixote, he therefore decides to go out of his house and look for wrongs to right. He then meets Sandra, whom he calls Wonder Woman, and together in an old car, the two friends begin their journey. Their adventures resemble various well-known episodes from *Don Quixote*, such as the scenes of the prisoners, the helmet of Mambrino, the magical balsam *Fierabrás*, and the burning of Don Quixote's books, among numerous others.[20] In this manner, Mitchell's story is an imitation of Cervantes's novel, a re-accentuation of Cervantine heroes, and a parody of comic books that incorporates a presentation and critique of the problems of twenty-first-century North America. As they travel around Canada and the US, the two protagonists witness various issues of the modern world and their effects on society, including corruption, entertainment, and substandard education. By merely presenting the images that the two protagonists see, Mitchell informs his readers of the prevailing reality, making them question what reality actually is. At the end of the novel, Donny Coyote and Sandra reach Las Vegas, where Donny volunteers to be the bodyguard of Ronald Reagan. As expected, he is rejected. He returns to Moose Jaw, where the novel concludes with remarks on Donny Coyote recuperating and contemplating his next journey; he still plans to make the world better, free from injustice or cruelty.

The protagonist of *Donny Coyote* is a clear re-accentuation of Don Quixote, embodying nearly all of the most prominent quixotic traits.

20 In his article "Don Quixote: Coming to America," Mancing provides an elaborate list of parallelisms found between *Don Quixote* and *Donny Coyote* (411-12).

As Mitchell asserts early in the novel, "Coyote's greatest skill . . . was his wild imagination" (4). He nurtures his imagination by reading incessantly and, similar to Don Quixote, the books he reads greatly influence him. In addition, Coyote's car, like Don Quixote's only means of transportation, is barely functional and serves, similar also to Father Quixote's, as a nod to Rocinante. Those who see him driving around in his old Pinto ask him whether he has gone mad. But Coyote is determined to use it to "fight injustice and evil" (21). With his re-accentuated Sancho, he sets off on the adventures that, again, echo *Don Quixote*, including the encounters of Coyote and Wonder Woman with Gino Pasamonte, the enchanted Maritornes, and Princess Micomicona.

Like his precursor, Donny Coyote is in love with a woman who he thinks is the most beautiful person in the world. Like the famous Princess Dulcinea, Princess Di is immaculate, beautiful, and ideal. However, as much as Coyote loves Princess Di, he does show interest in other women, which resembles several subtle implications of similar cases in *Don Quixote*.[21] One particular woman who captures Donny's attention is the perverse cowgirl, Marcella, a re-accentuated Marcela.[22] As opposed to the discreet shepherdess in Cervantes's novel, Mitchell's Marcella is bossy, loud, and spoiled. Donny Coyote becomes fond of

21 Although Don Quixote undoubtedly idealizes the image of his love, Dulcinea, and strongly believes in his imaginary creation, he still shows interest toward other women in the novel. Some of these instances appear to be sexual. For example, in the episode where Maritornes sneaks into the room where Don Quixote and others are sleeping, the knight insists that she sit next to him and refuses to let her go, which creates havoc and results in everyone being beaten. Other women who catch his attention are Altisidora and Marcela, the latter suggesting a less sexual connotation than the rest.

To compare with the above, Johnson shares an interesting conviction that Don Quixote also has women of unconfessed love near home. These are his housekeeper and his niece (*Madness* 79). Because the knight errant could not possibly have any relations with them, he seeks their image in other female characters of the novel (like the image of his niece in Marcela; 101). For more on sexuality and eroticism in several women characters and various scenes in *Don Quixote*, see Brewer.

22 Note the resemblance to the name of Cervantes's character Marcela, whose incorruptible image Mitchell parodies in his Marcella.

her, but deep inside he feels guilty for having Marcella, not his Princess Di, in his thoughts. In one post-fighting scene, for example, after he applies the Firebrass Balm to his face, he drifts into "a blissful sleep, hoping Marcella would appear riding a horse into his dream" (116).[23] Although the balm does not have any real effect on him, after using it, Coyote "is reported to feel 'recovered and well'" (Brink 34).

Re-accentuating most of the prominent characters in *Don Quixote* and recontextualizing these well-known quixotic episodes, Mitchell produces an excellent work that combines humor with social and political critique. While his adventurers make readers laugh at behavior that is marked as delusional, Mitchell raises questions about illegal immigration, the advantages and disadvantages of popular culture, and lack of tolerance for diversity, among other concerns. The issues his characters set out to fix deserve a critical approach and promise to shake the conformist tendencies of readers.

### The Poetics of Adventures

Roberto Bolaño, a Chilean author whose works exhibit complex polyphony, published *Detectives salvajes* (*The Savage Detectives*), "widely acclaimed as the exemplary text of the post-boom era," in 1998 (Aran-

23 Mitchell's Firebrass Balm resembles Cervantes' *Bálsamo de Fierabrás*; both are magical. As Donny claims: "Rawleigh's Firebrass Balm. You can use it for anything—burns or cough syrup, even on snake bites." . . . / "It's hard to find. I'm not even sure Rawleigh's make it any more. But one drop fixes anything. They kept a big five-gallon can of it at the Orange Home, and when I left, they gave me a jarful." / "Jeeze, whudja do with it?" / "I used it whenever I got the flu, or diarrhea, or when I had to cut off a wart. Good for pulled muscles, too, when I'm lifting weights. And once I caught my finger in a bike sprocket and sliced the tip right off. I picked it up from the ground and ran home and rubbed Firebrass balm on it, and stuck it back on and wrapped it in a cloth. It healed as good as new. See?" / "Yuk! What a scar." / "It's magic stuff. If some terrorist blew us up with dynamite, I could stick us together again with Firebrass." / "Better than Krazy Glue, eh?" / "Wish I had some now. Doc put mine somewhere for safekeeping. My skin feels like it's still burning up." / "Quit whining. Remember, a superhero has to take pain." / "Taking pain is different than liking it. It's better to slather ointment than just grin and bear it." (Mitchell 97)

cibia 210). It was translated into English in 2007. The novel relates the story of young poets who become part of a visceral realist poet group and spans the far-reaching boundaries of various geographic locations through some twenty years. It is divided into three parts, with the first and the third sections narrated by Juan García Madero. The latter identifies himself as a member of the visceral realist poet group, although others claim that he "never belonged to the group" (Bolaño, *Savage* 585). García Madero's narration encompasses the time period of 1975 to 1976 and relates his story of joining the mysterious group of poets, trying to formulate their mission, and his quest to find the Mother of the visceral realist poets, Cesárea Tinajero, a woman about whom "everyone says either wonderful or terrible things . . . but no one published her" (165). Fifty-three characters narrate the non-chronological second and largest part of the novel, creating an episode-driven structure that resonates with *Don Quixote*. In fact, Stavans claims that for narrative and other reasons, "Cervantes's masterpiece serves Bolaño as pretext and subtext. The entire book is episodic, alternating between discussions of literature, misadventures, and stories within stories" (*Critic's* 138). Together, the episodic narrative, multiple viewpoints, and polyphonic complexities of the intricate novel bring about a notable Cervantine air.

*Detectives salvajes* reads like a literary adventure, narrating the feats of young men eager to be integral in the visceral realist poets' society. Although García Madero's voice is the most persistent, he is rather peripheral in the circles of the visceral realists. Instead, Ulises Lima and Arturo Belano, who never narrate any part of the novel, are the central characters, accountable for most of the adventures. Ulises, one of the poets, undergoes a name change from "Alfredo Martínez, something like that" to Ulises because of his girlfriend, Laura Damián (Bolaño, *Savage* 34). Later, after meeting Arturo and founding the society of visceral realist poets,[24] the two are usually seen together, traveling, spending time with friends, and writing and reciting poems. Both he

24 Note the resemblance of Arturo Belano's name to Roberto Bolaño. The character inevitably reminds the reader of Bolaño, who was also from Chile, moved to Mexico, worked as a journalist, founded a literary society, and moved to Spain. For more, see Madariaga Caro.

and Arturo are aspiring intellectuals with a mutual interest in reading, especially poetry, and in literary discussions. Because they expose a deep interest in and understanding of literature, they inevitably evoke the trait of a quixotic reader. It is through literature that they are propelled to realize their dream, which becomes the adventurous quest to find the Mother of the poetic movement of visceral realism. Eventually, they are able to find Tinajero; however, they lose her again right away, since she is killed in a fight between the poets and a gang.[25] The achievement of their dream after numerous adventures is reminiscent of Don Quixote, as is the disillusionment that this ephemeral achievement inflicts upon them.

Ulises and Arturo's literary pursuit is partly experienced with their friend, García Madero, and Lupe, a prostitute they are trying to protect. The four set out on an adventurous quest on their way to find Tinajero, meanwhile also avoiding and escaping Alberto, Lupe's pimp, and his gang. Alongside their search for the Mother, Ulises and Arturo travel and undergo life adventures separately, even after witnessing her murder. As indicated by various narrators in the second part of the novel, the two quixotic characters are found traveling, meeting new literary personnel, and leading a bohemian lifestyle in Europe. While Arturo works as a war journalist in Angola, Liberia, and Rwanda, Ulises serves a sentence in Israel. While Arturo finds himself at a book festival in Spain in the midst of writers bragging about their work, Ulises stays in Israel and travels with his neo-Nazi spy friend. In the interim, both encounter various sexual and romantic partners, although none of their love subjects become reminiscent of Dulcinea.

Through their passion for literature, their dream to find the Mother of visceral realism, and the adventures they undergo together or alone as part of their literary journey, Ulises and Arturo make clear re-accentuated quixotic characters. They turn into each other's Don

25 Although Tinajero is omnipresent in the novel, she is only encountered for a fleeting moment at the end. According to Macarena Areco, her unavailability as the Mother of a movement, and in general, either the absence or the futility of parental figures of the young poets (such as the crazed figure of Quim and his unorthodox image of a parent) becomes a central point and even the reason why the young poets are prone to failure (220).

Quixote and Sancho Panza, the former through their salient quixotic traits and the latter through their roles as companion and friend. Their adventures mark the spirit of Bolaño's writing, like that of Cervantes. Bolaño compares his work to that of Twain, author of the quixotic adventures of Tom Sawyer and Huckleberry Finn, a staple of American Realism that has been approximated to *Don Quixote* in its own right; its protagonists too are trying to find their place in a mature world.[26] Bolaño writes:

> So *The Savage Detectives* is more or less forgotten. I can only venture a few thoughts about it. On the one hand I think I see it as a response, one of many, to *Huckleberry Finn*; the Mississippi of *The Savage Detectives* is the flow of voices in the second part of the novel. It's also the more or less faithful transcription of a segment of the life of the Mexican poet Mario Santiago, whose friend I was lucky enough to be. In this sense the novel tries to reflect a kind of generational defeat and also the happiness of a generation, a happiness that at times delineated courage and the limits of courage. To say that I'm permanently indebted to the work of Borges and Cortázar is obvious. I believe there are as many ways to read my novel as there are voices in it. It can be read as a deathbed lament. It can also be read as a game. (*Between* 353)

Similar to those of Twain and Cervantes, Bolaño's protagonists are crusaders for attempting to change the world (Soto and Bravo 45). They persist in their endeavors to achieve their goals and follow their dreams.

Cervantes's and Bolaño's novels represent the real history of the time, and both are representations of their generations (45). The Latin American writer also claims that it is nearly impossible to write a novel and not show the impact of Cervantes.[27] In an interview, Bolaño said: "I think all writers who write in Spanish have or should have a Cer-

26 See Ginés and Wonham for more on a reading of Twain in the context of *Don Quixote*.

27 In one of his interviews, Bolaño was asked if he was Chilean, Spanish, or Mexican. His answer was: "I'm Latin American" (Bolaño, *Between* 357).

vantean influence. We are all indebted to Cervantes, in large or small part, but we are all indebted" (quoted in Álvarez 86). Bolaño, in general, saw *Don Quixote* as a universal work and regarded anyone who achieved a writing style and structure like Cervantes's as successful. He states in an interview:

> . . . a work like *Don Quijote* can resist even the worst translator. As a matter of fact, it can resist mutilation, the loss of numerous pages and even a shit storm. Thus, with everything against it—bad translation, incomplete and ruined—any version of *Quijote* would still have very much to say to a Chinese or an African reader. And that is literature. We may lose a lot along the way. Without a doubt. But perhaps that was its destiny. Come what may. (Soto and Bravo 50)

With this in mind, Bolaño created his *Savage Detectives*, a quixotic story that would speak to any global reader acquainted with twentieth-century literary movements, including the Boom and Post-Boom era of Latin America, along with the political, social, and historical turmoil of the time. That is the reason Bolaño's novel is representative of his generation and all generations (45), as its characters, like Don Quixote, see the world through literature and as literature—something to be studied, bettered, corrected. Like one of his favorite novels of world literature,[28] Bolaño manages to write a work heavily influenced by a literary genre (visceral realism, a fictionalized version of infrarealism, the poetic movement in which Bolaño himself took part) that becomes a form of lifestyle and propels adventure. Influenced by *Don Quixote*, the narrative of *The Savage Detectives* can similarly "resist even the worst translator" (50), as Bolaño espouses a universal language—that of literature and literary meanings.

28 Bolaño was asked to name five books that have marked his life. *Don Quixote*, of course, was on the top of his list, followed by *Moby Dick*, another quixotic novel with a brilliant re-accentuation of a dreamer Quixote (Maristain, "The Last" 118).

## A Polyphony of Events

Fyodor Dostoevsky, one of the most eminent Russian writers, demonstrates the explicit influence of Cervantes's works, especially *Don Quixote*. It is known from the writer's diaries that he profoundly examined the structure and stylistics of Cervantes. In Dostoevsky's novels, one not only finds characters or ideas similar to those of *Don Quixote* but also polyphony—an abundance of dialogues and characters who, albeit secondary, play a prominent role in the development of the narration. *The Idiot* (1869), among all of his well-known works, is a unique novel that includes both nuances and characters grounded in *Don Quixote*.

In *The Idiot*, Prince Myshkin returns to St. Petersburg from Switzerland, where he spent four years in a clinic to be treated for epilepsy. In Russia, he only knows the Epanchin family. The Epanchins have three daughters, the youngest of whom is Aglaya. General Epanchin's assistant, Ganya, is in love with Aglaya; however, he proposes marriage to another woman, Nastasya Filippovna, after being promised 75,000 rubles to do so. Nastasya has another suitor, Rogozhin. On the day Ganya asks for her hand, Prince Myshkin suddenly does the same, and, of course, both of them are rejected. Although certain about her rejection of Ganya, Nastasya Fillippovna has second thoughts about Myshkin and cannot decide between him and Rogozhin. Meanwhile, Myshkin begins courting Aglaya, who does not seem indifferent. Aglaya then asks Nastasya to meet her and Myshkin and gives the Prince an ultimatum to choose between the two of them. This encounter results in Aglaya running away and Nastasya Filippovna moving in with Rogozhin. Chasing Nastasya down to St. Petersburg, Myshkin finds out that Rogozhin has killed her—news that causes him to lose his mind and return to the Swiss clinic.

Prince Myshkin recapitulates Don Quixote's adventurous spirit as he travels from Europe to Russia, misinterprets the social realities of the Russian aristocracy, and, overcome by the idea of love, naively persists in his quest until his misadventures result in his mental ruination. Furthermore, while Alonso Quijano, a simple *hidalgo*, claims to be a knight errant to be addressed as Don Quixote, Myshkin insists he is of noble descent and invites others to call him a prince. As Don Quixote likes to read chivalric romances, Myshkin reads Russian literature to bring him closer to Russian culture after his many years in Switzerland: "I studied constantly for four years, though not quite in a regular way, but by his special system, and I also managed to read a great many Russian books," says Myshkin (Dostoevsky 29). Finally, the Prince has two re-accentuated Dulcineas: Aglaya and Nastasya Filippovna. According to Mancing, Aglaya approximates Dulcinea better than any other character:

> In *The Idiot*, Aglaya Epanchin, the figure who most parallels D[ulcinea del] T[oboso], hastily places a note from the prince in a book and only later sees that the book is D[on] Q[uixote], an act that, like the chapter devoted to a discussion of Pushkin's ballad "Poor Knight" and D[on] Q[uixote] (where Aglaya says "the 'poor knight' is also a Don Quixote, only serious and not comic"), is an explicit allusion to one source of the protagonist's character. (*Encyclopedia I* 249)

Myshkin's love story, nonetheless, is complicated by his surprising proposal to Nastasya Filippovna, also a figure reminiscent of Dulcinea. Although it is hard to believe that Myshkin is in love with Nastasya, he claims that his proposal is not just to show his affection toward her but also to try to rectify the mess created by Ganya's financially-induced proposal. The act can thus be interpreted as chivalrous, a righting of Ganya's wrong deed, without considering the repercussions. Ludmilla Buketoff Turkevich believes that Myshkin is moved to act by a love that is fervent but not passionate: "Like Don Quixote, he is ignorant of women, except as aspects of his ideal. Physical love would have been just as great a betrayal of his ideal as it would have been in the case of Don Quixote" (129). Yet, unlike Don Quixote, it is not reading fiction that becomes the reason for Myshkin's loss of sanity; it is the death of Nastasya, a re-accentuated Dulcinea, that takes him back where his adventures commenced—the Swiss clinic.

Along with these resonances, there are several references to *Don Quixote* in *The Idiot.* For example, Aglaya accidentally puts her letters in a copy of *Don Quixote*, which suggests that she has read, will read, or is currently reading the novel: "And only a week later did she happen to notice what book it was. It was *Don Quixote de La Mancha*. Aglaya laughed terribly—no one knew why" (Dostoevsky 189). Myshkin is also compared to Cervantes's hero, the "poor knight," a direct reference to Don Quixote (247), but Myshkin does not seem to understand the reference. It is important to note that both "poor knights," Don Quixote and Myshkin, have a common objective, which is to make the surrounding world a better place. Don Quixote wants to be a knight errant and save the world from evil, and Myshkin wants to go back to his home country and be a positive change. Like Cervantes's protagonist, Myshkin's good intentions are misinterpreted in the Russia he encounters, and he is seen as a naive romantic, a Quixote.

Unlike Cervantes, whose characters are universally recognizable, Dostoevsky is perhaps better known among scholars for the multitude of voices present in most of his oeuvre. In *Problems of Dostoevsky's Poetics*, Bakhtin refers to the representation of all of his characters and their voices as one whole called "polyphony" (6).[29] Gary Morson perceptively points out that the concept of polyphony is often misunderstood and used as if it meant a mere plurality of voices (*Narrative* 91). Building upon Bakhtin's definition, he clarifies:[30]

> As Bakhtin coined the term, a polyphonic novel is one in which a special relation obtains between author and hero. That relation allows the hero to be truly free, capable of surprising not only other characters but also the author. In some crucial aspects, the poly-

29 See Chapter Three, note 23.

30 It is worth noting here that what Bakhtin refers to as a polyphonic novel, clarified further by Morson, is for Watt an example of a modern novel, clarified further by Allen: "The following are Ian Watt's criteria for characterizing the modern novel: (a) originality of plot, (b) realistic particularity of detail, (c) individual identity of characters, (d) and (e) particularized time and space, and (f) an authentic account of the actual experiences of individuals, achieved through referential (as opposed to strictly stylized) language. Which of these characteristics is lacking in *Don Quijote*? None, obviously" ("*Don Quijote* and the Origins" 126-27). Allen then notes that none of the characteristics of the modern novel proposed by Watt are lacking in *Don Quixote* (127).

> phonic author—not just the narrator—resembles just another character. (*Narrative* 91)

It is important to note that Cervantes's novel comports with the characterizations of a polyphonic narration well before the novels of Dostoevsky. We know that Dostoevsky was profoundly influenced by Cervantes, and it is very possible that the polyphony found in *The Idiot* reflects *Don Quixote*'s influence. What Dostoevsky also seems to have adopted from Cervantes is excellent narrative expertise, along with characters and episodes. Similar to his predecessor, Dostoevsky was able to balance the two extremes and create a brilliant Russian re-accentuation of Don Quixote under the identity of Prince Myshkin.

## Conclusion

"Every story is a travel story," says Adrian Arancibia (205). What the statement implies, however, is not that every story presents geographical travels, but that by reading we become travelers. Reading is traveling. Quixotic adventurers, who are avid travelers, often combine textual traveling with geographical movement. Don Quixote, one of the most fervent readers in literature, sees knowledge as shaped through reading and traveling (Cervantes 625). Parson Adams, one of his re-accentuated counterparts, also believes that traveling occurs while reading books, "the only way of travelling by which any Knowledge is to be acquired" (Fielding, *Joseph* 159). Yet Adams is out in the open, reading, adventuring, and learning with his travel companion, Joseph Andrews. In this manner, Don Quixote and re-accentuated adventurers like Adams connote journeys that are both literary and spatial. Going on a journey, according to Steven Hutchinson, means "moving in a space that's not one's own, it means having simultaneous but shifting relationships with more than one place, continually displacing oneself" (83). Cervantes took this Odyssean notion of displacement, added various literary traditions to it—from chivalric to picaresque to byzantine romances—and created a traveler who continuously needed to experiment with his environment, both textual and spatial. Together with his re-accentuated adventurers, Don Quixote thereby negotiates between text and space, navigates displacement, and makes sense of himself and his surroundings.

Quixotic adventurers do not adapt. They are inquisitive, nonconformist, and unattached to their time and space. They keep asking *what if.* Due to their experimental nature, they create and recreate; they go through *poiesis* and *autopoiesis.* And while these characters travel and recreate themselves in new places and times with every reading, so do their stories—"objects that do a lot of traveling: across space and especially across time" (Dimock 1061).

# 5
# Lovers

Don Quixote, as a lover, is controversial. Some scholars interpret his expression of love in the light of irony (Close), some view it as flawed and coming from a chivalrous need (Laguna), and others see it as the driving force of the novel (González Echevarría). Various readers have pondered if the hero's love entails loyal, idealized, and platonic feelings toward Dulcinea, or if his feelings are self-serving, forged, and dubious. While the Cervantine knight's definition of love resembles those highlighted in medieval romances and chivalric fictions, it ultimately falls short of becoming one like those, generating parody (rather than imitation). A beloved's ideal is of crucial role in Don Quixote's sense of what makes a successful knight errant. He acknowledges that his attempts to personify a knight errant would fail without a woman to whom he can pledge devotion. For this reason, he chooses Aldonza Lorenzo as the lady worthy of his love and names her Dulcinea of Toboso, "a name, to his mind, that was musical and beautiful and filled with significance" (Cervantes 24). Although Don Quixote never once encounters his beloved woman, the idea of her remains omnipresent throughout the novel. Her image serves Don Quixote as a muse, an angel, and in some ways, even as God.[1] And so, throughout the novel, the Spanish *hidalgo* adulates Dulcinea in so

1 Note the language used by Cervantes's knight errant as he evokes Dulcinea before his first adventures: "Oh lady of my soul, Dulcinea, flower of beauty, come to the aid of this thy knight, who, for the sake of thy great virtue, finds himself in grave peril!" (Cervantes 64).

many ways that he eventually generates a sort of Pygmalion-like fetish for the creation of his own imagination.

Writing a story of love, in the age of Cervantes, was no easy feat. As John Beusterien and Ana María Laguna note, "[t]raditional lifelines such as Petrarchan and Neoplatonic paradigms of love . . . were nearly completely spent and had begun to show clear signs of inadequacy and exhaustion;" readers were beginning to see "displacement of the theme of love as literary epicentre," while authors were suffering through the "tremendously complicated exercise" of writing about love (4, 6, 21). Cervantes ironically simplifies this task in his Prologue noting (in the words of the friend in the Prologue):

> If you write about love, with the couple of ounces of Tuscan that you know you'll run right into León de Hebreo, who will inflate your meters. And if you don't care to travel to foreign lands, right at home you have Foncseca's *Del amor de Dios*, which summarizes everything that you or the most ingenious writer might wish to know about the subject. (Cervantes 7)

But the different love tales told in the novel do not simply regurgitate these tired narratives. Rather, Cervantes parades various phases of the multifaceted concept of love that were still not widely explored in literary circles, going well beyond the traditions of Hebreo and Fonseca.[2] And so, Cervantes develops his main character, along with other secondary characters, who often "embody or exemplify a negative – even 'pestilent' (amorosa pestilencia) – outlook on the sentiment [of love]" (Cammarata and Laguna 34). This "pestilence" is described as comedy by Anthony Close, who bases his influential "Don Quixote's Love for

2 León de Hebreo (Leone Ebreo) was a philosopher who wrote a treatise titled *Dialoghi d'amore* (1535) in Italian. Cristóbal de Fonseca, a Spanish theologian, translated Hebreo's work into Spanish in 1596 and composed his own derivation from the latter's philosophy, titling it *Tratado del amor de Dios*. In both works, the authors engage with Neoplatonic and Catholic doctrines to discuss love. For details regarding Cervantes's references heeding or departing from Hebreo and Fonseca, see John Beusterien and Ana María Laguna's "Introduction," as well as Armando Maggi's "The End of the Renaissance Philosophy of Love."

Dulcinea" on "an examination of the comedy" of the knight's sentiment (238). But more often than not, as Wayne Booth suggests, we read Don Quixote's madness of excess idealism—in his interpretation of love or other ideals—in a forgiving way "convinced that his heart . . . is in the right place" (246). In this manner, we often understand quixotic love as something platonic, idealized, and dedicated, neglecting the flaws that Don Quixote bears as a lover (Laguna 252). It is, in Mandel's famous description, a soft approach to quixotic love. Looking deeper into this seemingly pure sentiment, however, the reader sees a rather complex muddle of emotions. After all, Don Quixote himself declares that he is in love "simply because it is obligatory for knights errant to be so," implying that for him, love is "a sort of professional obligation" (Cervantes 666; Close 246). Accordingly, we need to complicate how we understand quixotic love even more, viewing it as a sentiment that reinvigorates the typical love narrative by deftly combining traditional Neoplatonic lifelines with "pestilence," "comedy," and "irony."

Re-accentuating Don Quixote as a lover can be a complex task. It is because love on Don Quixote's terms can be polemical: idealized but ignorant, devoted but self-serving. When quixotic characters uncloak their romantic predilections, they often reveal problematic expressions of the sentiment, such as heedless devotion to an inamorato, like in Tolstoy's *Anna Karenina* (1877); gullible sentiment of attachment to one person, like in Vargas Llosa's *The Bad Girl* (2007); or pedophilia camouflaged as love, like in Nabokov's *Lolita* (1955). In addition, enamored characters or their sweethearts may be classified in a way that divulges affection as a gendered experience. It invites equivocal and problematic analyses when authors brand their characters as the "ruined woman" (as in *Anna Karenina* for the eponymous protagonist) or the "good boy" (as for Ricardo Somocurcio in *The Bad Girl*). A reading of re-accentuated romantics through the lens of gender studies might seem a logical route for this chapter, but a study of quixotic love as something polemic and perhaps even blight might offer new perspectives on this very complex sentiment in Cervantes and Cervantes-inspired fiction.

Just as Unamuno speaks of happiness as something that is designed to be "lived and felt and not something thought out and defined" (*Tragic* 111), so is love in *Don Quixote.* And when Cervantes throws down the gauntlet on the definitions of love outlined in Fonseca and Hebreo, he may be suggesting that as soon as passions leave the confines of the conventional, the defined, the accepted, they risk becoming what Joan Cammarata and Ana María Laguna view as pestilence. A superficial reading of the abovementioned novels may suggest that romantic yearning is a positive event functioning, for example, as the missing piece of Anna Karenina's life, the forever pledge that Don Quixote gives to his Dulcinea (also conferring on her the sweetest of sweet names), or the unwavering faithfulness Ricardo Somocurcio nurtures for Otilia. However, a more detailed reading of Cervantes's character and his re-accentuated counterparts can help uncover the flaws that love bears—its rough edges—and the consequences of its imperfections upon paramours. Devoted, platonic, and ideal on the surface, quixotic love can be as complex to analyze as the "complicated exercise" of writing it (Beusterien and Laguna 21).

Re-accentuated characters who exhibit the trait of the lover have in common the problematic, controversial, and abstruse sides of the sentiment of love, interrupted by ephemeral moments of romance. Most re-accentuated lovers, like Don Quixote, exhibit self-serving motives in their romantic feelings; they also often portray the dreamy, ideal, and illusionary perceptions of quixotic love. Perhaps romantic and feverish at first glance, re-accentuations of quixotic love prove to generate obsession and mania due to excessive idealization and possessive jealousy. In such novels as *Anna Karenina, Lolita,* and *The Bad Girl,* re-accentuated characters demonstrate the pitfalls of love, questioning its essence.

## Feelings Unrestrained

Leo Tolstoy, a contemporary of Fyodor Dostoevsky, gained renown for his realist novels. His works scrupulously represent his time and beliefs, depicting the life of Russian aristocrats, the working class, and villagers in the countryside. Reading Tolstoy is like reading Cervantes: one can learn about the class divisions of the era, the political structures, the lives of the wealthy and the poor, as well as discern details about geography, climate, places, and people of the area. Tolstoy and

Cervantes are among those pre-twentieth-century authors who observed and understood human nature and psychology deeply and depicted their characters as imperfect, flawed human beings, with their virtues and faults, fears and strengths. The Russian author's novel, like the work of his Spanish predecessor, "illustrates why we would be wise to proceed from experience up" (Morson, *Anna* 32). Tolstoy created and developed "prosaics in unforeseen directions" and offered "ways of comprehending not only individual lives but also general issues of social reform" (32), a statement that is true about Cervantes's work, as well.

*Anna Karenina*, one of the most read and analyzed works of Tolstoy, introduces a feminized re-accentuation of Don Quixote questioning the place of women in Russian aristocratic society from a viewpoint of love and sexuality. To a traditional reader, the eponymous heroine of the novel may seem to stand as the archetype of the anti-woman and anti-mother of the nineteenth-century Russian upper class because she succumbs to the allure of love, which is lacking in her marriage. Surrendering to her need for romance, this re-accentuation of Don Quixote in Russia has a fate similar to that of her Western predecessors Arabella, Catherine, and Emma as discussed in Chapter Two. Indeed, Tolstoy's novel has often been compared with *Madame Bovary* in the way that it exposes a non-stereotypical unity of a "terrible woman" and a "magnanimous husband" (Tolstoy 513). *Anna Karenina* also depicts the life of several families very different from each other. It is perhaps to juxtapose what is good with what is bad as perceived by Tolstoy and his contemporaries.[3] For example, Anna Karenina and her family can

3 Regarding the similarities between *Madame Bovary*, *Anna Karenina*, *Don Quixote*, as well as the polyphonic narration observed in the novels, it is highly relevant to take a look at Nabokov's *Lectures on Don Quixote* (1983). The writer states that: "*Madame Bovary*, for instance, is a one-track novel, with hardly any switches. *Anna Karenina* is a multi-track novel with major switches. What is *Don Quixote?* I should call it a one-and-a-half rack novel, with a few switches. Knight and squire are really one, and anyway the squire only plays up to his master; however, at a certain point in the second part they get separated. The switches are very crude, as the author shuttles self-consciously between Sancho's island and Don Quixote's castle,

be interpreted as examples of the degrading social system of Russia, while Konstantin Levin, a landowner, can be seen as someone who acts as the "spokesman for his creator," communicating the archetype of a virtuous Russian *muzhik* and the working class (ix).[4] Interweaving the stories of these two families, Tolstoy seems to offer a reading of good and bad, especially in terms of love as in *eros* (Anna: bad) and love as in *agape* (Levin: good). Anna's romantic ventures point to the dangers of feelings unrestrained, while the author explores the boundaries of quixotic love. Just like Anna's attractiveness, which she treasures as the warrant of her relationship with Count Vronsky, love as characterized by *eros* is depicted as ephemeral by Tolstoy.

Anna is married to General Karenin, and she and her family enjoy renown in the brittle hierarchies of nineteenth-century Russia. When

---

and it is a positive relief to everybody concerned—author, characters, and reader—when the two get together again and revert to their natural knight-and-squire combination" (10). Nabokov's perception of *Don Quixote* as a one-and-a-half faceted novel, as opposed to *Anna Karenina*, which is a novel with double switches, is somewhat problematic. While Tolstoy makes a clear distinction between the voices of the protagonists and the intersections of their lives, Cervantes masterfully unites the life paths of knight and squire and elevates the polyphony to a level where Don Quixote and Sancho leave an impression of inseparable unity. Still, they are independent characters whose personalities shine through even when they are separated from each other. Due to the fully developed and complex personalities that Don Quixote and Sancho exhibit, Cervantes's story flows freely and coherently, whether the protagonists are together or separated from each other. But a reader like Nabokov, subconsciously, is perhaps unable to separate them, which is a result of a monophonic approach to Cervantes's polyphonic creation. As Unamuno suggests: "The greatest . . . feature of their [Don Quixote's and Sancho's] common life is that we cannot conceive of the one without the other; and that . . . they were, not the two halves of a whole, but a single being viewed from either side" (*The Life* 150-51).

4 The term *muzhik* is now often used to mean "a man" in Russian. However, Tolstoy used this word to denote "a farmer" or "a peasant," reflecting the common terminology of his time to refer to men belonging to the working class.

Anna travels to help her brother's family,[5] her trip to change someone's life for the better clearly resonates with the purpose of Don Quixote's sallies. The Spanish knight errant, who sets off from his house to right all wrongs, encounters various incidents that he feels demand his intervention to be successfully resolved. As opposed to Don Quixote in his quests, Anna is able to have a positive impact on her brother's family. However, her marital life is soon to experience its own turmoil, as she falls for Count Vronsky. From this point on, love and lust outside of one's marital life become one of the primary ways that Tolstoy's novel engages with quixotism, displaying the re-accentuated trait of a lover in the capricious heroine of the novel.

Anna and Vronsky's love affair—irresistible for Anna and dishonoring for her husband General Karenin—causes scandal in their social circles. Her insatiate sentiments for Vronsky spellbind the heroine to such an extent that she takes advantage of any opportunity she can to keep seeing her beloved. Although mutual, Anna and Vronsky's love metamorphizes into an importunate nuisance for them and their acquaintances alike. Unable to face her adultery, the reproach of society, and her circumstances, Anna takes her own life.

The novel concludes not with Anna's death but with the reflections of Levin who goes through self-realization and comes into harmony with his Christian beliefs. In this manner, Tolstoy seems to juxtapose the adulterous image of Anna Karenina with the righteous figure of Konstantin Levin. According to Elisabeth Stenbock-Fermor, this opposition illustrates Tolstoy's own religious views, and also that "Anna belonged to the social group who lived in darkness and hypocrisy; when tempted by evil she could not resist and destroyed herself. Levin knew where the evil was and avoided it" (64). Sure, viewing this from a Christian perspective drawing from Tolstoy's own faith, Anna can be read as an exemplar of those facing evil and unable to resist it. But her predicament, like Don Quixote's, is her inability to bring herself into

5 Anna's brother Stiva was unfaithful to his wife Dolly, who was determined to leave him after finding out about his affair. Anna believes she should talk to Dolly to change her mind and save her brother's marriage.

harmony with her environment.[6] She is an outcast for wanting something that is defined as unorthodox. Her actions are seen as unjustified "not only because she becomes incapable of dialogic communication, but because her final self-dialogue is a 'rational' recognition and her suicide an action and work which she intends as a recognition of herself, as a self-objectification" (Jaanus and Kurrik 140).[7] And while Levin's example at the end of the novel can be interpreted as a moral lesson for the readers, Anna's ruin can be read as a warning against self-alienation by following passions unsupported by societal norms.

It is appropriate to describe what Anna and Don Quixote go through as *exotism*, a term coined by Bakhtin, defined as "*opposition of what is alien to what is one's own*, the otherness of what is foreign is emphasized, savored, as it were, and elaborately depicted against an implied background of one's own ordinary and familiar world" (*Dialogic* 101). What is familiar to both of the characters—their home life, social status, cultural situatedness, historical era, etc.—is also somewhat alien or alienating for them. Cervantes's and Tolstoy's protagonists both strive for something more, something different, which is utterly foreign in their surroundings. The two characters, exotic within their circumstances, struggle to maneuver between personal wishes and social demands. Again, Anna follows the paradigm of Don Quixote not because she is weak or unable to resist the charms of Vronsky, but because she, like her predecessor, fails to reconcile herself with her own identity. One of the problems that Anna faces is that she, like Don Quixote, is a victim of circumstances. But if Don Quixote can be interpreted to achieve different outcomes as one who perseveres in his quests (e.g., a madman who is, ultimately, a victim of practical jokes; a dreamer, who teaches others to dream with or like him; etc.), Anna's

6 It is what Ortega y Gasset aptly notes when he writes: "I am myself plus my circumstance, and if I do not save it, I cannot save myself" (45). Applying this to Anna Karenina, we can see how the heroine is unable to come to terms with her circumstances, thus unable to save herself.

7 Don Quixote goes through a somewhat similar process of self-recognition throughout the novel; while the reader can sense Don Quixote's self-realization at several points in Part II, he does not fully acknowledge and accept his *hidalgo* identity until the last moments of his life.

choice of following her emotions ends in a singular juncture, social disrespect (Welsh 163).

Anna Karenina's intents of self-fulfillment seem to fail because of her gender (Mandelker 50). Life at home feels monotonous to her. She yearns for more but also realizes that she will endanger the social image of herself and her family if she pursues that which she is lacking at home: love. Via Anna's sentiments throughout the novel, Tolstoy exposes the conflict between the social and personal image that many aristocratic families of the time endured. According to Mack Smith, *Anna Karenina* and *Don Quixote* both introduce protagonists in binary opposition to the "social and representational conventions" of their respective eras, and both face harsh realities only after undergoing unreal fancies (13). Their carefully fashioned and idealized worlds often collide with the actualities that their societies experience.[8] Anna's love-relation, for example, brings forth the social perception of her as a "ruined woman;" even Vronsky, who is involved in this very relationship, thinks that Anna is a woman of "non-existent honour" (Tolstoy 543, 305). The reader, then, may justifiably ask whether Tolstoy's intention was misogynist and sexist, attempting to bring to light the dangers that alienating oneself from domestic and marital life can pose (Mandelker 18). According to Morson, however, Tolstoy does not only question the role of women in a given society but also criticizes the "great man" as seen in the persona of General Karenin. He asserts that Tolstoy "has a point in suggesting . . . that negligence and inaction, rather than malice, cause much evil, he exaggerates in attributing most evil to negligence" (*Anna* 2). I do not think, however, that Tolstoy takes aim at gender or gender attributes in such characterization. Rather, I be-

8 Consider especially the love constructions of Don Quixote and Anna Karenina. "Well, well!" exclaims Sancho as he realizes who Dulcinea is. "Are you saying that Lorenzo Corchuelo's daughter . . . is the lady Dulcinea of Toboso? . . . I know her very well" (Cervantes 199). Armed with the knowledge of who the real Aldonza Lorenzo is, Sancho poses a challenge to Don Quixote's imagination of the princess, threatening to shatter all the convictions of Don Quixote's ideal world of knight errantry. Anna also holds a distorted version of life driven by her yearning for romance, in this way, defying extant social norms (Mandelker 80).

lieve it is what we know as quixotism that Tolstoy critiques. Additionally, it is the unorthodox love that becomes a reason Anna drifts away from the social responsibilities and expectations of her time and place, combined with her inability to adapt to her circumstances.

To come back to the conclusion of Tolstoy's work: we see quixotism (Anna Karenina) juxtaposed with heedfulness (Konstantin Levin) in the parallel worlds of turmoil and peace, aristocracy and the working class. Levin, who finds the perfect harmony between personal needs and societal expectations, is a polar opposite of Anna, who is unable to assess the consequences that her actions will bring. This quixotic negligence of seeing self under the direct scrutiny of the society is what causes Anna to succumb to her passions, stigmatizing her as a "ruined woman." By creating a feminized re-accentuation of Don Quixote, Tolstoy, like Cervantes, warns against quixotic love: love that is idealized more than it is felt, more self-serving than selfless, and frustrated as well as frustrating, experienced beyond the limits that the social standards are ready to support.

## A Reading of Love in Decay

The eminent Russian-American writer Vladimir Nabokov is the author of the celebrated yet controversial *Lolita* (1955). Soon after the publication of the novel, its protagonists, Humbert Humbert and especially his beloved Lolita, became popular literary-cultural images. A number of episodes from the book have been so popularized that even those who have not read it could still recognize aspects of Nabokovian personages.[9] Cervantes's protagonist precedes Lolita as a character easily recognizable by readers. Lolita and Don Quixote are two of the very few literary characters to enjoy recognition independently from their creators.[10] Cervantes is often named as one of Nabokov's most significant literary antecedents and the founder of a tradition that stretches from the year of publication of *Don Quixote* to "the self-referential metafiction of postmodernism" (Krabbenhoft 213). Nabokov himself

9 For example, the image of Lolita in the piazza or the girl wearing one sock might come to one's mind.

10 Other similar examples are Sherlock Holmes, Hamlet, and Robinson Crusoe.

notes that "*Don Quixote* is one of those books that are, perhaps, more important in eccentric diffusion than in their own intrinsic value" (*Lectures* 111). He later sets out to create this Cervantine eccentricity in his own novel.

Nabokov's composition of *Lolita* during his employment at Cornell University coincided with his delivery of a series of lectures on *Don Quixote*, which he later compiled in a book. In *Lectures on Don Quixote,* Nabokov studies in detail the violence and cruelty in Cervantes's novel. According to him, Cervantes's protagonists Don Quixote and Sancho Panza are exposed to excessive amounts of violence, mockery, and disrespect throughout their travels and adventures.[11] But it is quite noticeable that, ultimately, he incorporated these aspects of Cervantes's novel into his own (Krabbenhoft 214).

Nabokov's antagonist Humbert Humbert, a traumatized pedophile, embarks on a disturbingly obsessive love quest upon meeting Lolita, the daughter of his landlady and soon-to-be wife. Humbert rents a room across from Lolita's bedroom in her mother's house and pretends to establish a friendship with the girl. This friendship grows into a perturbed intimacy, seemingly unbothered by the death of Lolita's mother. Through their troubled relationship,[12] Humbert and Lolita lead their respective lives obtaining from each other whatever their needs dictate of them. Despite the polemical nature of Humbert's character, he embodies a quixotic lover. At first glance, it may seem gruesome to equate Cervantes's impulsive but well-intentioned knight errant with the "pathologically self-serving" antagonist of *Lolita* (214). However, an unorthodox approach to the sentiment of love unites the two figures, making Humbert a re-accentuation of Don Quixote.

According to Kenneth Krabbenhoft, Don Quixote and Humbert respond to similar impulses based on the premise that "both *Don*

11 See "Cruelty and Mystification" in Nabokov's *Lectures on Don Quixote*.

12 Humbert's manipulative maneuvers often trap Lolita in abuse. However, Lolita exhibits superb shrewdness for a teenage girl in several instances. For example, Lolita employs sexual favors to convince Humbert to let her act in a drama piece organized by her school. Her ability to conceal her contact with Quilty is another example of her wiles.

*Quixote* and *Lolita* are concerned with love, its definition, possibilities, and limitation" (216). He identifies these traits as follows: erotomania, disillusionment, and paranoia (216). The first two characterizations of Krabbenhoft are very prevalent in quixotic terms given the abundance of scholarship on *eros* in Cervantes; also ubiquitous is the sentiment of disillusion in the Spanish Golden Age in general. Still, erotomania may at first seem to be not applicable to Cervantes's protagonist because several episodes in the novel question his sexuality, suggesting his impotence.[13] As a result of this interpretation, Don Quixote's sexuality does not seem to be erotic mania or erotomania but rather a representation of erotic lack, or perhaps even of frustration. However, Don Quixote exposes sexual and frenzied behavior in several instances. For example, the episode with Maritornes, studied abundantly by Cervantes scholars, defines the erotic and manic inclinations of Don Quixote. Humbert, on the other hand, has a mind full of flagrant sexual desires. Humbert's plans and thoughts are grotesque, carnal, and sexual, while Don Quixote's ideas are generally spiritual and pure, although still driven by self-serving motives. For Humbert, sexual attachment to Lolita becomes a form of mania, but for Don Quixote, it is the image of Dulcinea and defending his own creation that turns him manic. Of course, the obsessiveness in both characters induces paranoia, given that both feel the need to protect, defend, and justify their love-choices. So too, both become disillusioned after these efforts and excesses give way to reality.

Humbert and Don Quixote both experience disillusion, according to Krabbenhoft. Humbert's erotomania and paranoia lead to his disenchantment. A catalyst to this sentiment becomes Lolita's disappearance, destroying Humbert's illusions. To compare, Don Quixote's disillusionments come from being unable to comply with the rules

13 Johnson, however, believes that Don Quixote is an old man with a problematic sexual background. According to him, the fact that he lives in a home where he is the only male and does not have sexual relations with anyone, shows his sexual repression. In addition, because the name Quixote may have been influenced by the word signifying a piece of armor that covers the thigh, Johnson asserts that Cervantes's character "would want to cover and protect his sexuality" fearing that "it was protruding" (*Madness* 68).

that he has set for himself, in addition to social standards deemed as excessive for his age and his times. A factor in both Don Quixote's and Humbert's disillusion is the role played by their doppelgangers, Sansón Carrasco and Clare Quilty, respectively.[14] Scham points out: "As in *Don Quijote*, *Lolita* combines the chivalric with the theme of the double. Quilty is described as a shape-changer as he pursues Humbert and Lolita cross-country . . . Sansón Carrasco pursues Don Quijote, appearing alternately as 'el Caballero de los Espejos' and 'de la Blanca Luna'" (84). Sansón Carrasco's intention is to imitate the chivalric world and mimic the knight to help bring him home. Through his imitation, Sansón embodies a shadow of Don Quixote, seen as his doppelganger or his reflection.[15] Don Quixote's defeat toward the end of the novel is, correspondingly, the victory of his doppelganger, as Don Quixote accepts his failure as a knight errant. This defeat is followed by a self-realization process before his death, in which Don Quixote rejects the illusionary world of chivalry and accepts his reality of being a *hidalgo* named Alonso Quijano. In a similar manner, Humbert's double, Clare Quilty, is the incarnation of his paranoia. Quilty's presence in Humbert's life makes increasingly unlikely the latter's prospects of a union with Lolita. Both Quilty and Humbert are manic and disturbed individuals. Here, as in *Don Quixote*, the doppelganger steals what is dear to Humbert.

Although carnal in nature, Humbert's love bears a striking resemblance to Don Quixote's feelings for Dulcinea. Lolita, an inspiration and ideal for Humbert, is comparable to Dulcinea, Don Quixote's muse, who also embodies an idealized woman and inspires the knight to engage in adventures. Nevertheless, as Krabbenhoft argues:

14 Another parallel, Quilty thwarts Humbert's goals by taking Lolita away from him. Like the image of Frestón in *Don Quixote*, Quilty appears as the figure of the evil enchanter who "steals" from Humbert his longed-for love.

15 In one instance, Sansón reveals his new identity as the Knight of the Mirrors, a name which suggests the act of mirroring or reflection. While Sansón mimics Don Quixote in knight errantry, Don Quixote is supposed to see his own reflection in Sansón.

> these loves have two fundamental aspects in common: they are both obsessive, and they are both frustrated by a society which views them as unorthodox. Don Quixote is mocked and ridiculed because his contemporaries consider courtly love an extravagance best confined to books, and Humbert is reviled and prosecuted because his contemporaries consider pedophilia a crime. (217)

It is true that their respective contemporaries would view Don Quixote's and Humbert's interpretations of love as eccentric and nonconformist. It is also true that what is rejected by their contemporaries is not their love subjects but the characters' unreasonable quixotism, which engenders excessive obsession and over idealization.[16] It is the exaltation of the "beauteous and peerless" Dulcinea by Don Quixote, as opposed to someone who "can throw a metal bar just as well as the brawniest lad in the village" and who is "as sturdy as a horse" (Cervantes 63, 199). And it is Humbert's obsession for an underage girl who "should wash her hair once in a while," who has a "strident voice" and "vulgar vocabulary" (Nabokov, *Lolita* 43, 65). The glaring discrepancies between the real and idealized selves of these women, Cervantes and Nabokov introduce unreliability into their narrative, a rhetorical strategy that has been studied minutely in these novels by various critics.[17]

*Lolita* is deeply infused with the spirit of *Don Quixote*, "especially its fantasy-reality theme and its insistence on its status as a true history" (Mancing, *Cervantes* 503). Cervantes's polyphonic narrative that is translated and rendered from the fictional Cide Hamete's original script, allegedly "without taking away or adding anything" (Cervantes 67-68), contrasts starkly with the monophonic auto-reflective narra-

---

16 Note that Humbert carefully conceals his identity as a pedophile, revealing it only in the story that he writes in jail, waiting for his trial for murder. Don Quixote, similarly, camouflages his and Dulcinea's real identities, but unlike Humbert, he brandishes his love sentiments towards Dulcinea publicly and flamboyantly.

17 See, for example, Filardo Llamas and Gutiérrez Rodríguez's "Lectures on *Lolita*: La influencia cervantina en Nabokov," Scham's "*Don Quijote* and *Lolita* Revisited," and Wood's "Cervantes Reads Borges and Nabokov."

tion of *Lolita*. The narrative truth, however, is lost in both cases—tangled in the polyphony of *Don Quixote* and questioned in the one-sided account of a pedophile in *Lolita*. That Humbert is the sole narrator of the novel casts doubts about the truth of his story. In effect, Humbert declares that his name is a pseudonym, carefully picked to "express the nastiness best" (Nabokov, *Lolita* 308). The reader does not know his real name, has no access to any other perspectives to his story, and yet, in effect, grants him credibility. As Lisa Zunshine points out: "The writer who creates an unreliable narrator runs an exciting and terrible risk: his or her readers may wind up believing the narrator's version of events" (100). Perhaps Nabokov wishes to achieve exactly that: readers' trust in Humbert's diegesis, leading to feelings of empathy for the "tenderhearted boy" who was destroyed by the "deadly daemon" (100). Michael Wood notes that "Humbert gives us every reason to distrust this text, but we end up . . . weirdly trusting it—the more so because he tells us when he feels the afterthoughts have crowded too thickly upon him . . ." (32). Propelled by the need to get the story "off his chest," Nabokov creates a piece influenced by Cervantes's work—from narrative technique to quixotic satire—with a style that "parodies everything it touches" (Rolo, "*Lolita*").

In sum, Humbert is a re-accentuation of Don Quixote, sharing various characteristics with him: obsessive love, self-deception, perseverance, and ultimately, disillusionment. Cervantes's and Nabokov's characters have unrealistic expectations of the world that surrounds them and embark on dangerous journeys driven by these expectations (Scham 81). Both characters fail in their respective quests. Humbert never gains Lolita's love and reminisces alone in his prison cell. Don Quixote fails in his dream to become an invincible knight errant, as well as in his fictional quest to disenchant Dulcinea and his real objective of perhaps meeting Aldonza Lorenzo. The failures that the two characters endure turn them into melancholic beings—Humbert falling into melancholia in prison, and Don Quixote representing "perhaps one of the most well-known melancholic characters in literature" (Filardo Llamas and Gutiérrez Rodríguez 418; my translation).

## The Bad Girl's Good Love

Published in 2006, *Travesuras de la niña mala* (*The Bad Girl,* 2007) by Mario Vargas Llosa is a recent Latin American quixotic achievement. The eccentric love story and the loyalty of the novel's protagonist quickly catch readers' attention and lead them through the lingering and problematic relationship of the main characters. The book has been compared to *Madame Bovary,* as it represents an unfaithful female character alongside a working, loving, and domesticated male character.[18] Like *Madame Bovary,* it also features various aspects of *Don Quixote.* Vargas Llosa's *The Bad Girl* is based on adventures, en-

18 Since it is well known that the Peruvian writer was influenced by Flaubert, especially his *Madame Bovary,* many claim that he began writing his novel with an intention to imitate Flaubertian concepts (Tajuddin 312). Kathryn Harrison, in her New York Times article "Dangerous Obsession," compares *The Bad Girl* to Flaubert's *Madame Bovary.* As noted in the article, Emma Bovary has fascinated the Peruvian writer since his first reading of the novel in 1959, when he had just moved to Paris. Reading Flaubert's work, Vargas Llosa's attention was immediately captured by the surreal and imaginary reality that Emma Bovary builds around herself, becoming so submerged in her own dreamlike life that opening her eyes to reality causes her to fall in deep distress. In *The Perpetual Orgy,* which was published in 1986, the Peruvian writer declares his love and fascination towards the Flaubertian revolutionary literary creation, Emma. Vargas Llosa, therefore, follows the example of the master of realism depicting an unreal love story in *The Bad Girl.* The beginning of his novel is comparable to Flaubert's, with descriptions of boyhood and the narration of "I." But as the story unfolds, readers find that the bovaresque character presented in *The Bad Girl* develops in other dimensions. Emma Bovary is able to realize and accept all the harm she has caused to others, namely to her husband, by cheating, lying, and stealing, a reality she is unable to cope with and prefers to bring to an end by taking her own life. The bad girl, on the other hand, suffers physically (and not as much mentally) as she manipulates others, especially Ricardo, making him endlessly worry and look after her. Nevertheless, she tries to soothe the harm she caused by giving Ricardo all her properties and belongings when she finds out she is going to die. With these and other Flaubertian influences observed in Vargas Llosa's novel, the Peruvian author also weaves a quixotic story that shifts the focus from the female to the enamored male character, Ricardo Somocurcio.

deavors, dreams, encounters, and abandonments, drawing a quixotic storyline and quixotic characters. Above all, however, it is quixotic love and the re-accentuated lover's journey that define the plot of the Peruvian writer's work.

*The Bad Girl* offers a linear narrative describing the amorous relationship between two people acquainted in the *barrio* of Miraflores in Lima, Peru. The first-person narrator and the protagonist of the novel is an average boy named Ricardo Somocurcio, who is born and raised in Lima. His childhood and teenage years conform with every other boy's in the neighborhood. One day, the teenagers in the *barrio* begin hustling and bustling regarding the arrival of two controversial Chilean girls. One of the girls immediately catches Ricardo's attention, and her mysterious parents, house, and daring behavior intrigue the inhabitants of the traditional Miraflores. As Ahmed Tajuddin observes, she "embodies everything that the other girls of Miraflores wanted to be but never dared to be" (313). A sweet love blooms between the two teenagers, but Ricardo soon realizes that his beloved is not at all who she claims to be. Otilia,[19] which the boy later finds out to be the real name of the girl, resembles Dulcinea in that her real self and his version of her differ from each other. Ricardo's enthrallment with Otilia resembles Don Quixote's enchantment with Dulcinea, while the duplicity of Otilia's identity parallels Dulcinea's inscrutable character. The reader begins to unveil Vargas Llosa's version of a quixotic love, juxtaposing Otilia's *exoticism* with her elusive image. Ricardo presents a re-accentuated quixotic figure in the Latin American novel,

19 In almost every chapter, the girl appears with a changed name. Ricardo becomes acquainted with Lily in Lima; she supposedly came to live in Miraflores from Chile. They later reconvene in Paris, where her name is Arlette. She then marries a French diplomat and is referred to as Madame Arnoux. Later, she appropriates the name Kuriko during her stay in Japan with Fukuda. Eventually, it becomes clear that the real name of Ricardo's beloved is Otilia (*ostilia–hostile*), but she is referred to as *la niña mala*, "the bad girl" for the rest of the narrative. As Ricardo contemplates: "Lily, the Chilean girl, Comrade Arlette, Madame Robert Arnoux, Mrs. Richardson, Kuriko, and Madame Ricardo Somocurcio was, in reality, named Otilia. Otilita. How funny" (Vargas Llosa, *The Bad* 234).

portraying unconditional yet frustrated love, and Otilia stands as his re-accentuated Dulcinea.

At first sight, *The Bad Girl* may look like a romantic adventure book, all the more so given that the full, literal English translation of its title is the "travesties of the bad girl" (from travesuras de la niña mala). The title promises a window into the "travesties" of the girl who later declares on her deathbed to her loyal devotee: ". . . you always wanted to be a writer and didn't have the courage. Now that you'll be all alone, you can make good use of the time, and you will not miss me so much. At least admit I've given you the subject for a novel. Haven't I, good boy?" (Vargas Llosa, *The Bad* 276). But to understand the novel as a story of travesties would be misleading, because the narrative develops into an exploration of love in its extremes: a tool to get by (Otilia) and heedless devotion (Ricardo).

Vargas Llosa's novel breaks through artificial definitions of love and shows the many ways the romanticized concept can be expressed and felt. On the one hand, Ricardo is devoted to his beloved woman whose image he has idealized. On the other, the bad girl obliterates all the labels of the stereotypical "domesticated" woman—who is free to love for money (French diplomat), personal benefits (Ricardo), and even what seems to have no good reason (Yakuza Fukuda). Some critics claim that the construction of this character defies the long-established stereotype of the domestic woman in Peru and Latin America in general (Felipe 96-97). But others take her sexual freedom and reputation as a bad girl to affirm that a woman should not challenge the social norms established by the patriarchy (Henighan 384). Otilia's suffering, brought about as a consequence of her lifestyle, may suggest that she is being punished for her "liberated sexuality and its possible relation with female emancipation" (Tajuddin 315). Conversely, *The Bad Girl* might very well represent a parody of conventional romantic literature exploring idealized love and its moral absolutes. While Vargas Llosa's intentions remain open to interpretation, what does seem sure is that the author reverses and questions gender roles in the romantic affair between "the good boy" and "the bad girl."

The love that Ricardo feels toward Otilia is quixotic. Ricardo, unlike Don Quixote, soon realizes that his feelings for Otilia are nothing more than a result of his own creation and that he might never be together with the woman he adores and idealizes. Nevertheless, he becomes incapable to repress his feelings for the bad girl every time she reappears in Ricardo's life, so much so that he asks her to marry him, explicitly comparing her with Dulcinea (Vargas Llosa, *The Bad* 204). The re-accentuated quixotic image lies in the amorous journey of Ricardo: his romanticized love towards the bad girl; his low income in contrast to his addiction to reading and translating novels; his trips to various places including Germany, England, Spain, Austria, Japan, and Russia; and his mundane dream of maintaining his modestly paid job and having Otilia by his side as his wife (Felipe 97). Ricardo's ideal world, like Don Quixote's, is meaningless without love. But Ricardo seems condemned to be alone; people leave him at various points in his life. Even when Otilia comes back to become that unblemished companion that Ricardo has never had, she does so with terminal cancer. Ricardo's quixotic dream, as in all previous instances, ends before it seems it is finally coming true. Ricardo shares with Don Quixote idealized yet unattainable sentiments, while Vargas Llosa puts forth the question: "why do we fall in love with the people we fall in love with" (Sánchez 110; my translation), and what are we prepared to undergo for the people we claim to love?

Ricardo is an exquisite example of a re-accentuated Quixote because he shares the four primary quixotic traits: reader, dreamer, adventurer, and lover. Like many other novels discussed in this book, *The Bad Girl* features strong and well-developed quixotic characteristics along with weak and subtle ones. Ricardo leaves Peru with a dream and his sallies are marked by intermittent affairs with Otilia. His life itself is a romantic adventure, featuring an invaded space when the bad girl is around and a feeling of emptiness when she leaves him with lengthy intermissions in order to undertake her own adventures. Ricardo's dream is to pursue Otilia. The Peruvian man's most well-elicited quixotic trait is the love he feels toward the bad girl. Similar to Don Quixote, who idealizes the image of Dulcinea and gives her an erroneous identity, Ricardo glorifies Otilia and selflessly helps her every time she reappears in his life with new urgencies.

Vargas Llosa's novel illustrates how being good leads to failure, a notion that noticeably carries through *Don Quixote* as well. In both instances, the protagonists of *Don Quixote* and *The Bad Girl* are "cryptic testimony on the alliance between the greatness and tragedy of the human condition" (Forgues 168). By depicting virtuous characters in unfavorable circumstances, Cervantes and Vargas Llosa posit a somewhat pessimistic view of the *causatum* of personal merits. It seems like both authors wondered: why is it bad to be good sometimes?

## Conclusion

*Anna Karenina*, *Lolita*, and *The Bad Girl* present different types of love stories. The protagonist of Tolstoy's novel shows the consequences of constant search for happiness in romance. What Anna Karenina shares with Don Quixote is idealized love. Anna, as we have seen, believes that Vronsky's affection is the source of her happiness. Similarly, the other re-accentuated lovers analyzed in this chapter seek mutual feelings from their beloveds. While Humbert cares less about the sincerity of Lolita's dedication, he is determined to keep her by his side. On the other hand, Ricardo's zeal to be forever united with Otilia is genuine and well-intentioned. All three re-accentuated protagonists are ardent lovers, and for all of them, love defines their journeys. Although the predecessor of Anna, Humbert, and Ricardo does not seem to necessitate reciprocated feelings from Dulcinea, he captures the irrationality of one-sided and monologic love. To readers, Anna might seem needy and discontent. In a similar manner, Humbert's love endeavors might bring about repugnance, and Ricardo might arouse pity. Like Don Quixote, the re-accentuated lovers Anna, Ricardo, and Humbert need the idea of a partner for various levels of self-fulfillment. All these trapped-in-passion characters fail in their quests for love, partly because they all refuse to accept the importance of the dialogic nature of the sentiment that is different from obsessive idealization and devoid of purely romantic definitions. Perhaps in this manner Cervantes, and later his disciples, aimed precisely at that: showing what is perceived as one of the most virtuous human sentiments in its vile and destructive extremes, punishing their characters for their versions of love in their individual contexts and experiencing love as a mode of punishment when it becomes antagonistic to what is normalized.

# Conclusion

As Cervantes's novel revives each time it is adapted, parodied, recreated, imitated, rewritten, or referenced, re-accentuations of its characters add intertextual significance to its literary legacy. Exploring quixotic novels and entering the world of quixotic meanings is fun, but it can also be confusing, as it connotes endless manners of quixotizing, deriving from Cervantes's complex and multifaceted work. Reading quixotic novels with an eye for re-accentuated readers, dreamers, adventurers, and lovers allows one to conceptualize the word quixotic and the world of quixotic notions based on salient characteristics of Don Quixote. Subsequently, re-accentuated Quixotes not only allow us to view Cervantes's hero through a well-recognized set of traits—much simpler than the pluralistic meanings of the word quixotic—but they also help us understand who Don Quixote can be and, consequently, understand in what essence quixotic characters are grounded.

Quixotic readers, dreamers, adventurers, and lovers are many—too many to reference in a single project (or even to be able to come across all of them in pursuit of a comprehensive study). It seems safe to assert that there is no other novel or character in literature that has generated as many re-accentuations as *Don Quixote* and its eponymous hero. Think of some of the greatest and most popular characters in fiction: (in no particular order) Hamlet, Jane Eyre, Odysseus, Robinson Crusoe, Emma Bovary, Jay Gatsby, Peter Pan, Anna Karenina, Captain Ahab, Hermione Granger, Scarlett O'Hara, Elizabeth Bennet, Scheherazade, Gandalf, Lemuel Gulliver, Sherlock Holmes, Alice, and so many others. None of them has generated literary procreation to the extent that Don Quixote has. One would hardly ever come across descriptions or denotations such as *hamletian* or *bennetian*, *ahabesque* or *hermionesque*, although some characters have transcended their literary confines into the linguistic world with such descriptions as *bovaresque*, *odyssean*, or *gargantuan*. Even then, adaptations, imitations, parodies, or re-accentuations of these characters are few, at best, and do not come anywhere close to what Cervantes has made possible to be achieved with his Don Quixote.

So, a logical question to ask is: what makes *Don Quixote* and its eponymous character so special—so generative, so popular, so relevant, and so timeless? There are various answers that can take different scopes, from the value of the novel in the literary world to the transcendental nature of the novel, filtered through various theories and philosophies—all viable and valuable to the extents they have been for over four centuries. However, when stripped of every literary approach or theory and viewed as a book that tells a story about humans, it is the characters and their worldliness that make Cervantes's work so special.

Cervantes did with his characters what no one before him was able to achieve, part of which is that he was able to capture in his characters what is universally human. With the extensive experiences the writer had communicating with people of different nations and backgrounds due to his lengthy travels as a soldier, a captive, a tax collector, and more, Cervantes was able to observe what connects all humans in the extremely divisive world of which he was part.[1] Cervantes could see that with all the diverse idiosyncrasies, worldviews, and lifestyles that humans live, they share feelings and wishes—even if for different things. And so, in his Quijano, Cervantes seeded the traits of the reader, dreamer, adventurer, and lover. These traits were transformative: Quijano became Quixote, a *hidalgo* became a knight errant, a

1 I refer to some events of Cervantes's life in the next few paragraphs without going much into detail. There are many accounts of Cervantes's life. For more detail, see some of the recent great pieces: *The Man Who Invented Fiction* (2016) by William Egginton, *No Ordinary Man* (2006) by Donald McCrory, and the *Biography* section of *The Oxford Handbook of Cervantes* (2021) edited by Aaron M. Kahn.

reader became a character—change seemed possible for someone with these traits for a moment. Reading *Don Quixote*, various authors have noticed not only the generative nature of Cervantes's characters, but also their transformative power, and re-accentuating the knight errant recapitulating these traits allowed for new intertextual quixotic births.

The trait of a reader, as seen in Don Quixote, speaks to the world because it connotes the obsessive nature that humans can develop. Promoting a rush of dopamine, any enjoyable act, especially one that promises some sort of instant gratification, can keep us wishing for more. That is the reason we humans often binge read, binge watch, binge eat or drink, or engage in some sort of shopping therapy, among other activities. It is a mode of escapism and allows for a break from one's quotidian life. Don Quixote is one of the first literary characters who so starkly captures this very human trait, not only exhibiting obsession and some form of escapism, but also promoting engagement and activism. It is through reading that Don Quixote experiences realities far from his own and is able to identify what he wishes his world represented. It is through reading that Don Quixote is moved, propelled to dream big; he sets out on adventures to change the world with a zeal to imitate his bookish ideals, which also include a pledge to a beloved woman. Of course, Cervantes depicts Don Quixote as an idealist whose bookish world is not feasible in seventeenth-century Spain, but that same idealist inspired many authors to create their own characters in his image because, simply, he is too relatable.

Cervantes was a dreamer, like most humans are, but he was disillusioned upon his return to Spain after his captivity and as a war hero. His absence from the motherland for over a decade undoubtedly inflicted upon him nostalgic thoughts about it—a construct that was probably more of an illusion than reality. Perhaps his personal experiences pushed him to present a literary dreamer to the world—a naive, well-meaning old man with a relentless belief that he can change his environment. But then, his creation, too, struggles to make his dream a reality, which makes him feel disillusioned. Authors influenced by *Don Quixote* have undoubtedly seen this melancholy in dreaming and captured it well in their own interpretations of a quixotic dreamer.

To dream is a mental activity, but once it awakens the physical need to act upon those dreams, it creates adventure. And what is adventure if not getting out of one's comfort zone and seeing what the result of the dream-inspired adventure would be? Cervantes experienced this firsthand by joining the fleet to fight in the Battle of Lepanto, dreaming of fame and the opportunity to go back home as a veteran with his honor restored.[2] His experiences during the battle, after victory, in captivity, and upon return to his homeland are a series of life journeys unlike any other world-renowned author's. While it was common in his contemporary Spain for veterans to write and publish testimonies or autobiographies describing their heroic deeds and experiences at war, Cervantes leaned towards creating a fictional account of a knight's adventures, remotely and metaphorically representing a soldier's experiences (Puchner 197).[3] A parody of chivalric romances, an allegory of disillusionment of fighting for a just cause, *Don Quixote*'s adventure-rich prose motivated many readers and introduced an alternative to an Odyssean hero, perhaps even an anti-hero, whose adventures result in more peril than triumph. Cervantes taught the literary world that journeys and adventures can be heroic, but they also can be picaresque; they can be carnivalesque, but also travel-inspired (byzantine). Above all, however, Cervantes showed that adventures are experiments—mad and unrealistic at times, inquisitive and revealing at others.

An avid reader, an aspiring dreamer, and an experienced adventurer himself, Cervantes understood that previous literary traditions sometimes lacked a candid presentation of universally human conditions. And perhaps one of the most universally experienced feelings is love. Cervantes felt the complications of love himself. It is unclear how certain advances took place in Cervantes's life, but we do know that he had an affair with a married woman, had an illegitimate daughter (who moved in with him after her mother's death), and later had a

---

2 He fled home due to his involvement in a duel, which was illegal at the time.

3 There are several autobiographical notes in *Don Quixote*, some of them presented in the Captive's Tale, others as references to Cervantes himself or his own work. For more on autobiographical references in Cervantes, see Garcés, Canavaggio's "La dimensión," and Rivers.

seemingly problematic marriage. (It is unclear if love formed part of that marriage.) What the literary world had inherited by Cervantes's time in terms of depictions of love were expressions of love in either moral or poetic realms (Cammarata and Laguna 36), and *Don Quixote* broke the literary norm by presenting love as an oxymoron—both beautiful and ugly—surely inspired by such mythologies as Galatea and Pygmalion.[4] One of the most idealized notions of life—love—took another form in Don Quixote; it could be viewed from different angles—from a point of view of an idealized platonic feeling to a narcissistic, self-serving need. Quixotic lovers sprung up fast in subsequent literary works, ready to endanger their reputations, health, or familiar relations. A most complicated and complex trait, this quixotic feature has made room for discussion of love as cacoethes.

Although I focused primarily on re-accentuations of Don Quixote in this book, authors who show influence of Cervantes are usually inspired by other characters, as well. And so, re-accentuated Quixotes often come accompanied with re-accentuated Sanchos, Dulcineas, Rocinantes, and even Marcelas and Carrascos. Various quixotic novels introduce the image of a friend, an adviser, and an accompanying figure, who resembles Sancho; an idealized woman or an object of adoration, who reminds of Dulcinea. In several cases, there is even a means of transportation, intended to represent the image of Rocinante. Those novels that integrate re-accentuated images of Don Quixote, Sancho Panza, Dulcinea, and others present a quixotic community. In some of the novels discussed in the previous chapters, the presence of such a community is evident, while in others it is either not prominent or entirely absent.

The significant impact that *Don Quixote* has had on the dynamics of the novelistic genre is undeniable. The works where Don Quixote revives with a new twist in a new context suggest various interpretations of why this character continuously demonstrates a trend of re-accentuation. In eighteenth and nineteenth-century Europe, Don Quixote has come dressed, for instance, as a woman reader. The re-

4 It is noteworthy that Cervantes authored a pastoral novel titled *La Galatea*. His first work, it was published in 1585, twenty years before the first part of *Don Quixote* hit the market.

accentuated feminized Quixotes in the works of Lennox, Austen, and Flaubert, for example, serve as warnings against certain types of reading that consequently needs a cure. As Gordon points out:

> The "reality" to which cured female Quixotes return involves courtship, marriage, and a productive domestic life: orthodox Quixote narratives treat courtship and marriage as the trajectory that all young women would follow naturally had their weak imagination, enthralled by fictions, not embraced mistaken expectations and (mis)perceived world. This account of female Quixote narratives differs from most recent readings of this genre that depict the practice of quixotism as a strategy that enables young women to voice their resistance to eighteenth-century patriarchy. (38)

And in general, if Don Quixote's vagaries, be it through his characteristics of a reader, dreamer, adventurer, or a lover, have adverse outcomes for him, female re-accentuations of Don Quixote are patronized even more harshly in their contexts. Thinking of Anna Karenina (Chapter Five), Otilia (Chapter Five), Emma (Chapter Two), or Catherine (Chapter Two), among others, it becomes clear that quixotism is a punishable act for these women; none of these women belong in a patriarchal society unless they are willing to succumb to its norms. It seems like the re-accentuated feminized image of Don Quixote serves to show the only two possible solutions a non-stereotypical and unconventional woman can find in a patriarchal society: be domesticized and marry or become another case of a Bovary or Karenina.

It is also thought-provoking to see how various authors have elevated the quixotic trait of the lover in their protagonists. The re-accentuated Quixotes discussed in the previous chapters very often present love as obsession and idealization, a trait comparable to Cervantes's knight errant. As known, Don Quixote never encounters his love *tête-à-tête* in the novel. He simply chooses a peasant woman named Aldonza Lorenzo "with whom he had once been in love" (Cervantes 23), gives her the name Dulcinea, and pledges love and commitment to her to comply with the expectations of knight errantry described in chivalric romances. The reader then learns that Dulcinea may not at all be what Don Quixote pictures her to be. Sancho, for example, finds her rather unappealing. Parallel to Don Quixote's idealized image of Dulcinea stand the characters of Daisy, perfected in the mind of Jay Gatsby (Chapter Three); Otilia, romanticized by Ricardo Somocurcio (Chapter Five); and various characters like Rebeca, Remedios, and others held as flawless exemplars of women in the minds of several characters in *One Hundred Years of Solitude* (Chapter Three).

Re-accentuated Quixotes also depict deep obsession with their respective quests. For example, Melville's protagonist Captain Ahab (Chapter Three) is looking for the white whale so obsessively that he endangers the lives of his own crew during his quest. In a similar manner, Daniel Quinn (Chapter Three), immersed in a self-oblivious quest, does not perceive any indications that clearly lead him to a dead end in his quest. Both Jay Gatsby (Chapter Three) and Humbert Humbert (Chapter Five) are obsessed by the image of the woman they compulsively love, while Donny Coyote (Chapter Four) sets out on an impossible pursuit pretending to be a superhero. It is notable that most of the quixotic quests that re-accentuated protagonists undertake end up with the protagonists failing, dying, or renouncing their ideals. This type of conclusion is a clear derivative of *Don Quixote*. What does Don Quixote's story look like? As J. J. Allen points out: "Within the novel, it is Don Quixote's undisciplined egocentricity, and Part II is the story of his recovery" (*Don Quixote, Hero* 201). Nearly every re-accentuated character mentioned above follows a comparable trajectory, beginning with self-negation and a lack of awareness of their surroundings due to their obsessive pursuits. This phase is succeeded by self-realization and recovery, frequently accompanied by disillusionment.

The images of Arabella, Catherine, Emma, Prince Myshkin, Anna, Jay, Ahab, Humbert, Monsignor Quixote, Daniel, Ricardo, all Buendías, Dr. Francia, and innumerable others are vivid examples of various transformations that Don Quixote can undergo. These illustrations and other quixotic works prove once again that "*Don Quixote* is the archetypal novel that seems to encompass the range of what would be written afterward" (Alter 29). Quixotic novels demonstrate a continuous attempt to revive the "theory" introduced by Cervantes, and quixotic characters elevate the Cervantine "practice" (Bayliss 167).

The terms "theory" and "practice," coined by Robert Bayliss, are meant to describe what *Don Quixote* "theory" and Don Quixote "practice" have brought to the academic, cultural, and literary worlds (167). And we continue reading and rereading *Don Quixote* because, as Paul Armstrong states, we "have not yet exhausted its capacity to be understood in new and perhaps unexpected ways" (21). *Don Quixote* falls into the category of such novels that keep being discovered and rediscovered in a variety of manners, opening numerous possibilities for new interpretations, criticism, and analyses. The "theory" and the "practice" of Cervantes's genius have been ongoing for over four hundred years, and that will continue as readers read, authors cite, and writers re-accentuate every valuable piece of *Don Quixote*.

Jacques Lezra opens his *Contra todos los fueros de la muerte* (2016) unexpectedly: "A Cervantes, manosearlo. El toqueteo, la falta de respeto," which translated and paraphrased calls for a prerequisite to have a grip on Cervantes's work—by reading and rereading it—because surface dissection of his work is mere disrespect (13).[5] I would like to close this book with a similar message. Cervantes is not an author who should be read once. *Don Quixote* is not a novel to glance through once. It is a novel that not only became canonical in world literature, but also inspired other canonical works. Very few authors in all human history could achieve such influence. And maybe when *Don Quixote* seems to have exhausted its answers to an inquisitive reader, we could turn to *Quixote*-inspired literature to find how other authors have answered questions like ours. Then, perhaps, we can endeavor to perceive *Don Quixote* and its characters through various lenses, gleaning from these readings a common thread, like the one I have discerned that gave birth to this book: the identification of quixotic readers, dream-

5 Lezra's book title comes from a quote from *Don Quixote*: "For me alone was Don Quixote born, and I for him; . . . and you will warn him, if you ever happen to meet him, to let the weary and crumbling bones of Don Quixote rest in the grave, and not attempt, *contrary to all the statutes of death*, to carry them off to Castilla la Vieja, removing him from the tomb where he really and truly lies, incapable of undertaking a third journey or a new sally . . . (Cervantes 939; emphasis added to indicate the translation from Spanish into English).

ers, adventurers, and lovers—quixotic essences re-accentuated in hundreds of works, of which I presented to you a synechdochal few. So, yes read and reread, think and rethink Cervantes and *Don Quixote*, but also turn to literature that was influenced by the first modern novel and its author, as each inspired work is its own reading of Cervantes that informs the world of Cervantine meanings, intertextual realms, quixotic works, and re-accentuated characters.

## Works Cited


Aguilera Serey, Juan. "Movimiento, espacio y lenguaje en *Ciudad de Cristal* de Paul Auster." *Alpha*, vol. 1, no. 42, July 2016, pp. 77-92.

Allen, John Jay. *Don Quixote: Hero or Fool? A Study in Narrative Technique*. U of Florida P, 1979.

———. "*Don Quijote* and the Origins of the Novel." *Cervantes and the Renaissance*, edited by Michael D. McGaha, Juan de la Cuesta, 1978, pp. 125-40.

———. "Smiles and Laughter in *Don Quixote*." *Comparative Literature Studies*, vol. 43, no. 4, 2006, pp. 515-31.

Alter, Robert. *Partial Magic: The Novel as a Self-Conscious Genre.* U of California P, 1975.

Álvarez, Eliseo. Interview. "Positions are Positions and Sex is Sex." Maristain, pp. 69-91.

Andrade, Max Ubelaker. "*Don Quixote*: Pain, Space, and Artifice." *Cervantes: Bulletin of the Cervantes Society of America*, vol. 32, no. 2, Fall 2012, pp. 81-121.

Arancibia, Adrian. "Postmodernity and the Latin American City: Mexico City and *The Savage Detectives*." *Black Renaissance*, vol. 2, no. 3, Winter 2009, pp. 204-19.

Areco, Macarena. "Las ciudades, los tiempos, las trayectorias y los géneros de *Los detectives salvajes*." *Anales de literatura chilena*, vol. 10, no. 11, June 2009, pp. 213-25.

Armstrong, Paul B. *Conflicting Readings: Variety and Validity in Interpretation*. U of North Carolina P, 1990.

Austen, Jane. *Northanger Abbey*. Edited by Barbara M. Benedict and Deirdre Le Faye, Cambridge UP, 2006.

Auster, Paul. *The Art of Hunger: Essays, Prefaces, Interviews; And, The Red Notebook*. Penguin, 1993.

———. *City of Glass*. Sun and Moon P, 1985.

Bakhtin, M. M. *The Dialogic Imagination: Four Essays*. Edited by Michael Holquist, translated by Caryl Emerson and Michael Holquist, U of Texas P, 1982.

———. *Problems of Dostoevsky's Poetics*. Edited and translated by Caryl Emerson, Introduction by Wayne C. Booth, U of Minnesota P, 1984.

———. *Rabelais and His World*. Translated by Helene Islowsky, Indiana UP, 2009.

———. *Speech Genres and Other Late Essays*. Edited by Caryl Emerson and Michael Holquist, translated by Vern W. McGee, U of Texas P, 1986.

Bandera, Cesáreo. *The Humble Story of Don Quixote: Reflections on the Birth of the Modern Novel*. Catholic U of America P, 2006.

Barrio Marco, José Manuel, and María José Crespo Allué, editors. *La huella de Cervantes y del Quijote en la cultura anglosajona*. Secretario de Publicaciones, 2007.

Bartolomeo, Joseph F. *Matched Pairs: Gender and Intertextual Dialogue in Eighteenth-Century Fiction*. U of Delaware P, 2002.

Bayliss, Robert. "A Tale of Two Quixotes: *Don Quixote* Today, in Theory and in Practice." Don Quixote: *Interdisciplinary Connections*, edited by James A. Parr and Matthew D. Warshawsky, Juan de la Cuesta, 2013, pp. 165-83.

Beaumont, Francis. *The Knight of the Burning Pestle*. Edited by Todd H. J. Pettigrew, Broadview, 2023.

Bell, Michael. "The Cervantean Turn: *One Hundred Years of Solitude*." *Bloom's Modern Critical Interpretations: One Hundred Years of Solitude*, edited and Introduction by Harold Bloom, Infobase, 2009, pp. 99-126.

Bernández Rodal, Asunción. "Las mujeres lectoras en el *Quijote*." *El* Quijote *en clave de mujer/es*, edited by Fanny Rubio, Editorial Complutense, 2005, pp. 283-304.

Beusterien, John, and Ana María Laguna. "Introduction." Laguna and Beusterien, pp. 3-29.

Blackmur, R. P. "Madame Bovary: Beauty out of Place." *The Kenyon Review*, vol. 13, no. 3, Summer 1951, pp. 475-503.

Bloom, Harold. *Gabriel García Márquez's* One Hundred Years of Solitude. Chelsea House, 2006.

———. *How to Read and Why*. Scribner, 2000.

———. *A Map of Misreading*. Oxford UP, 1975.

Bolaño, Roberto. *Between Parentheses: Essays, Articles, and Speeches, 1998-2003*. Edited by Ignacio Echevarría, translated by Natasha Wimmer, New Directions, 2004.

———. *The Savage Detectives.* Translated by Natasha Wimmer, Straus, 2007.

Booth, Wayne C. *The Rhetoric of Fiction.* 2nd edition, U of Chicago P, 1983.

Borges, Jorge Luis. "Pierre Menard, Author of the *Quixote*." *Collected Fictions*, translated by Andrew Hurley, Penguin, 1999, pp. 88-95.

Borgmeier, Raimund. "Henry Fielding and his Spanish Model: 'Our English Cervantes.'" Fernández-Morera and Hanke, pp. 43-64.

Boyd, Diane E., and Marta Kvande. "Introduction: Reading Women, Reading Public and Private." *Everyday Revolutions: Eighteenth-Century Women Transforming Public and Private*, edited by Diane E. Boyd and Marta Kvande, U of Delaware P, 2008, pp. 17-29.

Brantlinger, Patrick. *The Reading Lesson: The Threat of Mass Literacy in Nineteenth-Century British Fiction.* Indiana UP, 1998.

Brewer, Brian. "Comic Exaggeration, Eroticism, and Character in *Don Quijote*: Maritornes, Doña Rodríguez, Altisidora." *Cervantes: Bulletin of the Cervantes Society of America*, vol. 42, no. 1, Spring 2022, pp. 35-55.

Brink, André. *The Novel: Language and Narrative from Cervantes to Calvino.* New York UP, 1998.

Cain, William E. "American Dreaming: Really Reading *The Great Gatsby*." *Society*, vol. 57, no. 4, 2020, pp. 453-70.

Cammarata, Joan, and Ana María Laguna. "Egocentricity versus Persuasion: Eros, Logos and Pathos in Cervantes's Marcela and Grisóstomo Episode." Laguna and Beusterien, pp. 33-52.

Campbell, Joseph. *The Hero with a Thousand Faces*. Princeton UP, 1972.

Canavaggio, Jean. "La dimensión autobiográfica del *Viaje del Parnaso.*" *Cervantes: Bulletin of the Cervantes Society of America*, vol. 1, no. 1-2, 1981, pp. 29-41.

———. *Don Quijote, del libro al mito.* Translated by Mauro Armiño, Espasa, 2006.

Caso, Antonio. "Cervantes." *Don Quijote: Meditaciones hispanoamericanas*, vol. 1, Prologue by Frederick Viña, UP of America, 1988, pp. 60-62.

Cervantes, Miguel de. *Don Quijote de la Mancha*. Edited by John Jay Allen, 2 vols, Cátedra, 2009.

———. *Don Quixote*. Translated by Edith Grossman, Introduction by Harold Bloom, Harper Collins, 2003.

———. *La Galatea*. Edited by Juan Bautista Bergua, Ediciones Ibéricas, 2011.

Church, Margaret. *Structure and Theme: "Don Quixote" to James Joyce.* Ohio State UP, 1983.

Clignet, Remi. "*Madame Bovary* and *Lady Chatterley's Lover* as Social Problems: The 'Natural History' of Immoral Novels." *Social Problems*, vol. 28, no. 3, February 1981, pp. 290-307.

Close, Anthony J. "Don Quixote's Love for Dulcinea: A Study of Cervantine Irony." *Bulletin of Hispanic Studies*, vol. 50, no. 3, 1973, pp. 237-55.

Da Rosa, Doris C. "*Yo el Supremo* and Augusto Roa Bastos's Search for the Future of Paraguay." *Discurso literario,* vol. 1, no. 2, 1984, pp. 169-76.

Dahl, Roald. *Matilda*. Illustrated by Quentin Blake, Puffin Books, 1991.

Dale, Amelia. *The Printed Reader: Gender, Quixotism, and Textual Bodies in Eighteenth-Century Britain*. Bucknell UP, 2019.

D'haen, Theo, and Reindert Dhondt, editors. *International Quixote.* Rodopi, 2009.

Dimock, Wai Chee. "A Theory of Resonance." *PMLA*, vol. 112, no. 5, Oct. 1997, pp. 1060-71.

Donaldson, Scott, editor. *Critical Essays on F. Scott Fitzgerald's* The Great Gatsby. G. K. Hall, 1984.

———. "The Trouble with Nick." Donaldson, pp. 131-39.

Dostoevsky, Fyodor. *The Idiot*. Translated by Richard Pevear and Larissa Volokhonsky, Introduction by Richard Pevear, Everyman, 2002.

Doubinsky, Sébastien. "'In the Mind of the Bourgeois Reader': An Essay on Reading as an Uncomfortable Experience." *Reading Literature Today: Two Complementary Essays and a Conversation* by Tabish Khair and Sébastien Doubinsky, SAGE, 2011, pp. 83-121.

Drumm, Elizabeth. "Foucault's Madmen and Poets: Don Quixote and Daniel Quinn's Quest for a Unitary Sign." *Cervantes: Bulletin of the Cervantes Society of America*, vol. 42, no. 2, Fall 2022, pp. 11-31.

Durán, Leopoldo. *Graham Greene: amigo y hermano.* Espasa, 1996.

Durán, Manuel, and Fay R. Rogg. *Fighting Windmills: Encounters with Don Quixote*. Yale UP, 2006.

Ebreo, Leone. *Dialogues of Love*. Translated by Damian Bacich and Rossella Pescatori, edited by Rossella Pescatori, U of Toronto P, 2009.

Egginton, William. *The Man Who Invented Fiction: How Cervantes Ushered in the Modern World*. Bloomsbury, 2016.

Espejo, Ramón. "Coping with the Postmodern: Paul Auster's *New York Trilogy*." *Journal of American Studies*, vol. 48, no. 1, February 2014, pp. 147-71.

Estébanez Estébanez, Cayetano. "Don Quijote, de hidalgo de la Mancha a monseñor: Cervantes, Graham Greene y Rodney Bennet." Barrio Marco and Crespo Allué, pp. 301-10.

Felipe, Pedro de. "Un cuarto de siglo en la búsqueda de la felicidad en tres novelas de Mario Vargas Llosa. *La ciudad y los perros* (1963), *La tía Julia y el escribidor* (1977) y *Las travesuras de la niña mala* (2006)." *Contexto*, vol. 16, no. 18, 2012, pp. 88-101.

Fernández, Jerónimo. *Historia del magnánimo, valiente e invencible caballero Don Belianís de Grecia, I*. Edited by Lilia E. F. de Orduna, Reichenberger, 1997.

Fernández de Lizardi, José Joaquín. *La educación de las mujeres; o la Quijotita y su prima; historia muy cierta con apariencias de novela.* Cámara Mexicana Del Libro, 1942.

Fernández-Morera, Darío, and Michael Hanke, editors. *Cervantes in the English-Speaking World: New Essays.* Reichenberger, 2005.

Fiedler, Leslie A. "The Death and Rebirth of the Novel." *The Theory of the Novel*, edited by John Halperin, Oxford UP, 1974, pp. 189-209.

Fielding, Henry. *Joseph Andrews*. Edited by Martin C. Battestin, Wesleyan UP, 1967.

———. *Tom Jones*. Edited by Sheridan Baker, 2nd edition, Norton, 1994.

Filardo Llamas, Laura, and Marta M. Gutiérrez Rodríguez. "Lectures on *Lolita*: La influencia cervantina en Nabokov." Barrio Marco and Crespo Allué, pp. 407-20.

Fitzgerald, F. Scott. *The Great Gatsby*. Preface and Notes by Matthew J. Bruccoli, Scribner, 2003.

Flaubert, Gustave. *Madame Bovary*. Translated by Margaret Mauldon, Introduction by Malcolm Bowie, Notes by Mark Overstall, Oxford UP, 2008.

Flores, Angel, and M. J. Benardete, editors. *Cervantes Across the Centuries*. Gordian, 1969.

Fonseca, Cristóbal de. *Tratado del amor de Dios*. Guillermo Foquel, 1592.

Forgues, Roland. "Humanism and Criticism: The Presence of French Culture in Vargas Llosa's Utopia." *Vargas Llosa and Latin American Politics*, edited by Juan E. de Castro and Nicholas Birns, Palgrave, 2010, pp. 159-72.

Fox, Soledad. *Flaubert and Don Quijote: The Influence of Cervantes on Madame Bovary*. Sussex, 2010.

Fuentes, Carlos. "New Novel, New World." *The Modern Language Review*, vol. 84, no. 4, Oct 1989, pp. xxxi-xlii.

Furui, Yoshiaki. "Lonely Individualism in *Moby-Dick*." *Criticism*, vol. 62, no. 4, Fall 2020, pp. 599-623.

Fussell, Edwin. "Moby-Dick and the American West." Hayes, pp. 99-117.

Gallo, Marta. "Pasión del texto: muerte y resurrección en *Yo el Supremo*." *Homenaje a Ana María Barrenechea*, edited by Lia Shwartz Lerner and Isaias Lerner, Castalia, 1984, pp. 431-38.

*Game of Thrones*. Directed by Alan Taylor et al., written by David Benioff and D.B. Weiss, HBO, 2011-2018.

Garcés, María Antonia. *Cervantes in Algiers: A Captive's Tale.* Vanderbilt UP, 2002.
García Márquez, Gabriel. *One Hundred Years of Solitude.* Translated by Gregory Rabassa, Penguin, 2000.
Garrido Ardila, J. A. *Cervantes en inglaterra: El* Quijote *y la novela inglesa del siglo XVIII.* Centro de estudios cervantinos, 2014.
———, editor. *The Cervantean Heritage: Reception and Influence of Cervantes in Britain.* Legenda, 2009.
———. "Cervantes y la novela moderna: Literatura experimental y realismo en el *Quijote.*" *Cervantes: Bulletin of the Cervantes Society of America,* vol. 33, no. 2, Fall 2013, pp. 145-72.
———. *A History of the Spanish Novel.* Oxford UP, 2015.
Garrigós, Cristina. "Las mujeres quijotes y los efectos perniciosos de la lectura en *The Female Quixote* de Charlotte Lennox y *Female Quixotism* de Tabitha Tenney." Barrio Marco and Crespo Allué, pp. 457-66.
Gersdorf, Catrin. "Postmodern Aventiure: *Don Quijote* in Amerika." *Zeitschrift für Anglistik und Amerikanistik,* vol. 46, no. 2, 1998, pp. 142-56.
Ginés, Montserrat. *The Southern Inheritors of Don Quixote.* Luisiana State UP, 2000.
Girard, René. *Deceit, Desire, and the Novel.* Translated by Yvonne Freccero, Johns Hopkins UP, 1965.
Gleim, William S. *The Meaning of Moby Dick.* Russel, 1962.
González Echevarría, Roberto. *Love and the Law in Cervantes.* Yale UP, 2005.
Gordon, Scott Paul. *The Practice of Quixotism: Postmodern Theory and Eighteenth-Century Women's Writing.* Macmillan, 2006.
Gratchev, Slav N., and Howard Mancing, editors. *Don Quixote: The Re-Accentuation of the World's Greatest Literary Hero.* Bucknell UP, 2017.
Greene, Graham. *Monsignor Quixote.* Simon and Schuster, 1982.
Greer, Andrew Sean. *Less.* Lee Boudreaux Books, 2017.
Griboyedov, Alexander. *Woe from Wit.* Bilingual edition, translated by Bernard Pares, edited by Anita Belotserkovskaya, Russian Information Services, 2017.

Groes, Sebastian. "Memory, Materiality and the Ethics of Reading in the Digital Age." *Memory in the Twenty-First Century: New Critical Perspectives from the Arts, Humanities, and Sciences*, edited by Sebastian Groes, Palgrave, 2016, pp. 130-37.

Gyulamiryan, Tatevik. "On Re-accentuation, Adaptation, and Imitation of Don Quixote." Gratchev and Mancing, pp. 11-22.

———. "Toward a Poetics of Re-accentuation: Don Quixote and His Female Mimeses." *Cervantes ilimitado: Cuatrocientos años del Quijote*, special issue of *ALDEEU*, edited by Nuria Morgado, 2016, pp. 51-73.

Hammond, Brean. "The Cervantic Legacy in the Eighteenth-Century Novel." Garrido Ardila, pp. 96-103.

Hanlon, Aaron R. "Toward a Counter-Poetics of Quixotism." *Studies in the Novel*, vol. 46, no. 2, Summer 2014, pp. 141-58.

———. *A World of Disorderly Notions: Quixote and the Logic of Exceptionalism*. U of Virginia P, 2019.

Harrison, Kathryn. "Dangerous Obsession." *New York Times*, 14 Oct. 2007, www.nytimes.com/2007/10/14/books/review/Harrison.html?pagewanted=1&_r. Accessed 1 March 2023.

Hayes, Kevin J., editor. *The Critical Response to Herman Melville's "Moby Dick."* Greenwood, 1994.

Henighan, Stephen. "Nuevas versiones de lo femenino en *La Fiesta del Chivo, El paraíso en la otra esquina* y *Travesuras de la Niña Mala*." *Hispanic Review*, vol. 77, no. 3, Summer 2009, pp. 369-88.

Hennings, Terri Jane. *Writing Against Aesthetic Ideology*. Traugott Bautz Verlag, 2016.

Henríquez Jiménez, Santiago J. "*Don Quijote de la Mancha* y *Monsignor Quixote*: la inspiración castellana de Graham Greene en el clásico español de Cervantes." Barrio Marco and Crespo Allué, pp. 311-18.

Homer. *The Odyssey*. Translated by Robert Fagles, Introduction and Notes by Bernard Knox, Viking, 1996.

Honeyman, Gail. *Eleanor Oliphant Is Completely Fine*. Penguin, 2017.

Howard, Jacqueline. *Reading Gothic Fiction: A Bakhtinian Approach*. Clarendon P, 1994.

Hutcheon, Linda. *A Theory of Adaptation*. Routledge, 2006.

———. *A Theory of Parody: The Teachings of Twentieth-Century Art Forms*. Methuen, 1985.

Hutchinson, Steven. *Cervantine Journeys*. U of Wisconsin P, 1992.

Iser, Wolfgang. *Prospecting: From Reader Response to Literary Anthropology*. The John Hopkins UP, 1989.

———. "The Reading Process: A Phenomenological Approach." *Reader-Response Criticism: From Formalism to Post-Structuralism*, edited by Jane P. Tompkins, The John Hopkins UP, 1980, pp. 50-69.

Jaanus, Maire, and Kurrik J. Maire. *Literature and Negation*. Columbia UP, 1988.

Jefferson, D. W. "*Tristram Shandy* and the Tradition of Learned Wit." *Tristram Shandy,* edited by Melvyn New, St. Martin's P, 1992, pp. 17-35.

Jehenson, Myriam Yvonne, and Peter N. Dunn. *The Utopian Nexus in Don Quixote.* Vanderbilt UP, 2006.

Jofré, Manuel. "Don Quijote de la Mancha: Dialogismo y carnavalización, diálogo socrático y sátira menipea." *Revista chilena de literatura,* vol. 67, Nov. 2005, pp. 113-29.

Johnson, Carroll B. *Don Quixote: The Quest for Modern Fiction*. Twayne, 1990.

———. *Madness and Lust: A Psychological Approach to Don Quixote.* U of California P, 1983.

Johnson, Carroll B., and Joe Brockmeier. "Ricote the *Morisco* and Capital Formation." *Cervantes and the Material World*, U of Illinois P, 2000, pp. 51-68.

Jonson, Benjamin. *The Alchemist*. Edited by Elizabeth Cook, Norton, 2010.

Kahn, Aaron M., editor. *The Oxford Handbook of Cervantes*. Oxford UP, 2021.

Krabbenhoft, Kenneth. "Don Quixote and Lolita." *Atlantis,* vol. 18, no. 1, June-December 1996, pp. 213-27.

Kropf, C. R. "Educational Theory and Human Nature in Fielding's Works." *PMLA,* vol. 89, no. 1, Jan. 1974, pp. 113-20.

Kubayanda, J. Bekunuru. "Sin razón de la razón: *Yo el supremo* como paradoja." *Las voces del karaí: estudios sobre Augusto Roa Bastos*, edited by Fernando Burgos, Edelsa, 1988, pp. 119-26.

La Calprenède, Gauthier de Costes. *Cassandra; the Fam'd Romance*. 1663, https://quod.lib.umich.edu/e/eebo/A47682.0001.001?view=toc. Accessed 5 March 2023.

Laguna, Ana María. "The Unromantic Approach to Don Quixote: Cervantine Love in the Spanish Post-War Age." Laguna and Beusterien, pp. 247-69.

Laguna, Ana María, and John Beusterien, editors. *Goodbye Eros: Recasting Forms and Norms of Love in the Age of Cervantes*. U of Toronto P, 2020.

LaLonde, Suzanne. "Don Quixote's Quixotic Trauma Therapy: A Reassessment of Cervantes's Canonical Novel and Trauma Studies." *Open Cultural Studies,* vol. 1, no. 1, 2017, pp. 244-56.

Langbauer, Laurie. "Diverting Romance: Charlotte Lennox's *The Female Quixote*." *Women and Romance: The Consolations of Gender in the English Novel*, edited by Laurie Langbauer et al., Cornell UP, 1990, pp. 62-92.

———. "Romance Revised: Charlotte Lennox's *The Female Quixote*." *Novel: A Forum on Fiction*, vol. 18, no. 1, 1984, pp. 29-49.

Lavender, William. "The Novel of Critical Engagement: Paul Auster's *City of Glass*." *Contemporary Literature*, vol. 34, no. 2, Summer 1993, pp. 219-39.

*Lazarillo de Tormes*. Edited by Francisco Rico, Cátedra, 2008.

Lázaro Lafuente, Alberto. "Estampas del *Quijote* en la novela británica contemporánea." Barrio Marco and Crespo Allué, pp. 253-77.

Lázaro Larraz, María Luisa. "La incuestionable impronta cervantina en la narrativa de Paul Auster." Barrio Marco and Crespo Allué, pp. 437-43.

Lehman, B. H. "Of Time, Personality, and the Author: A Study of *Tristram Shandy*: Comedy." Spector, pp. 165-84.

Lennox, Charlotte. *The Female Quixote, or, The Adventures of Arabella*. Edited by Margaret Dalziel, Introduction by Margaret Anne Doody, Oxford UP, 2008.

Lezra, Jacques. *"Contra todos los fueros de la muerte": El suceso cervantino*. La Cebra, 2016.

Lombardi, Elena. *Imagining the Woman Reader in the Age of Dante.* Oxford UP, 2018.

López Navia, Santiago Alfonso. *Inspiración y pretexto II: Nuevos estudios sobre Cervantes, su obra y su recepción*. Iberoamericana—Vervuert, 2021.

Lynn, David H. *The Hero's Tale: Narrators in the Early Modern Novel.* St. Martin's P, 1989.

Madariaga Caro, Montserrat. *Bolaño Infra 1975-1977: Los años que inspiraron* Los detectives salvajes. RIL editores, 2013.

Maggi, Armando. "The End of the Renaissance Philosophy of Love: Cristóbal de Fonseca and León Hebreo in *Los trabajos de Persiles y Sigismunda*." *Bulletin of Hispanic Studies*, vol. 84, no. 6, 2007, pp. 761-77.

Mancing, Howard. "Bakhtin, Spanish Literature, and Cervantes." *Cervantes for the 21st Century/Cervantes para el siglo XXI: Studies in Honor of Edward Dudley*, edited by Edward Dudley and Francisco La Rubia Prado, Juan de la Cuesta, 2000, pp. 141-62.

———. *The Cervantes Encyclopedia*. 2 vols, Greenwood, 2004.

———. *The Chivalric World of Don Quijote: Style, Structure, and Narrative Technique*. U of Missouri P, 1982.

———. "Don Quixote: Coming to America." *Cervantes y su mundo*, edited by A. Robert Lauer and Kurt Reichenberger, Reichenberger, 2005, pp. 397-419.

———. "Embodied Cognition and Autopoiesis in *Don Quixote*." *Cognitive Approaches to Early Modern Spanish Literature*, edited by Isabel Jaén and Julien Jacques Simon, Oxford UP, 2016, pp. 37-52.

Mandel, Oscar. "The Function of the Norm in *Don Quixote*." *Modern Philology*, vol. 55, 1958, pp. 154-63.

Mandelker, Amy. *Framing* Anna Karenina*: Tolstoy, the Woman Question, and the Victorian Novel*. Ohio State UP, 1993.

Manuel, Don Juan. *Count Lucanor: The Fifty Pleasant Stories of Patronio*. Translated by James York, UP of the Pacific, 2002.

Maravall, José Antonio. *Utopia and Counterutopia in the Quixote*. Translated by Robert W. Felkel, Wayne State UP, 1991.

Maristain, Mónica. Interview. "The Last Interview." Maristain, pp. 93-123.

———, editor. *Roberto Bolaño: The Last Interview and Other Conversations*. Melville House, 2009.

Martín, Adrienne L. "Humor and Violence in Cervantes." *The Cambridge Companion to Cervantes*, edited by Anthony J. Cascardi, Cambridge UP, 2002, pp. 160-85.

Martin, Gerald. *Journeys through the Labyrinth: Latin American Fiction in the Twentieth Century*. Verso, 1989.

Martinez-Bonati, Felix. *"Don Quixote" and the Poetics of the Novel*. Cornell UP, 2019.

Matooka, Wendy. *The Age of Reasons: Quixotism, Sentimentalism and Political Economy in Eighteenth-Century Britain*. Routledge, 1998.

Maturana, Humberto R., and Francisco J. Varela. *Autopoiesis and Cognition: The Realization of the Living*. Reidel, 1980.

McCrory, Donald P. *No Ordinary Man: The Life and Times of Miguel de Cervantes*. Dover, 2006.

McFarlane, Brian. "It Wasn't Like That in the Book..." *The Literature/film Reader: Issues of Adaptation*, edited by Peter Lev and James Michael Welsh, Scarecrow P, 2007, pp. 3-14.

———. *Novel to Film: An Introduction to the Theory of Adaptation*. Clarendon P, 1996.

Meehan, Adam. "Repetition, Race, and Desire in The Great Gatsby." *Journal of Modern Literature*, vol. 37, no. 2, 2014, pp. 76-91.

Melville, Herman. *Moby Dick*. Introduction by Brian Busby, Arcturus, 2018.

Mitchell, Ken. *The Heroic Adventures of Donny Coyote*. Fitzhenry, 2003.

Morrison, Paul. "Enclosed Openness: *Northanger Abbey* and the Domestic Carceral." *Texas Studies in Literature and Language*, vol. 33, no. 1, Spring 1991, pp. 1-23.

Morson, Gary S. *Anna Karenina in Our Time: Seeing More Wisely*. Yale UP, 2007.

———. *Narrative and Freedom: The Shadows of Time*. Yale UP, 1994.

Musarra-Schronder, Ulla. "Cervantes in Paul Auster's *New York Trilogy.*" D'haen and Dhondt, pp. 219-35.

Nabokov, Vladimir. *Lectures on Don Quixote.* Edited by Fredson Bowers, Introduction by Guy Davenport, Weidenfeld, 1983.

———. *The Annotated Lolita.* Introduction and Notes by Alfred Appel, Vintage, 1991.

Nadeau, Carolyn A. *Women of the Prologue: Imitation, Myth, and Magic in Don Quixote I.* Bucknell UP, 2002.

Narozny, Christopher, and Diana de Armas Wilson. "Heroic Failure: Novelistic Importance in *Don Quixote* and *Tristram Shandy.*" Garrido Ardila, pp. 142-50.

Neill, Natalie. "'the trash with which the press now groans': *Northanger Abbey* and the Gothic Best Sellers of the 1790s." *The Eighteenth-Century Novel,* vol. 4, edited by Albert J. Rivero, George Justice, and Margo Collins, AMS, 2004, pp. 163-92.

Nicolás Román, Susana. "English Quixotes in the Eighteenth-century: Major and Minor Imitators of the Spanish Knight." Barrio Marco and Crespo Allué, pp. 159-65.

Ortega y Gasset, José. *Meditations on Quixote.* Introduction by Julián Marías, translated by Evelyn Rugg and Diego Marín, Norton, 1961.

Parker, A.A. "Fielding and the Structure of *Don Quixote.*" *Bulletin of Hispanic Studies,* vol. 33, no. 1, Sep. 2007, pp. 1-16.

Paulson, Ronald. *Don Quixote in England: The Aesthetics of Laughter.* John Hopkins UP, 1998.

Pawl, Amy J. "Feminine Transformation of the *Quixote* in Eighteenth-Century England: Lennox's *Female Quixote* and Her Sister." Garrido Ardila, pp. 166-75.

Perdou de Subligny, Adrien Thomas. *The Mock-Clelia: Being a Comical History of French Gallantries and Novels, in Imitation of* Don Quixote. 1678, https://quod.lib.umich.edu/e/eebo2/A61927.0001.001?view=toc. Accessed 1 March 2023.

Philbrick, Nathaniel. *In the Heart of the Sea.* Penguin, 2001.

Presa Díaz, José Carlos. "Del sentimiento de desengaño como 'género' de la literatura española." *Hipertexto,* vol. 3, Winter 2006, pp. 72-80.

Puchner, Martin. *The Written World: The Power of Stories to Shape People, History, Civilization*. Random House, 2017.

*Quixote*. Directed by Steven Ritz-Barr and Hoku Uchiyama, Classics in Miniature, 2010.

Radcliffe, Ann. *The Mysteries of Udolpho*. Penguin Classics, 2001.

Rader, Ralph W. "The Emergence of the Novel in England: Genre in History vs History in Genre." *Narrative*, vol. 1, no. 1, Jan. 1993, pp. 69-83.

Randall, Dale B. J., and Jackson C. Boswell. *Cervantes in Seventeenth-Century England: The Tapestry Turned*, Oxford UP, 2009.

Raúl, Dorra. "Yo el supremo: la circular perpetua." *Texto crítico*, vol. 9, 1978, pp. 58-70.

Richardson, Samuel. *Pamela: Or, Virtue Rewarded*. Edited by Peter Sabor, Introduction by Margaret Anne Doody, Penguin Classics, 1981.

Ritz-Barr, Steven. "Extracting the Essence of *Don Quixote* for a Puppet Film." Gratchev and Mancing, pp. 205-18.

Rivas, Vladimiro. *Mundo tatuado*. Paradiso, 2003.

Rivers, Elias L. "Cervantes' Journey to Parnassus." *MLN*, vol. 85, no. 2, 1970, 243-48.

Roa Bastos, Augusto. *I the Supreme*. Translated by Helen Lane, Vintage, 2018.

Rodríguez Alcalá de Gonzales Oddone, Beatriz, et al. *Comentarios sobre* Yo el Supremo. Club del Libro N1, 1975.

Rodríguez de Montalvo, Garci. *Amadís de Gaula*. Juan Cromberger, 1531, *Library of Congress*, www.loc.gov/item/2021666763/. Accessed 1 March 2023.

Rojas, Fernando de. *Celestina*. Translated by Peter Bush, Introduction by Juan Goytisolo, Penguin Classics, 2009.

Rolo, Charles J. "*Lolita*, by Vladimir Nabokov." *The Atlantic*, Sep. 1958, www.theatlantic.com/magazine/archive/1958/09/lolita-by-vladimir-nabokov/304639/. Accessed 24 March 2023.

Rowe, William, and Teresa Whitfield. "Thresholds of Identity: Literature and Exile in Latin America." *Third World Quarterly*, vol. 9, no. 1, Jan 1987, pp. 229-45.

Sánchez, Luis Rafael. "Dos novelas de ahora mismo: *Son de Almendra*, de Mayra Montero, y *Travesuras de la niña mala*, de Mario Vargas Llosa." *Hispamérica*, vol. 36, no. 106, April 2007, pp. 103-11.

Sánchez Sarmiento, Rafael. "Revisión del *Quijote*: Ilusión, desengaño, nostalgia." *Actas del II Coloquio Internacional de la Asociación de Cervantes*, 1990, pp. 567-74.

Scham, Michael. "*Don Quijote* and *Lolita* Revisited." *Cervantes: Bulletin of the Cervantes Society of America*, vol. 26, no. 1, Spring-Fall 2006, pp. 79-101.

Schmidt, Rachel. *Forms of Modernity: Don Quixote and Modern Theories of the Novel.* U of Toronto P, 2011.

Scudéry, Madeleine de. *Artamenes, or, The Grand Cyrus.* 1653-1655, https://quod.lib.umich.edu/e/eebo/A70988.0001.001. Accessed 2 March 2023.

———. *Clelia.* 1678, https://quod.lib.umich.edu/cgi/t/text/text-idx?c=eebo;idno=A58876.0001.001, Accessed 2 March 2023.

Selig, Karl-Ludwig. "*Don Quixote* and *The Great Gatsby*." *Revista Hispánica Moderna*, vol. 3, no. 4, 1978-1979, pp. 128-29.

Sijie, Dai. *Balzac and the Little Chinese Seamstress.* Translated by Ina Rilke, Anchor Books, 2002.

Slochewer, Harry. *Mythopoesis: Mythic Patterns in the Literary Classics.* Wayne State UP, 1970.

Smith, Henry Nash. "The Madness of Ahab." Hayes, pp. 183-200.

Smith, Mack. *Literary Realism and the Ekphrastic Tradition.* Pennsylvania State UP, 1995.

Soto, Héctor, and Matías Bravo. Interview. "Literature is Not Made from Words Alone." Maristain, pp. 41-50.

Spector, Donald Robert, editor. *Essays on the Eighteenth-Century Novel.* Indiana UP, 1966.

Spilka, Mark. "Comic Resolution in Fielding's *Joseph Andrews*." Spector, pp. 78-91.

Spitzer, Leo. "On the Significance of *Don Quijote*." *MLN*, vol. 77, no. 2, March 1962, pp. 113-29.

Stavans, Ilan. *A Critic's Journey*. U of Michigan P, 2010.

———. *Gabriel García Márquez: The Early Years*. Palgrave Macmillan, 2010.

Staves, Susan. "Don Quixote in Eighteenth-Century England." *Comparative Literature*, vol. 24, no. 3, Summer 1972, pp. 193-215.
Stenbock-Fermor, Elisabeth. *The Architecture of Anna Karenina: A History of Its Writing, Structure and Message*. John Benjamins, 1975.
Sterne, Laurence. *The Life and Opinions of Tristram Shandy, Gentleman*. Edited by James Aiken Work, Odyssey, 1940.
Stoopen, María. "Cervantine Instances of Unreliability in Ricardo Piglia's 'Assumed Name.'" D'haen and Dhondt, pp. 109-35.
Tabbi, Joseph. *Cognitive Fictions*. U of Minnesota P, 2002.
Tajuddin, Ahmed. "In 'Prison-House of Love': *The Bad Girl* and Bad Girls of Mario Vargas Llosa." *Rupkatha Journal on Interdisciplinary Studies in Humanities*, vol. 2, no. 3, 2010, pp. 312-18.
Tandon, Bharat. *Jane Austen and the Morality of Conversation*. Anthem P, 2003.
Tolstoy, Leo. *Anna Karenina*. Translated by Richard Pevear and Larissa Volokhonsky, Introduction by Richard Pevear, Penguin, 2002.
Tovar, Francisco. *Las historias del dictador* Yo el Supremo*, de Augusto Roa Bastos*. Ediciones del Mall, 1987.
Trilling, Lionel. "F. Scott Fitzgerald." Donaldson, pp. 13-20.
Triplette, Stacey. *Chivalry, Reading, and Women's Culture in Early Modern Spain: From* Amadís de Gaula *to* Don Quixote. Amsterdam UP, 2018.
Turkevich, Ludmilla Buketoff. *Cervantes in Russia*. Gordian, 1975.
Twain, Mark. *Adventures of Huckleberry Finn*. Oxford UP, 1996.
———. *The Adventures of Tom Sawyer.* Illustrations by Paul Geiger, Afterword by Bernard DeVoto, Reader's Digest, 1985.
Unamuno, Miguel de. *The Life of Don Quixote and Sancho*. Translated by Homer P. Earle, Alfred A Knopf, 1927.
———. *The Tragic Sense of Life in Men and Nations*. Translated by Anthony Kerrigan, Princeton UP, 1972.
Urbina, Eduardo. *La ficción que no cesa: Paul Auster y Cervantes*. Academia del Hispanismo, 2007.
Van Doren, Carl. "Mr. Melville's *Moby Dick*." Hayes, pp. 56-60.
Vargas Llosa, Mario. *The Bad Girl*. Translated by Edith Grossman, Farrar, 2007.

———. *The Perpetual Orgy: Flaubert and* Madame Bovary. Translated by Helen Lane, Farrar, 2011.

Voegeli, William. "Gatsby and the Pursuit of Happiness." *Claremont Review of Books*, Winter 2003, pp. 69-71.

Vollendorf, Lisa. *"Cervantes and His Women Readers." Romance Quarterly*, vol. 52, no. 4, 2005, pp. 312-27.

Wasserman, Dale. *Man of La Mancha*. Directed by Arthur Hiller, MGM Home Video, 2004.

Watt, Ian P. *The Rise of the Novel: Studies in Defoe, Richardson and Fielding*. U of California P, 1957.

Weldt-Basson, Helene Carol. *Augusto Roa Bastos's* I the Supreme: *A Dialogic Perspective*. U of Missouri P, 1993.

Welsh, Alexander. *Reflections on the Hero as Quixote*. Princeton UP, 1981.

Williamson, Edwin, editor. *Cervantes and the Modernistas: The Question of Influence*. Tamesis, 1994.

———. "The Quixotic Roots of Magic Realism: History and Fiction from Alejo Carpentier to Gabriel García Márquez." Williamson, pp. 103-20.

Wilson, Diana de Armas. "Where Does the Novel Rise? Cultural Hybrids and Cervantine Heresies." *Cervantes and His Postmodern Constituencies*, edited by Anne J. Cruz and Carroll B. Johnson, Garland, 1999, pp. 43-67.

Wonham, Henry B. "Mark Twain: The American Cervantes." Fernández-Morera and Hanke, pp. 159-68.

Wood, Michael. "Cervantes Reads Borges and Nabokov." Williamson, pp. 29-41.

Ziolkowski, Eric J. *The Sanctification of Don Quixote: From Hidalgo to Priest*. Pennsylvania State UP, 1991.

Zunshine, Lisa. *Why We Read Fiction: Theory of Mind and the Novel*. Ohio State UP, 2006.

## Index


Abraham Adams (Parson), 32n8, 104-108, 130

accent, 25. *See also* accentuate

accentuate, 25, 35, 41

adaptation, 20, 24-25, 29, 33-35, 95, 154

adventure(s), 16, 19, 21, 28, 32, 37, 39-40, 43-46, 50n1, 53, 58-60, 65, 73, 75-76, 78, 84n18, 85-86n19, 96-97, 100-102, 106-109, 110-11, 113, 115-26, 128, 132n1, 142, 144, 147, 149-50, 155-56. *See also* journey; quest

adventurer(s), 16, 19-22, 24, 29, 32n8, 33, 35, 38-39, 43, 45, 48-49, 53, 55, 80, 100-104, 106, 116, 119, 122, 130-31, 150, 153-54, 156, 158, 161

*agape*, 137

Aglaya Epanchin, 127-29

Aldonza Lorenzo, 46-47, 106, 117n16, 132, 140n8, 146, 158. *See also* Dulcinea del Toboso

Alfredo Stroessner, 88

Alice, 153

Allen, John Jay, 77n10, 100, 101n1, 129n30, 159

Alonso Quijano, 13-14n4, 42, 60, 85-86, 94-95, 113, 127, 144, 154. *See also* Don Quixote

Alter, Robert, 11, 15, 62, 111

Altisidora, 113, 121n21

Amadís de Gaula, 33, 52-53, 65, 77n9

Amaranta Úrsula, 96

American Dream, 78-80, 82, 99

Andrade, Max Ubelaker, 65n16

Andrés, 34, 108

Angola, 124

Anna Karenina, 47, 135-41, 151, 153, 158-59

anti-literature, 64

Arabella, 41, 55, 57-60, 63, 65n16, 67-70, 136, 159

Arancibia, Adrian, 130

Areco, Macarena, 124n25

arms and letters, 91

Armstrong, Paul, 160

Arturo Belano, 123-24

Asia, 38

Aureliano Buendía, 96-97

Austen, Jane, 31, 41, 54n9, 55-56, 60-63, 68-70, 158; *Northanger Abbey*, 31-32, 41, 54n9, 55, 60, 62-63, 67, 69

Auster, Paul, 43, 51n2, 74n6, 83-88; *City of Glass*, 43, 51n2, 74n6, 83-86, 98; *The New York Trilogy*, 83

Auster-author, 83-85, 87

Austria, 150

author(s), 12, 13n3, 15-16, 19, 21, 23-26, 28-30, 32n7, 33-36, 39, 45, 52, 56, 58n13, 63, 65-67, 70-72, 74, 75n8, 83-89, 94n28, 97, 107, 112, 114, 116, 122, 125, 129-30, 133-34, 136-37, 141, 147n18, 149, 151, 155-158, 160-61

autobiographical, 12, 156n3

autobiography, 109

*autopoiesis*, 13, 15, 24, 102, 131. *See also* self-growth

*baciyelmo*, 44

Bakhtin, Mikhail, 12-14, 21n7, 23-26, 28-29, 31, 35, 49, 50n1, 71n2, 87n20, 88n21, 89-90n23, 112-13, 129, 139; *The Dialogic Imagination*, 25, 50n1; *Problems of Dostoevsky's Poetics*, 89n23, 129; *Speech Genres*, 21n7. *See also* Bakhtinian, carnival; dialogic; dialogism; exotism: heteroglossia; heteroglot; homecoming festivals; monologic; polyphonic; polyphony; re-accentuate; re-accentuation

Bakhtinian, 15, 17, 19, 24, 28-29, 39, 49, 55. *See also* Bakhtin, Mikhail

*Bálsamo de Fierabrás*, 120, 122n23

Bandera, Cesáreo, 77

barber (*Don Quixote* character), 44

*barrio*, 148

Bartolomeo, Joseph, 108

Bath, 61, 67

Bayliss, Robert, 159

Beaumont, Francis, 56n10; *The Knight of the Burning Pestle*, 56n10

Belianís de Grecia, 53, 65

Bell, Michael, 94n28, 98

beloved, 43, 46-48, 80-82, 105-106, 118, 132, 138, 141, 148-49, 155

Benardete, M. J., 18; *Cervantes Across the Centuries*, 18. *See also* Flores, Angel

Bernández Rodal, Asunción, 54n7

Beusterien, John, 133

bibliophile(s), 40, 51, 53-54, 56, 63. *See also* reader

*Bildüngsroman(e)*, 13-14n4, 113

Bloom, Harold, 32n7, 78, 95

Bolaño, Roberto, 45, 102, 122-23, 125-26; *Detectives Salvajes* (*The Savage Detectives*), 45, 122-23, 125-26

booklovers, 41, 53

Boom (literary), 88, 126

Booth, Wayne, 112n10, 134

Borges, Jorge Luis, 29-30, 125; "Pierre Menard, Author of *Don Quixote*," 29-30

Borgmeier, Raimund, 106

Boswell, Jackson, 56n10; *Cervantes in Seventeenth-Century England*, 56n10. *See also*, Randall, Dale

Brantlinger, Patrick, 56, 61

Brewer, Brian, 121n21

Britain, 17, 68, 107; British, 57

Brockmeier, Joe, 71n1

byzantine (fiction), 32, 130, 156

Cain, William, 82

Cammarata, Joan, 135

Campbell, Joseph, 22n8, 45n20, 101; *The Hero with a Thousand Faces*, 22n8. *See also* hero's journey

Canada, 119-20; Canadian, 119

Canavaggio, Jean, 106, 156n3

Captain Ahab, 32, 43, 73-79, 82, 153, 159

Caraculiambro, 104

carnival, 15, 71n2, 88n21, 112n9. *See also* Bakhtin, Mikhail

carnivalesque, 112, 156

Caso, Antonio, 79n13

Catherine Morland, 31, 55, 60-63, 65n16, 67-70, 136, 158-59

Cervantean, 17, 94-95n28, 112n8. *See also* Cervantine

Cervantes, Miguel de, 11, 12, 15-19, 21-22, 24-25, 27n3, 28-41, 44, 46, 48-49, 51-52 54n7, 55-58, 60, 65-67, 71-72, 74-75, 78-84, 86, 88-92, 94-95, 97-98, 100-10, 112-23, 125-27, 129-30, 132-37, 139, 141-43, 145-46, 151, 153-61; characters 11, 15, 19, 22n8, 33n10, 36-41, 44, 46, 48-49, 51-52, 56, 58, 65, 72, 75, 78, 80, 91, 97, 100, 101n1, 103-06, 117-19, 121n22, 129, 132n1, 135, 141-43, 146, 153, 155; *La Galatea*, 157n4; scholars, 8, 143; scholarship 17, 34, 36, 101; work 11-12, 15-19, 21, 24-25, 29-30, 31n5, 32n7, 34-35, 37, 39, 48-49, 51n3, 56, 78-79, 84, 90-91, 94-95, 102, 104, 116-21, 125, 127, 130, 136, 142, 146, 153-54, 160. *See also Don Quixote*

Cervantic[k], 112. *See also* Cervantine

Cervantine, 17, 24, 28, 32-33, 39, 63, 75, 93, 102-103, 106-107, 112n8, 120, 123, 132, 142, 159, 161. *See also* Cervantic[k]; Cervantean

Cesárea Tinajero, 123-24

Chile, 123n24, 148n19; Chilean, 122, 125n27, 148

China, 50

chivalric, 13, 15, 31-33, 40-42, 44, 46, 50-53, 57, 66-67, 72, 77n9, 102, 117n17, 119, 128, 130, 132, 144, 156, 158

chivalrous, 75, 92, 100, 128, 132

chivalry, 15, 40-41, 52, 71, 73, 87-88, 101, 111, 144

Christian, 118, 138

Church, Margaret, 104-106

Cide Hamete Benengeli, 75n8, 91, 116n13, 145

Clare Quilty, 142n12, 144
Clignet, Remi, 65
Close, Anthony, 133
Colombia, 98; Colombian, 94, 98
Colonel Auerliano Buendía, 96-97
comedy, 133-34
comic (books), 32, 120
conservatism, 71
conventionalism, 71
Cortázar, Julio, 88, 125
Count Vronsky, 137-40, 151
counterutopia, 72, 74, 86, 98
Countess Trifaldi, 26-27
Da Rosa, Doris, 93
Dahl, Roald, 51n2, 54n9; *Matilda*, 51n2, 54n9
Daisy Buchanan, 43, 74, 80-82, 159
Dale, Amelia, 56
Daniel Quinn, 43, 74, 83-88, 159
deconstruction, 86
Defoe, Daniel, 12, 15, 102
*desengaño*, 72. *See also* disenchantment; disillusion; *engaño*
dialogic, 14, 23-24, 33, 47, 139, 151. *See also* Bakhtin, Mikhail
dialogism, 14, 31. *See also* Bakhtin, Mikhail
dialogue, 31, 35-36, 84, 93
Didapper, 104
discourse, 25-28, 35, 36n13, 91n25, 106; in the novel, 25. *See also* Bakhtin, Mikhail; re-accentuation
disenchantment, 78, 80, 143. *See also desengaño*
disillusion, 72, 143-44; disillusionment, 72, 74, 80, 82, 99, 124, 143, 146, 156, 159. *See also desengaño*
Dolly Oblonsky, 138n5
Don Quixote (character), 11n1, 13-14n4, 16, 18-21, 22n8, 23-24, 28-30, 33-53, 55-67, 69-89, 91-96, 98-102, 104-106, 108-10, 112-14, 116-21, 124-30, 132-46, 148, 150-51, 153-55, 157-60. *See also* Alonso Quijano; *hidalgo*; knight errant
*Don Quixote*, 11-12, 14-22, 24, 26-37, 39, 40n17, 43, 48, 50n1, 51, 54n7, 55, 61-62, 64-68, 71n1-2, 75n8, 76-79, 82-86, 88-95, 97, 99-108, 110-23, 125-30, 135, 136-37n3, 140-47, 151, 153-57, 159-61; first modern novel, 11-12, 102, 161. *See also* Cervantes, Miguel de
Donny Coyote, 119-22, 159
Dostoevsky, Fyodor, 89-90n23, 127, 129-30, 135; *The Idiot*, 127-28, 130
Dr. Francia, 74, 88-94, 99, 159
dreamer(s), 16, 18n6, 19-20, 22, 29, 32n8, 33, 38, 41-43, 48-49, 53, 55, 58, 71-75, 77, 80-83, 86-87, 92, 98-99, 102, 106, 119, 126n28, 139, 150, 153-56, 158
Drumm, Elizabeth, 83n15, 87n20

Duke and Duchess (*Don Quixote* characters), 26, 44, 55n3, 105n5

Dulcinea del Toboso, 24, 33-34, 39, 42, 46-47, 59n15, 79n13, 82, 87, 106, 113, 117n16, 118-21, 124, 128, 132, 134-35, 140n8, 143-46, 148-51, 157-59. *See also* Aldonza Lorenzo

Dunn, Peter N., 71n1; *The Utopian Nexus in Don Quixote*, 71n1. *See also* Jehenson, Myriam Yvonne

Durán, Leopoldo, 117n15; *Graham Greene: amigo y hermano*, 117n15

Durán, Manuel, 18; *Fighting Windmills: Encounters with Don Quixote*, 18. *See also* Rogg, Fay R.

education, 41, 52-53, 62, 107, 114, 120

Egginton, William, 154n1; *The Man Who Invented Fiction*, 154n1

El Toboso, 46, 117, 119, 132, 140n8

Eleanor Oliphant, 38

Elizabeth Bennet, 153

Emma Bovary (Madame), 33, 37, 54, 63-67, 69-70, 136, 147n18, 153, 158-59

enchantment, 82, 148. *See also engaño*

*engaño*, 72. *See also desengaño*; enchantment

England, 17, 31, 56n10, 70, 102-103, 107, 116, 150; English, 12, 17, 33, 56, 60-62, 67-68, 88, 102-103, 107, 123, 149, 160n5. *See also* English novel, the

English novel, the, 17, 62, 102-103, 107

Epicureanism, 77-78n11

*eros*, 137, 143

eroticism, 121n21

escapism, 51, 69, 155

escapist, 12, 61

Espejo, Ramón, 83n15

Estébanez Estebanez, Cayetano, 116n14

Europe, 17, 38, 124, 127, 157; European, 12-14, 89-90n23

*exempla*, 73n5

exotism, 139. *See also* Bakhtin, Mikhail

Faceless Man, the, 49n24.

fanatism, 75, 97

Fanny (Frances Goodwill), 105-106, 108

fantasy, 55, 69, 71n2

Father Quixote (Monsignor), 28, 117-119, 121, 159

Fernández, Jerónimo, 53n6; *Belianís de Grecia*, 53n6

Fernández-Morera, Darío, 18; *Cervantes in the English-Speaking World: New Essays*, 18. *See also* Hanke, Michael

fiction, 13, 17, 19, 21, 25-26, 28-32, 36n13, 40n17, 41-42, 50-54, 56, 59n14, 60-62, 64, 66, 69-70,

83n17, 85, 88, 95, 98, 114, 117n17, 119-20, 128, 134, 153

fictional, 15, 21, 28, 30, 40, 50-52, 57-58, 60, 65-66, 78-79, 84-85, 87-89, 94-95, 117n17, 145-46, 156; fictionality, 15

fidelity critics, 34-35

Fiedler, Leslie, 12

Fielding, Henry, 12, 15, 32-33, 61, 68, 102-104, 106-109, 114, 116; *Joseph Andrews*, 12, 32-33, 103-104, 106-109, 116; *Tom Jones*, 12, 103

Filardo Llamas, Laura, 145n17

Firebrass Balm, 122

Fitzgerald, F. Scott, 43, 74n6, 79-82; *The Great Gatsby*, 43, 74n6, 79, 81-82

Flask, 77-78n11

Flaubert, Gustave, 33, 41, 54n9, 55-56, 63-66, 68, 70, 147n18, 158; *Madame Bovary*, 33, 41, 54n9, 55-56, 63-67, 136, 147

Flaubertian, 147n18

Flores, Angel, 17; *Cervantes Across the Centuries*, 18. *See also* Benardete, M. J.

Fonseca, Cristóbal de, 133, 135; *Tratado del amor de Dios*, 133n2

formal realism, 12. *See also* Watt, Ian

Fox, Soledad, 64, 66-67

France, 33, 65, 70, 114; French, 56-57, 68, 148n19, 149

Frestón, 144n14

Fuentes, Carlos, 12

Galaor, 52-53

Galatea, 157

Gandalf, 153

Ganya (Gavril Ivolgin), 127-28

Garcés, María Antonia, 156n3

García Márquez, Gabriel, 74n6, 88, 94-98; *Cien años de soledad* (*One Hundred Years of Solitude*), 74n6, 88, 94-95, 97-99, 159

gargantuan, 154

Garrido Ardila, John, 12, 17, 19, 36, 51n4, 102, 103n3; *The Cervantean Heritage: Reception and Influence of Cervantes in Britain*, 17; *Cervantes en Inglaterra: El Quijote y la novela inglesa del siglo XVIII*, 17, 103n3; *A History of the Spanish Novel*, 103n3

Garrigós, Cristina, 58n13

General Epanchin, 127

General Karenin, 137-38, 140

Germany, 150

Ginés de Pasamonte, 113

Ginés, Montserrat, 125n26

Gino Pasamonte, 121

Girard, René, 77n9. *See also mimetic desire*

Gleim, William, 77-78

Golden Age (Spanish), 11-12, 72-73, 82, 143. *See also* Spain

Gordon, Scott Paul, 57, 158

gothic, 31-32, 60-63, 67-69

Greene, Graham, 28, 116-19; *Monsignor Quixote*, 28-29, 39, 116-19
Griboyedov, Alexander, 44
Groes, Sebastian, 81
Grossman, Edith, 27n2
*Guardia Civil*, 116, 118
Gutiérrez Rodríguez, Marta M., 145
Hamlet, 141n10, 153
Hammond, Brean, 68
Hanke, Michael, 18; *Cervantes in the English-Speaking World: New Essays*, 18. *See also* Fernández-Morera, Darío
Hanlon, Aaron, 18-19, 72-73, 110; *A World of Disorderly Notions*, 110n6
Harrison, Kathryn, 147n18
Hebreo, León de, 133, 135; *Dialoghi d'amore*, 133n2
Helmet of Mambrino, 119-20
Henry Tilney, 60-62, 69
Hermione Granger, 153
hero's journey, 45n20, 101. *See also* Campbell, Joseph
heroine(s), 31, 33n10, 41, 50n1, 55-60, 62-63, 66, 68-69, 136, 138-39
heteroglossia, 13, 15, 35. *See also* Bakhtin, Mikhail
heteroglot, 13-14, 25. *See also* Bakhtin, Mikhail
*hidalgo*, 13-14n4, 21, 29, 41-42, 44, 46-47, 53, 60, 74, 81, 85, 94, 109, 117n17, 127, 132, 139n7, 144, 154. *See also* Don Quixote
Hispanic, 95, 98
homecoming festivals, 21, 22n7, 49, 57. *See also* Bakhtin, Mikhail
Homer, 48
Honeyman, Gail, 38-39; *Eleanor Oliphant is Completely Fine*, 38
honor, 15, 156
housekeeper (*Don Quixote* character), 44, 64, 121n21
Huckleberry Finn, 125
Humbert Humbert, 47, 141-46, 151, 159
Hutcheon, Linda, 30-31, 34n11, 35, 63; *A Theory of Adaptation*, 34n11. *See also* ironic inversion
Hutchinson, Steven, 130
*idea*, 23
ideal, 46-48, 59n15, 61, 63, 65, 72-73, 75, 78-81, 88, 121, 128, 132, 135, 140n8, 144, 150
idealism, 21, 37, 71, 134
idealization, 21, 82, 99, 135, 145, 151, 158
illusion(s), 43, 55, 62, 65-66, 69, 72-73, 143, 155
image, 24-26, 28-31, 33, 35, 39, 42, 45-49, 51, 56, 58-59, 61-65, 67-68, 70-72, 80, 82, 86, 91-93, 95, 97-99, 106, 112, 119-21, 124n25, 132, 138, 140-41, 143-44, 148-50, 155, 157-59

imagination, 20, 39, 44, 46, 57, 62, 69, 87, 96, 98, 121, 133, 140n8, 158

imitation, 12, 20, 24-25, 27, 29-30, 32-33, 35-36, 50n1, 51, 62, 66, 68, 91, 101, 103-104, 106-107, 114, 119-20, 132, 144; satiric, 106

injustice, 100, 120-21

Inquisition, 108, 119

insanity, 37, 77

intertextual, 24-26, 29, 32n7, 33, 37, 38-39n16, 153, 155, 161

ironic inversion, 30-31. *See also* Hutcheon, Linda

irony, 12, 31, 74, 132, 134; comical, 36

irrationality, 18n6, 37, 87, 151

Isabella Thorpe, 61

Iser, Wolfgang, 52n5, 53-54

Ishmael, 75

Israel, 124

Jane Eyre, 153

Japan, 30, 148n19, 150

Jay Gatsby (Great Gatsby), 43, 74, 80-83, 153, 159

Jefferson, D. W., 110

Jehenson, Myriam Yvonne, 71n1; *The Utopian Nexus in Don Quixote*, 71n1. *See also* Dunn, Peter N.

John Thorpe, 61

Johnson, Carroll B., 18, 46n21, 71n1, 75n7, 121n21, 143n13; *Don Quixote: The Quest for Modern Fiction*, 18; *Madness and Lust: A Psychological Approach to Don Quixote*, 46n21

Jonson, Benjamin, 56n10; *The Alchemist*, 56n10

José Arcadio Buendía, 96-97

José Arcadio Segundo, 96

José Gaspar Rodríguez Francia. *See* Dr. Francia

Joseph Andrews, 32n8, 104-108, 130

journey, 13-14n4, 21, 45n20, 46, 101-102, 113, 118, 120, 124, 130, 148, 150, 160n5. *See also* hero's journey

Juan García Madero, 123-24

Juan Haldudo, 108

Kahn, Aaron M., 154n1; *The Oxford Handbook of Cervantes*, 154n1

Kingdom of Candaya, 101

knight errant, 13-14n4, 21, 32, 33n10, 35, 38-44, 46-48, 50, 52, 72-75, 77n9, 81, 87, 91, 97, 100-101, 109, 112, 118, 121n21, 127, 129, 132, 134, 138, 142, 144, 146, 154-56, 158. *See also* Don Quixote

Knight of the Mirrors (Caballero de los espejos), 42n19, 86, 144

Konstantin Levin, 137-39, 141

Krabbenhoft, Kenneth, 142-44

Kropf, C. R., 107-108

Kubayanda, J. Bekunuru, 94n27

La Calprenède, Gauthier de Costes, 58n12; *Cassandra; the Fam'd Romance*, 58n12

*La Celestina*, 102
La Mancha, 13-14n4, 35, 42, 46, 53, 64, 103, 117, 119. *See also* Manchegan
Laguna, Ana María, 133, 135
LaLonde, Suzanne, 38n16
Langbauer, Laurie, 56-57, 59n14
Las Vegas, 120
Latin, 41, 50, 105, 109
Latin America, 95, 149; Latin American, 88, 94, 125-26, 147-48
laughter, 41, 77, 104, 108, 114; philosophic, 114
Laura Damián, 123
Lavender, William, 84
*Lazarillo de Tormes*, 13-14n4
Lazarillo de Tormes, 13-14n4
Lázaro Lafuente, Alberto, 117n15
Lehman, B. H., 114-15. *See also* laughter (philosophic)
Lemuel Gulliver, 153
Lennox, Charlotte, 41, 51n2, 55-59, 68-70, 158; *The Female Quixote*, 41, 50n1, 52n2, 55-57, 63, 67-68
Leonora, 103
Lepanto, Battle of, 89, 113n11, 156
Lezra, Jacques, 160
Liberia, 124
Lima (Peru), 148
linguistic, 13-14n4, 14n5, 18, 21-22n21, 23, 25, 39, 41, 93, 101n2, 106, 154; linguistics, 25
Little Seamstress, 54
Lolita, 141-46, 151
Lombardi, Elena, 54n7
López Navia, Santiago Alfonso, 37; *Inspiración y pretexto II: Nuevos estudios sobre Cervantes, su obra y su recepción*, 37n14
Lorenzo Corchuelo, 140n8
love (sentiment), 15-16, 21, 31, 37-38, 42, 47-48, 73, 80-82, 93n26, 96, 99, 105, 107, 111, 121n21, 127-28, 132-38, 140-52, 156-58; idealized, 38, 106, 149, 151; platonic, 37; quixotic, 21, 47, 134-35, 137, 141, 148
lover(s), 16, 19-22, 24, 29, 32n8, 33, 38, 45-49, 53, 55, 58, 80, 82, 95, 102, 106, 119, 132, 134-35, 138, 142, 148, 150-51, 153-54, 157-58, 161
Lupe, 124
Macondo, 96
Madame Bovary senior, 161
Madariaga Caro, Montserrat, 123n24
madman, 50, 58n13, 65, 67, 98, 119, 139
madness, 44, 56, 59n14, 70, 77-78, 86, 134
Maggi, Armando, 133n2
Manchegan, 84n18. *See also* La Mancha
Mancing, Howard, 13-14n4, 15, 19, 36, 110-11, 120n20, 128

Mandel, Oscar, 100, 101n1, 134

mania, 21, 47, 135, 143. *See also* obsession

Manuel, Don Juan, 73n5; *Count Lucanor*, 73n5

Maravall, José Antonio, 71-73, 86, 98; *Utopia and Counterutopia in* Don Quixote, 71

Marcela, 121

Marcella, 121-22

Maritornes, 105n5, 113, 121, 143

Matilda, 54

Matooka, Wendy, 36n13

Maturana, Humberto, 13-14n4. *See also autopoiesis*; Varela, Francisco

Max Work, 87

McCrory, Donald, 154n1; *No Ordinary Man*, 154n1

McFarlane, Brian, 34n11; *Novel to Film*, 34n11

medieval, 40, 46, 53, 71, 101, 132

Meehan, Adam, 81

Melquíades, 74, 96-97

Melville, Herman, 32n7, 43, 73, 75-78, 80, 82, 159; *Moby Dick*, 32n7, 43, 73, 75, 77-79, 82, 126n28

Merriam-Webster, 38n15

metafiction, 15, 40n17, 141

Mexico, 50, 123n24; Mexican, 125

Michael Saavedra, 83

Micomicona, 44, 104, 121

*mimetic desire*, 77. *See also* Girard, René

Miraflores, 148

Mitchell, Ken, 32, 45, 102, 119-22; *The Heroic Adventures of Donny Coyote*, 32, 45, 119

Moby Dick, 43, 74-77

*modus operandi*, 44

monologic, 14, 47, 89-90n23, 151. *See also* Bakhtin, Mikhail

Moose Jaw, 119-20

Morisco, 108

Morrison, Paul, 68

Morson, Gary, 129, 140

Mr. Glanville, 58

Mrs. Tilney, 60, 68

Mrs. Wadman, 110-11, 113

muse, 46, 132, 144

Myshkin (Prince, Lev), 127-30, 159

Nabokov, Vladimir, 47, 134, 136-37n3, 141-42, 145-46; *Lectures on Don Quixote*, 136-37n3, 142; *Lolita*, 47, 134-35, 141-46, 151

Napoleon III, 65

narrative(s), 13n3, 15, 24-26, 31-33, 36, 40, 43, 45n20, 55, 58, 60, 74, 75n8, 78, 84, 86, 89n22, 90-91, 94-95, 98, 103-104, 106-107, 110, 113, 115, 119, 123, 126, 130, 133-34, 145-46, 148-49, 158

narrator(s), 12-13, 75, 78, 81-82, 90-92, 102, 109-10, 115-16, 124, 130, 146, 148; unreliable, 12, 78, 146

Nastasya Filippovna, 127-28
Neill, Natalie, 60, 67n17, 69
Neoplatonic, 133-34
Nick Carraway, 82
Nicolás Román, Susana, 62
niece (*Don Quixote* character), 44, 121n21
No-man, 48
North America, 120; North American, 75, 119
Northanger Abbey, 60, 67
novel (genre), 11-15, 25-26, 49, 50n1, 51n4, 86, 102-104, 129n30; history of, 12; modern, 11-12, 14, 104n4, 129n30; two stylistic lines, 12-14; the first line, 14; the second line, 14. *See also* Bakhtin, Mikhail
novel(s) (work of fiction), 11-18, 20-22, 25-39, 41-48, 50n1, 51n3, 52-67, 69-70, 72, 74, 75n8, 77-81, 83-110, 113-21, 123-27, 129-30, 132-33, 135-51, 153-54, 157-61
novelist(s), 12, 15, 75n7, 85, 89, 98
novelistic, 11-12, 14, 26, 28-29, 49, 50n1, 52, 54, 66, 95, 102, 157
obsession(s), 21, 41, 45, 48, 56-58, 60, 75, 80-81, 86, 96-99, 109-11, 135, 145, 155, 158-59. *See also* mania
Odysseus, 153; Odyssean, 101, 130, 154, 156
optimism, 42
Ortega y Gasset, José, 63, 139n6
*othering*, 44
Otilia Somocurcio, 38, 135, 148-51, 158-59
palimpsest, 94, 97
Paraguay, 88, 90-91n24, 91-92; Paraguayan, 88-89, 93
paranoia, 143-44
Parfyon Rogozhin, 127
Paris, 147n18, 148n19
Parker, A. A., 104n4
parody, 17, 19-20, 24-25, 27n3, 29-33, 35-36, 48, 56, 62-63, 66, 101, 106, 120, 132, 149, 156; satiric, 31n5
pastoral (fiction), 13, 15, 32, 50n1, 102, 157n4
Paulson, Ronald, 59n15, 104
Pawl, Amy, 57, 67
Peña Pobre, 33
Perdou de Subligny, Adrien Thomas, 56; *Mock-Clelia, or Madam Quixote*, 56
*peripeteia*, 43, 69, 74
perspectivism, 101
Peru, 148-50; Peruvian, 147n18, 148, 150
pestilence, 133-35; *amorosa pestilencia*, 133
Peter Pan, 153
Peter Stillman Jr., 43, 74, 83-85, 87
Peter Stillman Sr., 43
*pharmakon*, 56
Philbrick, Nathaniel, 78n12; *In the Heart of the Sea*, 78n12

picaresque (fiction), 13-14n4, 15, 32, 50n1, 67, 102, 113-14, 130, 156
Pierre Menard, 29-30
Pinto, 121
Platonism, 77-78n11
poem(s), 15, 31n6, 123; epic, 31n6
*poiesis*, 131. *See also autopoiesis*
Policarpo Patiño, 89-90, 92-93
polyphonic, 14, 18, 25, 89-90, 123, 129-30, 136-37n3, 145. *See also* Bakhtin, Mikhail
polyphony, 14, 89-90, 106, 122, 127, 129-30, 136-37n3, 146. *See also* Bakhtin, Mikhail
Post-Boom, 122, 126
postmodern (fiction), 36, 50, 83, 86, 88
*pragma*, 23
Presa Díaz, José Carlos, 72n3
priest (*Don Quixote* character), 44, 51n3, 61
Princess Di, 120-22
psychology, 98, 136; psychological, 12, 47, 73, 99, 106
Pygmalion, 157
pygmalionism, 46
quest(s), 20-21, 43-45, 65, 71, 73-74, 80-81, 83, 86-87, 92, 96, 101-102, 120, 123-24, 127, 138-39, 142, 146, 151, 159. *See also* adventure; journey
Quim Font (Joaquín), 124n25
Quinn-Auster, 83n16, 84-85
quixotic, 16-21, 24, 28-29, 31n5, 32n8, 33, 36-43, 45, 47-57, 59n15, 60, 62, 64, 67-70, 72-75, 80, 82-83, 88, 92-93, 95-99, 102-104, 106, 109-12, 116-17, 119-20, 122, 124-26, 130-31, 134-35, 137, 141-43, 146-48, 150, 153, 155, 157-61
quixotism, 18-19, 36n13, 56-57, 60, 63, 67-68, 72, 75, 95-96, 99, 138, 141, 145, 158; cyclical, 95
Radcliffe, Ann, 60; *The Mysteries of Udolpho*, 60-61
Rader, Ralph W., 12
Randall, Dale, 56n10; *Cervantes in Seventeenth-Century England*, 56n10. *See also*, Boswell, Jackson
re-accentuate, 17, 25-26, 28, 33n10, 35, 37, 45, 48, 56, 73, 101, 160; re-accentuated, 16, 19-21, 24, 26, 28-30, 36, 38-39, 41-43, 45, 47-48, 51, 54-55, 60, 67, 69-70, 73-74, 79, 81-83, 86, 88, 92, 98-99, 101-103, 106, 110-13, 116, 118-21, 124, 128, 130, 134-35, 138, 148-51, 153, 157-59, 161. *See also* Bakhtin, Mikhail; re-accentuation
re-accentuation(s), 16-17, 19-21, 23-30, 32-39, 41, 49-50, 53, 55, 57, 63, 72, 75, 77, 80, 82, 87n20, 91, 96, 99, 120, 126n28, 130, 135-36, 141-42, 146, 153-54, 157-58; discourse, 25-26, 28, 35. *See also* Bakhtin, Mikhail; re-accentuate
reader(s), 11, 13-14n4, 16, 19-20, 22, 25-26, 28-30, 32-33, 37-41, 44, 48-61, 63, 65-67, 69-70, 75n8, 77-79, 82-83, 86, 88, 91-93, 98-

104, 106-107, 109-10, 112-15, 119-20, 122-24, 126, 130, 132-34, 136-37, 139-41, 146-48, 150-51, 153-58, 160; uncritical, 65; women, 54-56, 67, 69. *See also* bibliophile; booklover; reading

reader-response criticism, 51

reading, 12, 15-17, 20, 24, 28, 30, 38-41, 48, 50-70, 79, 82, 87n20, 96-97, 104, 109, 111, 113, 116, 120-21, 124-25, 128-31, 134-35, 137, 141, 147n18, 150, 153, 155, 158, 160-61; miseducated, 63; savvy, 63; uncritical, 20, 55, 66-67; unguided, 62; unrestricted, 41. *See also* reader

realism, 12, 124-26, 147n18; American, 125; visceral, 124, 126

reality, 15, 21, 25, 31, 40-41, 43-44, 55-56, 59, 66-67, 74, 76-78, 80, 83, 85, 87, 95, 97-98, 111, 117n17, 120, 143-44, 147n18, 148n19, 155, 158

Rebeca, 159

recreation(s), 16, 37, 117n15

Remedios Moscote, 96, 159

repetition, 34-35, 81

rewriting, 19, 29-30, 35, 90

Ricardo Somocurcio, 38, 47, 134-35, 147n18, 148-51, 159

Richardson, Samuel, 12, 15, 102

Ricote, 108

Ritz-Barr, Steven, 34; *Quixote*, 34-35. *See also* Uchiyama, Hoku

Rivas, Vladimiro, 79

Rivers, Elias L., 156n3

Roa Bastos, Augusto, 74n6, 88-94; *Yo el Supremo* (*I the Supreme*), 74n6, 88, 90-94, 99

Robinson Crusoe, 141n10, 153

Rocinante, 28, 39, 105n5, 111, 114, 118, 121, 157

Rodríguez de Montalvo, Garci, 33n9; *Amadís de Gaula*, 31n5, 40n18, 52, 105n5

Rogg, Fay R., 18; *Fighting Windmills: Encounters with Don Quixote*, 18. *See also* Durán, Manuel

romance (genre), 12, 50n1, 102

romance (love), 81, 135-36, 140n8, 151

romance (novelistic subgenre), 31, 33, 50, 56-57, 59n14, 62, 68

romance(s) (work of fiction), 31-33, 40-42, 46, 50-51, 55-58, 60-61, 66-68, 77n9, 101, 111, 119, 128, 130, 132, 156, 158

Ronald Reagan, 120

Russia, 30, 127, 129, 136-37, 150; Russian, 21-22n7, 23, 89-90n23, 127-28, 130, 135-37

Rwanda, 124

Sánchez Sarmiento, Rafael, 72n3

Sancho Panza, 24, 27-28, 36, 39, 46, 47n23, 53, 76, 79n13, 84n18, 87, 92-93, 105-106, 108, 111, 113, 116, 118-19, 121, 125, 136-37n3, 140n8, 142, 157, 159

Sancho Zancas, 28, 117-19

Sandra Dollar (Wonder Woman), 119-20

sanity, 44, 58, 128

Sansón Carrasco, 42n19, 51n3, 84n18, 144

*Santa Hermandad*, 118

Saskatchewan, 119

satire, 20, 31, 56, 63, 65-67, 106, 110, 114, 146

Scarlett O'Hara, 153

Scham, Michael, 31, 144, 145n17

Scheherazade, 153

Schmidt, Rachel, 31n5

Scudéry, Madeleine de, 58n12; *Artamenes; or, The Grand Cyrus*, 58n12; *Clelia*, 58n12

SEAT 600, 28, 118

self-growth, 13. *See also autopoiesis*

sensibility, 37, 60

sentimental (fiction), 13-14, 50n1, 66, 102

Shakespeare, William, 56n10, 89-90n23; *Cardenno*, 56n10

Sherlock Holmes, 141n10, 153

sidekick, 76, 84n18

Sijie, Dai, 51n2, 54n9; *Balzac and the Little Chinese Seamstress*, 51n2, 54n9

Slipslop, 104, 105n5

Slochewer, Harry, 78

Smith, Mack, 140

sonnet, 31n6

South American, 99

Spain, 28, 30, 48, 68, 72, 79, 92, 100, 102, 108, 116-19, 123n24, 124, 150, 155-56; early modern, 30, 72; post-Franco, 28, 116; Spanish 11-12, 15, 21, 29, 32n7, 38-40, 42-46, 50-51, 53, 56, 66, 72, 82, 89, 95, 109, 113n11, 117-18, 125, 132, 133n2, 136, 138, 143, 160n5

Spilka, Mark, 104, 107-108

Spitzer, Leo, 101

squire, 26-28, 42, 73, 79, 84n18, 87, 105n5, 115, 118, 136-37n3

St. Petersburg, 127

Starbuck, 76, 77-78n11

Stavans, Ilan, 95, 97, 123

Staves, Susan, 56, 57n11, 67n17

Stenbock-Fermor, Elisabeth, 138

Sterne, Laurence, 102, 109-13, 115-16; *The Life and Opinions of Tristram Shandy, Gentleman*, 103, 109-16

Stiva Oblonsky, 138n5

Stoicism, 77-78n11

Stoopen, María, 11

Stubb, 77-78n11

superhero(es), 32, 102, 119-20, 122n23, 159

Switzerland, 127-28; Swiss, 127-28

Tabbi, Joseph, 83n17

Tajuddin, Ahmed, 147n18, 148

Toledo, 116n13

Tolstoy, Leo, 47, 134-41, 151; *Anna Karenina*, 47, 134-37, 151
Tom Buchanan, 80
Tom Sawyer, 125
Trilling, Lionel, 81n14
Trim, 109, 112-13
Triplette, Stacey, 54n7
Tristram Shandy, 109-12, 114-16
Turkevich, Ludmilla Buketoff, 32n7, 128
Twain, Mark, 45, 125; *The Adventures of Huckleberry Finn*, 45, 125; *The Adventures of Tom Sawyer*, 45
Uchiyama, Hoku, 34; *Quixote*, 34-35. *See also* Ritz-Barr, Steven
Ulises Lima, 123-24
Unamuno, Miguel de, 101, 134, 136-37n3
Uncle Toby, 109-13
United States of America (US), 80, 98, 120
unreliability, 145
Urbina, Eduardo, 83n15, 86
utopia, 71-72, 86, 98
utopianism, 71
Van Doren, Carl, 76
Varela, Francisco, 13-14n4. *See also* Maturana, Humberto; *autopoiesis*
Vargas Llosa, Mario, 38, 47, 134, 147-51; *The Perpetual Orgy*, 147n18; *Travesuras de la niña mala* (*The Bad Girl*), 38, 47, 134-35, 147-51
Voegeli, William, 82
Vollendorf, Lisa, 54n7
Walter Shandy, 110-12
Wasserman, Dale, 20, 34; *Man of La Mancha*, 34
Watt, Ian, 12, 102, 129n30; *The Rise of the Novel*, 12. *See also* formal realism
Weldt-Basson, Helene Carol, 90-91n24, 93-94
William Wilson, 85
Williamson, Edwin, 97
Wilson, Diana de Armas, 15
windmills, 43, 76, 101, 118
Wonham, Henry B., 125n26
Wood, Michael, 145n17, 146
Yorick, 111
Zunshine, Lisa, 146